Modern

Modern Druidism

An Introduction

Yowann Byghan

McFarland & Company, Inc., Publishers
Jefferson, North Carolina

LIBRARY OF CONGRESS CATALOGUING-IN-PUBLICATION DATA

Names: Byghan, Yowann, 1948– author.
Title: Modern Druidism : an introduction / Yowann Byghan.
Description: Jefferson, North Carolina : McFarland & Company, Inc.,
    Publishers, 2018. | Includes bibliographical references and index.
Identifiers: LCCN 2018022828 | ISBN 9781476673141 (softcover :
    acid free paper) ∞
Subjects: LCSH: Druids and druidism. | Neopaganism.
Classification: LCC BL910 .B94 2018 | DDC 299/.16—dc23
LC record available at https://lccn.loc.gov/2018022828

BRITISH LIBRARY CATALOGUING DATA ARE AVAILABLE

ISBN (print) 978-1-4766-7314-1
ISBN (ebook) 978-1-4766-3178-3

Front cover: The Callanish II stones at sunset, with the Callanish I
stones on the horizon, July 2017 (Neil Pitchford of Awen Photos)

Printed in the United States of America

McFarland & Company, Inc., Publishers
    Box 611, Jefferson, North Carolina 28640
    www.mcfarlandpub.com

Acknowledgments

I am grateful to Neil Pitchford, Trustee, Treasurer and Inter Faith Network UK representative of the Druid Network (and outstanding natural photographer), for his close reading of the draft manuscript and his many helpful observations and suggestions. My fellow Cornish Bard, eminent archaeologist and author Craig Weatherhill, was also kind enough to review the draft and provide helpful feedback. I am equally grateful to my longstanding Irish-Cornish friend, Anne K. Kennedy Truscott, for her help with Irish Gaelic (Gaeilge) to complement my Scottish Gaelic (Gàidhlig). I am grateful to Greg Hill and Lee Davies of Dun Brython for permission to use their beautiful invocation poems in Chapter 11, and to Jenni Hunt of Ár nDraíocht Féin for permission to use her ritual text in Chapter 12. Philip Carr-Gomm, Chief Druid of the Order of Bards, Ovates and Druids and a widely published authority on Druidism, was also kind enough to read the final draft and offer many helpful corrections and suggestions. Ellen Evert Hopman, who has written widely about Druidism and related topics, and who is as helpful and kindly as she is authoritative and widely respected, also reviewed the draft and provided a stronger American perspective as well as lots of very useful and detailed general guidance. I thank my wife, Siaron Dolan-Powers (who is also American), not only for her specific suggestions and comments on the draft text and her help with finding illustrations, but more generally for her years-long tolerance of my distraction, absorption and frequent journeys into other worlds, the prerogatives of writers and Druids alike.

To Siaron,
light of my life, joy of my heart.

Modern Druidism
An Introduction

YOWANN BYGHAN

McFarland & Company, Inc., Publishers

Jefferson, North Carolina

LIBRARY OF CONGRESS CATALOGUING-IN-PUBLICATION DATA

Names: Byghan, Yowann, 1948– author.
Title: Modern Druidism : an introduction / Yowann Byghan.
Description: Jefferson, North Carolina : McFarland & Company, Inc.,
    Publishers, 2018. | Includes bibliographical references and index.
Identifiers: LCCN 2018022828 | ISBN 9781476673141 (softcover :
    acid free paper) ∞
Subjects: LCSH: Druids and druidism. | Neopaganism.
Classification: LCC BL910 .B94 2018 | DDC 299/.16—dc23
LC record available at https://lccn.loc.gov/2018022828

BRITISH LIBRARY CATALOGUING DATA ARE AVAILABLE

ISBN (print) 978-1-4766-7314-1
ISBN (ebook) 978-1-4766-3178-3

Front cover: The Callanish II stones at sunset, with the Callanish I
stones on the horizon, July 2017 (Neil Pitchford of Awen Photos)

Printed in the United States of America

McFarland & Company, Inc., Publishers
    Box 611, Jefferson, North Carolina 28640
        www.mcfarlandpub.com

Table of Contents

Acknowledgments   vi

Preface   1

I • INTRODUCTION TO DRUIDIC PHILOSOPHY AND RELIGION

  1. The Universe and the World   3

  2. Moral Philosophy   23

II • THE HISTORY OF DRUIDISM

  3. Ancient Celtic Druidism   37

  4. Classical Druidic Roles and Responsibilities   56

  5. Some Famous Druids in History and Legend   70

III • MODERN DRUIDISM

  6. The Romantic Revival   89

  7. Some Modern Groups and Organizations   100

  8. Some Modern Druids   114

IV • LORE AND RITUAL

  9. Sacred Sites   145

  10. The Tree Alphabet and Calendar   176

  11. Modern Rituals and Liturgy   193

  12. Sample Rites and Texts   208

Appendix A: Glossary   221

Appendix B: Contact Information   224

Chapter Notes   227

Bibliography   231

Index   235

Alterius non sit qui suus esse potest.

(Let no man belong to another
who can belong to himself.)
—motto of Paracelsus

Mock not the wife.
—motto of Siaron Dolan-Powers

Preface

Many books have been written about the ancient Celts in general and ancient Celtic Druidism in particular. I have written a couple of them myself. During the Romantic Revival of the 18th century, the supposed tenets of ancient Druidism were elevated to impossible heights of sanctity and wisdom, and were often forced into unlikely alliances with a presumed or imagined primitive, universal, pre–Christian religion, claimed by Stukeley, Higgins and others to have originated either in India or in Atlantis. The obvious differences between the patriarchal religions of Christianity, Judaism and Islam and the Pagan religion of Druidism were ignored or explained away in increasingly unlikely and fanciful theories, many of which simply seem bizarre today.

Then came Darwin, and modern scientific method, and especially (for our purposes) modern archaeology, which began to generate vast amounts of new information about the world in which ancient Druidism thrived. At the same time, the vernacular Irish and Welsh texts which had captured what survived of so-called Dark Age mythology, even though most of the British texts were not written down until the 11th and 12th centuries, began to become much more widely available in English translation. The combination allowed a new Druidism to grow, slowly at first, but inexorably, and today we have a modern philosophy or religion (followers think of it in both ways), called Druidism in America by and large, and Druidry mostly in Britain. Modern Druidism or Druidry is still exploring its connections and relations to ancient Druidism. It is still very much a minority religion or philosophy, but it is nevertheless a real, coherent and viable movement, despite (or, some would argue, because of) its remarkable diversity and the flexible nature of its central ideas.

This modern Druidism is the topic of this book. Most books about modern Druidism fall into one of two categories: they are either academically authoritative, but sometimes narrowly focused, often heavily dependent on historical or archaeological analysis (this is the minor category), or they are friendly, accessible, intuitive, informal and intended to help those who are exploring the modern Druid path to continue learning and practicing their faith or philosophy, either alone or with others (the major category). This book attempts to provide a slightly more comprehensive and informative background to the development of modern Druidism than some others, but also to be accessible and useful to the many potential readers in that major category who are not solely interested in the academic and historical background, but also might be interested in living and practicing Druidism, either as beginners, or as current practitioners, but more fully and effectively.

Some readers will perhaps already be familiar with some aspects of Druidism, while for others this will be a completely new adventure. Inevitably (at least I hope so), some of the reader's initial beliefs and attitudes may be challenged. Modern Druidism thrives on curiosity, independent thinking, and flexibility. It is surely the least dogmatic of all religions or philosophies. We do well to remember that we each perceive the world and the universe around us differently, and that we can only believe what we believe. I am reminded of a charming little story that I first heard spoken in Gàidhlig (Scottish Gaelic), a story that illustrates how easily misconceptions and misperceptions can lead us to false conclusions:

> An old farmer and his wife had lived all their lives on a tiny, remote island in the Hebrides. Life was so simple and plain there that neither of them had ever seen a mirror. The farmer's brother had left the island and moved to the mainland many years previously. When the brother died, the farmer crossed over for the funeral and found himself for the first time in the little ferry town, which seemed to him like a great city. In a shop window, he saw a mirror. Not knowing what it was, he peered closer. Seeing his reflection, he cried (in Gàidhlig, of course), "Good God! It is a painting of my grandfather!" He went inside and bought the mirror, bringing it home with him when he returned to the island. He put it in a drawer in the bedroom, and brought it out from time to time, when he would mutter a few words of fond remembrance to what he thought was the picture of his grandfather. One day, when the farmer was out working in the fields, his wife could no longer contain her curiosity. She opened the drawer, took out the mirror, and saw, of course, her own reflection. "Ah!" she cried. "I knew there was another woman. But why he has kept this painting of her I cannot tell, for she is the ugliest old biddy I ever saw!"

1. The Universe and the World

What Is Druidism?

Druidism is both a religion and a philosophy, and it is full of contrasts. It is an ancient, tribal, Pagan religion, often associated in the public mind with bloody animal and human sacrifices and terrible barbarity, but many of its modern-day adherents are vegetarians or vegans and wouldn't dream of harming a fly, let alone making blood sacrifices. It is a religion packed with Gods, Goddesses, heroes and spirits, but it serves nonetheless as a simple philosophical path for many, a way to lead a good and useful life without necessarily getting involved with occult or spiritual questions. It was originally shaped by the ancient Celtic tribal society in which it developed, but its modern supporters are now often open to other deities from other cultures: there are modern Druids who worship not only Celtic deities but also the Gods and Goddesses of the North, like Odin, Thor and Freyja, or who are also Christians. It boasts a magnificent mythology packed with magic, miracles and astonishing events, but it also attracts believers in scientific method, empiricists who need hard facts and demonstrable proofs. Modern Druids come from all classes and walks of life, from plumbers to professors, from bus drivers to botanists. We love Nature, so we sometimes deprecate high technology (or rather the *dependence* on high technology) and mechanistic attitudes, but many of us are also geeks, technophiles and quite the opposite of Luddites. For modern Druids, God can be just a concept, or a male presence, as in other religions, but God can also be a female presence or Goddess, or many Gods and Goddesses, and for many practitioners there is a genuine, new and refreshing freedom and power in the feminism and the polytheism of Druidism.

Druidism or Druidry therefore sometimes gives the impression of being all things to all people, a religion whose vagueness and contradictions allow believers to believe whatever they like and cherry-pick the ideas and practices that are most appealing. Some modern Druid groups or organizations (for example, Ár nDraíocht Féin, the Order of WhiteOak and Tribe of the Oak) are very structured, with strict protocols for induction, education and advancement, and with a great deal of importance paid to rank and seniority. As we shall see in more detail later, classical ancient Druidism provides plenty of exemplary material for rigorous and structured approaches: the training was long (nineteen or twenty years, according to Caesar), extremely arduous (Bards were expected to learn 20,000 verses of poetry, for example) and extremely rewarding—the ransom price for a Druid was the same as for a king or queen, and their social status was high. But in modern Druidism, rigidity and emphasis on rank, structure and organization are the exception, rather than the rule. If you're looking for a religion where all the work is already done for you and you simply have to learn what to say and when to say it, then Druidism is probably not for you. Modern Druids tend to be free-wheeling, free-thinking, tolerant, open-minded, eclectic, curious, independent, sometimes argumentative (in a friendly way), and above all creative—as we shall see shortly, being creative is almost a requirement of membership. Many, like myself, are solitary Druids, meeting with others on an *ad hoc* basis, and enjoying that fellowship when it happens, but not very good with rules and regulations and not really very interested in any permanent arrangement. Others do belong to groups (usually called either "henge" or "grove") and enjoy the fellowship, the group rituals and the supporting structure. Quite a few groups have a system of progression towards full qualification as a Druid, through a combination of education and progressive induction. But there are no standard religious texts or holy writ for Druidism (although there are countless stories and poems from Celtic vernacular literature). There are also no universal fixed rituals (although there are many common practices, especially at calendar festivals; many individuals and groups have created their own group rituals; and there are some examples of ritual formats and ritual texts at the end of this book).

Druidism's origins are Pagan, a word that still arouses negative expectations. The Latin root, *paganus*, simply meant "rustic," "of the countryside." Margot Adler's seminal *Drawing Down the Moon* was first published in 1979, but it was based on very extensive research and experience, and still says a lot that is true and wise about modern Paganism:

> The thousands of people in the United States today who call themselves Pagans or Neo-Pagans ... consider themselves part of a religious movement that antedates Christianity and monotheism. By *Pagan* they usually mean the pre–Christian nature religions of the West, and their own attempts to revive them or to re-create them in new forms.... The many hundreds of Pagan religious groups, by and large, stand in contrast and opposition to ... authoritarian movements. The Pagan vision is one which says that neither doctrine nor dogma nor asceticism nor rule by masters is necessary for the visionary experience, and that ecstasy *and* freedom are both possible.[1]

So, with all these contrasts and contradictions, with all this freedom and no central doctrine or dogma, is it possible even to say what modern Druidism is, or what it signifies?

The answer is yes. There is a clear and distinctive common core of Druidic belief, which connects ancient Druidism and modern Druidism, which projects a powerful and worthy moral philosophy for a troubled world, and which provides a sustaining philosophical and spiritual experience for its adherents. Unlike some other religions, where schism may be common, Druids from widely different backgrounds meet frequently and share ideas, experiences, and even rituals, mostly without friction. Historically, even when groups have split and created new groups, the friendliness and solidarity between individuals have tended to remain. Modern Druids respect all religions, including their own, and believe that friendship, respect and responsibility far outweigh dogma and ritual protocol. The Druid Network, in the foreword to its constitution, uses the elegant term "coherence" to describe the mechanism by which so many disparate paths connect with each other, and correctly identifies reverence for nature and all living things as the common ground where those paths always meet: "Coherence is brought to Druidism upon the spiritual foundations of its reverence for nature."[2]

The purpose of this book is to try to describe that common core of modern Druidic belief in a way that is both reasonably comprehensive yet still accessible. My purpose is emphatically *not* to persuade anybody that they should become a Druid. We do not proselytize, partly on principle, but also because people very often simply discover for themselves that Druidism fits what they believe and have always believed: many new members of the community have described it as "coming home"—you don't so much decide to become a Druid as discover that you are a Druid, and always have been, even if you didn't know it before.

Because modern Druidism is so diverse and eclectic, and because I am following nobody's rules and instincts but my own, the views I express here may frequently be different from those of other Druids. However, most if not all other Druids will forgive that, because we know and understand the great paradox that (a) nothing is more important than telling the truth and (b) any two people of the highest character and purest moral intent may still perceive a single truth differently, because they may be looking at it from different places. (An anecdote I saw on Facebook: A woman wrote to her brother, asking for some technical help with her *dy* computer. The brother had never heard of the make. He asked for a screenshot of the maker's logo, which she duly sent. Only after staring at it for several seconds did he realize that he was looking at *hp*, for Hewlett Packard, upside down and backwards.)

So let's dive off the high-board and plunge straight towards a modern Druidic picture of the Universe and the World. What is that viewpoint like?

Anam, Identity and Purpose

Anam is an Irish word. Literally, it means "soul," "spirit" or "life." It is related to the Latin words *anima* ("breath," "physical life") and *animus* ("soul," "mind" or "sensibility"), from the Greek root ανμι (*anmi*), literally "that which breathes," and of course the English word "animal," which literally means "living thing." In Druidism, *anam* describes identity, which almost by definition defines purpose. For Druids, all things have *anam*. All things. Not just humans, not just animals, but also rocks, streams, pebbles, grains of dirt, stars. Everything is alive. Everything has consciousness. Everything connects. Everything relates. The entire Universe is alive and has purpose. When Druids talk with trees (as many of us do on a daily basis), we are connecting and merging our individual and collective identity with the individual and collective identity of another species, and real conversations take place. (Trees are especially important to Druids, as we shall see later.) These notions of belonging, connecting and communicating are central to Druidism, as they are to many other religions, especially Earth-based or indigenous religions such as those found among American Indians, the Maori peoples of New Zealand, or Australian aborigines. When modern Druids talk about God, or the Goddess, or all the Gods and Goddesses, we are not talking about a distant, separate entity or entities: we are talking about a living, vibrant entity or group of entities that is or are immanent in all things, from quarks to constellations, always accessible through prayer, if we can find the right prayers, or through contemplation. For modern Druids, therefore, there is no real distinction between sacred and secular, or spiritual and material. Modern western society has so compartmentalized and confined God to very limited territories and responsibilities that this concept of universal sacredness or sanctity in all things seems very alien, but in fact the concept is far from new. It is how the Universe was generally perceived in many ancient religions, and is still perceived in many indigenous cultures.

Modern Druids, and Pagans in general, think of the material world, and of our bodies within the world, in a different way to most other religions. We do not move away from the world and away from our bodies towards a distant Heaven: to the contrary, we move and delve into the physical world around us, right now and here, and the reality of our own physical existence, in a constantly evolving exploration, driven by a curiosity which has no end and a hope and sense of purpose which stands its ground. Graham Harvey writes:

> At the root of the difference between Paganism and many other religions is a very different way of relating to the Earth and the body. Pagans say Earth is home and are finding ways to *be* at home in Earth and in bodies. Other religions say Earth is not home and the body is not the true person. Various more important—more holy, more pure, more spiritual or more ultimate—destinations are advertised, such as heaven, nirvana

or enlightenment. Various other parts of the person are more essential, e.g. the spirit, soul or Buddha nature. These locations of virtue and hope define much of what religious people do, say and believe.[3]

For Druids, Heaven and eternity are right here in this table leg, this grain of salt, this thumbnail, this single strand of hair. This sense of the numinous in all things, this profound universal religious awareness, is the exception rather than the rule in the modern, increasingly materialist western world, but it was the absolute foundation rock of the Celtic tribal society from which Druidism first emerged. The Druidism of ancient Britain (and of Gaul too originally) was so universal and potent that a number of classical commentators commented on it. Caesar tells us that Druid leaders met every four years at an international gathering in Britain, probably in Wales, which would have served to standardize and consolidate belief and practice.[4] The Druidic priesthood was universally held in very high regard and esteem, as well as in fear. Druids were reputedly able to kill or cripple people simply by lampooning or satirizing them, so great was the power of true and correct Druidic utterance. Even worse, perhaps, the Irish tradition says that Druids could induce instant insanity by use of the *dlui fulla*, the "madman's wisp," a little wisp of straw or grass into which they had whispered powerful incantations. Druids also used the "stink eye"—like the Irish God Balor, they could maim, blind or even kill someone by staring fixedly at them. The worst civil punishment (perhaps even worse than death) was to be publicly excommunicated or excluded from religious observances. As Caesar describes it:

> This with them is the most severe punishment. Whosoever are so interdicted, are ranked in the number of the impious and the wicked; all forsake them, and shun their company and conversation, lest they should suffer disadvantage from contagion with them: nor is legal right rendered to them when they sue it, nor any honor conferred upon them.[5]

Modern Druidism has nothing to do with deadly satires or curses or ritual excommunication. It is generally a friendly, broad-minded and welcoming religion, which places a great deal of emphasis on healthy, healing and harmonious relationships. What it does share with its ancient original (as well as with many other religions) is the belief that religion or spirituality, or even just philosophy for those who perceive it that way, is not something separate from life. Nor is it a specialized compartment of life that is only accessed or opened on limited, specific occasions, but rather an engagement which is 24/7. It is a way of perceiving and being and relating which never goes away, and which underpins every moment of our existence, the trivial as well as the grandiose.

I said we were diving off the high-board, and I may have induced some dizziness or panic already. Talking with trees? Conscious pebbles? Dirt with a sense of purpose? Well, if we're talking just about philosophy, we have already flown way past the empirical threshold, the line in the sand that says, "Where's your proof?" or "How do you demonstrate this experimentally?" For a few modern Druids, the little I have said is already too much, but— perversely, perhaps—they may just shrug and move on, and still describe themselves as Druids. (In the same way, many Christians may take the story of Adam and Eve as symbolically but not literally true, but that doesn't pre- vent them from maintaining their general Christian belief.) Nevertheless, for most Druids, the nature of matter, of energy, of time and space, is very flexible and still very much to be explored, and science is telling us more and more to keep our eyes and minds open. Quite a few scientists would agree. We have long since left Newton behind, and even Einstein is no longer infallible. Quantum physics and mechanics, recent discoveries in particle physics, and modern cosmogony continue to introduce us to new, sometimes bizarre con- ceptions of how the Universe is put together. We don't know for sure whether there is Dark Matter or not, and even though there is agreement that the Universe is still expanding at a literally astronomical rate, even the Big Bang theory is now in question. Scientists (and particularly mathematicians) talk about multiple or possibly infinite alternative universes, in which an infinite number of realities are possible. In this changed historical context, ontological discussions are no longer so sharply divided between materialists and non- materialists, since the very nature of material, or substance, or reality, has become so complex and multi-dimensional.

For Druids, *anam* is in everything. For the ancient Greeks and Romans, it was ανμω or *animus* that made a thing alive, aware. And, as many religions describe in one form or another, this *animus* or soul can live beyond physical death. Since, for most modern Druids, this means that animals have souls just as much as humans do, many are vegetarians or vegans. Even those who are meat eaters try to do so with respect and reverence, and are concerned to promote humane animal welfare and ethical farming practices.

Gaia, the Environment, Holy Places

This notion of life in all things leads to what is perhaps the most uni- versal characteristic of all modern Druidic individuals, groups and organi- zations: a profound commitment to environmentalism, protection of the Earth, and reverence for all living beings. The Gaia hypothesis, formulated by James Lovelock and Lynn Margulis in the 1970s, suggests that the entire planet of Earth has a system of self-correction to maintain its equilibrium (for example in global temperature and ocean salinity), which amounts, in effect, to a kind of self-consciousness or awareness. That is a step too far for most hard scientists, but there is general acknowledgment that the Earth does make adjustments to itself, even if there is no consciousness (as it is understood scientifically) involved. A prime directive, if you like, for philosophical modern Druids is to be aware of the Earth, to be good stewards of the environment, locally, regionally and globally, and to respect and honor nature deeply. For religious Druids, it is even simpler: the Earth is our Mother.

The Irish word *tuath* (pronounced approximately *too-uh*) means "tribe," "people" or "territory." The Tuatha Dè Danann (pronounced approximately *too-uh-ha-day-dawn-an*), meaning "Peoples of the Gods of Danu") were the Gods and Goddesses who populated Ireland before Christianity, and who still, as fairies or other spirit beings, frequent places which are still holy or magical to Druids and other Pagans to this day. For most practical purposes, our *tuath* as humans (and especially as Druids) is the whole Universe, and within that the totality of our planet or Mother Earth and all things on and in it, with specific *tuatha* or tribes or groups nested inside each other: air, land and ocean, seas, lakes, rivers, mountains, plains, rocks, all vegetation, all animals, humans, ethnic group, nation, region, community, locality, extended family (living and dead), nuclear family, self. Emma Restall Orr describes one of the common core beliefs of modern Druidism as, "honoring of the ancestors and honoring of the land."[6]

The ancient Druids conducted their ceremonies in different places, possibly including wooden halls or temples, but the evidence suggests that most if not all ceremonial took place in the open air. Since certain places themselves were especially charged with their own spiritual energy, it was in such places that ritual most likely took place most frequently. It was not Druids who built the stone circles and alignments found extensively in Britain and elsewhere in Europe—they predate the Druids by centuries if not millennia—but Druids almost certainly used them, since they seem to have been aware of their calendrical significance and they definitely could not have failed to recognize their spiritual potency. Lakes, rivers, springs and wells were also powerful places. The word *nemeton* comes from Old Irish *nemed*, via Latin *nemus* and Greek νεμω or *nemoo*, meaning "grove" or "wood with grazing land." It is usually translated as "grove," implying a clearing in the forest, but "grove" has limited meaning, and estuaries, ridges, hills, escarpments, even individual rocks and trees would also all have had their own *anam* or identity, and open-air worship may have taken place in a wide variety of locations and settings.

That is still true of modern Druidism. By and large, we do not meet in churches, temples, halls, or religious buildings. Most ceremonial is conducted outdoors, usually in a natural setting, and usually in close proximity to water, rocks, trees, or any combination of those. For some groups, a ritual is not valid unless a living tree makes up part of the sacred ceremonial space or *nemeton*. Sometimes we make do with somebody's back garden. Many Druids, myself included, have several different regular places for prayer and contemplation, and visit them in rotation. I have the great good fortune to live on a tiny island in the Inner Hebrides of Scotland, a rugged place surrounded by the Atlantic Ocean, where there are many suitable prayer sites to choose from. People living in the inner city may be restricted to a particular lawn or tree or even a window box, but Gaia is always there to be found, even if only in a single blade of grass.

Famous Sacred Sites

Since classical Druidism appears to have either originated in Britain, or to have established early prominence there, some of Britain's many ancient sites have strong and ancient Druidic connections, and have become famous as a result. The most famous, of course, is Stonehenge. As we shall discuss in more detail in Chapter 6, the antiquarian William Stukeley denied that Stonehenge was ever used by Pagans, believing its creators to have been Biblical patriarchs. The current Druids using and preserving Stonehenge are the Grove of Aes Dana, whose up-to-date information can be accessed online at www.stonehenge-druids.org. (A list of group contact information is given in Appendix B.) Aes Dana have made a strong connection with the Amauta people of Bolivia, so as well as its general attraction as an international tourist destination, modern Druids are keeping this world-famous sacred site in touch with other indigenous spiritual cultures.

Nearby Avebury, which is physically much larger than Stonehenge (it is so large that a village sits inside the main stone circle) is actually three stone circles, built in the Neolithic or New Stone Age period. In May 2008, the British Druid Order and friends from the Order of Bards, Ovates and Druids (OBOD) conducted ceremonies at Avebury, including a ritual of the World Drum, a project founded in Norway in October 2006, with focus on peace and environmental issues. The World Drum itself is a shaman drum made in Sami (indigenous people of Finland and Norway) traditional style, intended to bring people together across race, religion, borders, cultures, ethnicity, or political conviction in a common struggle for humanity and Mother Earth. Further details are available at http://www.theworlddrum.com.

How many modern Druids are there? Philip Carr-Gomm, Chief of the British-based Order of Bards, Ovates and Druids (OBOD), which he claims is the largest single Druid organization in the world, says that OBOD itself has 20,000 individual members, and over 175 Groves and Seed Groups of the Order across the world.[7] That would make the total number of modern Druids probably well over 50,000 and perhaps closer to 100,000. Markale would consider even that number a gross underestimation: he unequivocally claims that there are "perhaps a million people throughout the entire world, principally in Europe, America and Australia, who claim to be Druids or affiliated to Druidic orders or brotherhoods."[8]

Almost all of the well-known sacred sites in the USA are Native American. They include: Cahokia Mounds in Missouri, where a wooden circle called Woodhenge imitates the Woodhenge near Stonehenge in England; Crater Lake in Oregon, which is sacred to the Klamath nation; Mount Shasta in California, a still potentially active volcano sacred to several Native American nations; Devil's Tower in Wyoming, which featured in the film *Close Encounters of the Third Kind*; Bighorn Medicine Wheel in the Bighorn National Forest, Wyoming, which functions as an astronomical alignment in the same way as many of Britain's ancient stone circles; and Sedona in Arizona, which has been the spiritual center for many Native American nations, including the Hohokam, the Sinagua, the Yavapai and the Apache. There may well be interactions between Native Americans and Druidic groups and individuals at these and many other sites, but those interactions will typically go unrecorded. For example, my American wife (who now lives with me in Scotland and who, rather extraordinarily, is part Cherokee but also speaks Welsh) was for some years the fire maker and guardian for a group in Oregon (our "prayer family") who still hold regular prayer meetings and sweat lodges which combine Celtic Druidic and Native American traditions. We shall return to the American scene in greater detail in later chapters.

World Connections

We will look in detail at the Celtic pantheon of Gods and Goddesses in Chapter 3, but here I am simply describing some of the possible connections between modern Druidism and other traditions and religions. Revived or modern Druidism is just one of many reconstructions or adaptations of religions from other times and other places. Pagan spirituality comes in many forms. Because modern Druids are endlessly curious as well as (usually) very open-minded, many have taken an interest in all other religions, and some have taken into their worship and rituals deities and themes from other traditions, the three main sources being: the Greek and Roman classical pantheons; the traditional Northern pantheon, which includes both Norse and Germanic deities; and indigenous native pantheons, such as those of the Maori people in New Zealand or the Aborigine peoples of Australia, or nature-based and ancestor-based religions in South America, Asia and Africa. There is not space here to detail any more than a few of these, but the examples will illustrate the possible connections.

Hellenic polytheism is based on the Greek pantheon. Its principal Gods are generally well known in western culture: Cronos, the father of time; Zeus, father and king of the Gods; Hera, his wife and queen; Poseidon, brother of Zeus, God of the sea; Hades, also Zeus's brother, God of the Underworld, husband of Persephone, the queen of the dead; Athena or Athene, also called Pallas Athene, Goddess of wisdom, whose totem animal is the owl, and who gives her name to the city of Athens; Hermes, son of Zeus, messenger of the Gods; Ares, the God of war; Aphrodite, the Goddess of love, who was born of sea-foam; Artemis, Goddess of the moon and the hunt; Apollo, brother of Artemis, God of the sun, and of wisdom, poetry and music. These Greek Gods (there are hundreds more) were later adopted by the Romans. *Religio Romana* is a modern Pagan religion based specifically on the Roman pantheon. The Roman equivalents of the Greek Gods listed above are: Saturn for Cronos; Jupiter or Juppiter for Zeus; Neptune for Poseidon; Dis or Pluto for Hades; Minerva for Athene; Mercury for Hermes; Mars for Ares; Venus for Aphrodite; Diana for Artemis; and Apollo remains Apollo.

The Northern or Germanic Gods also define themselves either by family position and connection, or by specific area of responsibility or expertise. Many of the reconstructionist Pagan groups who follow the Northern path, most of them now in the United States, use the name Ásatrú, which means followers of the Æsir, the senior Gods of the Norse pantheon. Practitioners are known as Ásatrúer or Ásatrúar. Odinism, Wotanism and Heathenry (adherents prefer the title "Heathen" to "Pagan") are other names for the movement. Again, through popular culture, quite a few of the Northern Gods are generally quite well known: Odin, Woden or Wotan, known as Allfather, father and king of the Gods; Frigg or Frigga, mother and queen of the Gods, Goddess of fertility; Thor, son of Odin, God of thunder and war; Tir, Tyr or Tiw, also a God of war; Freyja, Goddess of love; Baldur, God of beauty, innocence and peace; Loki, God of mischief and harm; Éostre, Goddess of spring, after whom Easter is named, whose totem animal was the hare or rabbit, from which the Easter Bunny is derived (she is also related to the Sumerian Goddess Ishtar or Inanna, who was crucified on a stake and ascended from the Underworld after her death); Heimdall, gatekeeper of Asgard, home of the Gods. Four of these Gods are so deeply embedded in English-speaking cultures that we name days of the week after them: Tuesday is Tiw's Day, Wednesday is Woden's or Odin's Day, Thursday is Thor's Day, and Friday is Frigg's Day.

Unfortunately, some American Nordic Pagan groups have been tainted by racism and far-right political activism. Some of the groups are also heavily dominated by men and by anti-feminist sentiments. At the time of writing (2017), the Ásatrú Folk Assembly or AFA, which calls itself a "folkish Heathen" group, has been banned from Facebook for posting racially charged and homophobic material, including reference to "our feminine ladies, our masculine gentlemen and, above all, our beautiful white children."[9] In an attempt to distance themselves from the misogynist and right-wing elements, there are now Heathen groups who call themselves Vanatrú ("those who honor the Vanir," the Vanir being the deities who make up the other half of the pantheon). There are even some Heathens who call themselves Dísitrú ("those who honor the Goddess").[10] The vast majority of Pagan groups are tolerant, anti-homophobic and anti-racist, and are embarrassed, discomfited and saddened by these disputes and value clashes.

Witchcraft of one form or another has a long history in different parts of the world. The name Wicca is given to many modern groups whose religion and practices are based on revivals or reconstructions of the ancient witchcraft traditions. The modern movement began in Britain with Gerald Gardner in the 1950s, and we will look at that development in more detail in Chapter 7. Gardner himself used the term "witchcraft," or simply, "the craft," but since centuries of persecution and vilification have loaded the word "witch" with sinister or evil connotations, the name Wicca, derived from the Old English words *wicce* and *wicca*, meaning male witch and female witch respectively, was adopted and promoted by Gardner in the 1960s and has now become very widely accepted and understood. Many Wiccans associate *wicce* and *wicca* with the ancient word-root *wit*, meaning wisdom, in the same way that some Druids believe the origin of the word "druid" to be *deru-* or *derow-wit*, meaning "oak wisdom," but the more likely root is Proto-Indo-European *wic*, which means bending, shaping, changing or molding. Many Wiccans refer to Wicca as "the Craft of the Wise," also "Wisecraft" and "Wiccacreaft." Wicca has a pantheon of just two Gods, the Great God, sometimes described as the Horned God, and the Great Goddess or Mother Goddess. Some modern Druids are also Wiccans, but Wicca places more emphasis on magic and manipulation of events, and is different from Druidism in other ways. However, as we shall discuss later, Philip Carr-Gomm believes that Druidism and Wicca have a great deal in common, so much so that the OBOD program incorporates some elements of Wicca, and Carr-Gomm introduced the term "Druidcraft" to encapsulate that connection.[11] Stregheria, which is an Italian variant of Wicca, is also called *La Vecchia Religione* in Italian, simply meaning "the old religion"; it traces its reconstruction to roots in pre–Christian Italy and central Europe.

Even if Wicca is close to Druidism in many respects, it is still very different, in my view, despite Philip Carr-Gomm's beliefs. Dr. Ronald Hutton, a professor of history at the University of Bristol in England and renowned expert on Druidism, explains the differences he sees, at least as far as Britain is concerned:

> British Wicca is much longer-established than British Druidry, and its identity is far more fixed: conversely, it lacks some of the raw energy of the younger movement, being

rather less prone to flexibility, experimentation and adaptation. It is much more strongly a mystery religion, carried on in private and with only initiates present except at specific more open festivals. Druidry by contrast courts public attention and involvement, holds daylight rituals as prominently as those of night and the tween-times, and (save in the higher grades of the mystic Orders) is much more open to friends and relatives (including children) of members. Ritual is central to Wicca and peripheral or occasional in some Druid Orders and costume is definitive for most Druids. Wicca normally creates a level of intensity of experience rare in Druidry, and has a more pronounced sense of creating and controlling its sacred space; it is also inclined to be far more risqué and dramatic, incorporating nudity and sexuality and achieving altered states of consciousness in a way which is also unusual among Druids. Druidry has very little sense of working magic, and energy is only regularly raised through the "awen" chant: magic and energy raising are integral to Wicca. Druidry is far more concerned with healing the ills of its members, the land, and the planet, and is proportionately now much more mixed up with radical politics than Wicca. It is also more closely aligned to "alternative" lifestyles and the New Age. It is also more concerned to produce literature, art, and music.[12]

The Gods of the Maori tradition are called the *atua*. Ranginui is the Sky Father and Papatūānuku is the Earth Mother. From their eternal embrace or love-making, all other Gods were created. The main Gods reflect the most immediate areas of concern for ordinary people: Tangaroa is God of the sea; Tāwhirimātea is God of the sky and the wind; Tāne is God of the forest; Haumia is God of the wild harvest, natural fruits and vegetables; Rongo is God of cultivated foods and animal husbandry. Tāne, God of the forest, shaped the first woman and first human, Hineahuone, from earth, and took her as his wife, and all humans are descended from them.

The culture of the Australian aborigines is the oldest continuously maintained human culture in the world (along with Canada's First Nations and America's Native American tribal nations, perhaps). Aborigines settled in Australia some 40,000 years ago (recent research suggests perhaps more than 80,000 years ago), and their religion and traditions have therefore developed over a tremendously long period of time. The center-point of Australian aboriginal religion is the Dreaming. The Universe and the Earth, and everything in them, were created by a divine act of imagination or dreaming which has no time, and therefore comes from an eternal past, continues into the present, and will extend into an eternal future. Through rites of passage and through prayer, humans can connect to the eternal Dreaming, and our lives, thoughts and actions become part of the Dreaming after we are gone. Like the ancient Druids, and like most Native Americans, Aborigines connect their "songlines" or religious stories to specific places within a landscape perceived to be sacred and alive. Uluru, which sits massively right in the heart of Australia, is a famous example of a site of huge religious and spiritual significance. (The indigenous Aborigines call it by its ancient name, Uluru, and deride its "official" map name Ayers Rock as a recent, colonialist imposition.) Following decades of evangelical proselytizing, about two thirds of Australian aboriginal people now describe themselves as Christian, although the traditional religion remains deeply embedded in their culture.

Africa is a vast continent of many countries, with a huge range of languages, cultures and religions. The dominant African religions today are Christianity and Islam, but the most enduring and influential ancient African religion came from Egypt. There were followers of Egyptian religion among the Roman troops who occupied Britain for the first four centuries of the Common Era (although they were a very small minority), and modern Druids who also invoke Egyptian deities are part of a very long tradition of Egyptology. There are over 2,000 named Gods in the Egyptian pantheon. The main or best-known are: Osiris, God of life, death and resurrection; Isis, Goddess of nature, health, magic and wisdom, still very widely worshipped to this day by Pagans in many different traditions; Horus, God of the sky, portrayed with the head of a falcon, with whom many Egyptian kings or pharaohs identified themselves (and who, according to legend, was born on the 25th of December, as was also Mithras, the sun–God of Mithraism); Ra, the God of the sun, later combined with Amun to become Amun-Ra, father and king of the Gods; Bastet, daughter of Ra and Goddess of protection, portrayed as a cat (cats were sacred animals in Egypt); Anubis, God of mummification and the dead, portrayed with the head of a jackal; Hathor, Goddess of love, beauty, music and dance; Sekmet, Goddess of war, portrayed with the head of a lioness; Thoth, God of wisdom and writing. Many of the British Druids who were active in the Romantic Revival of the 18th and 19th centuries were keen Egyptologists, as we shall see in more detail in Chapter 6.

Decades and in some cases centuries of missionary influence have brought Christianity, Islam and Judaism to many African countries, but there are still estimated to be 100 million people in Africa following ancient national or tribal religions.[13] Mantric drumming and singing, which are also popular with many modern Druids, are commonly used in rituals in many African religions, since drums and simple flutes are the most ancient musical instruments. Respect is paid to the ancestors, with libations or regular offerings to the dead featuring in many traditions. Some African native religions are monotheistic: for example, the Kikuyu and Kamba worship a father-God whom they call Ngai. Mungu, Murungu and Mulungu are variant names for the father-God used by many nations and languages, including Yao, Swahili and the Zambese of Zambia. Unkulunkulu is a Zulu alternative. As in early Celtic mythology, animals often have totemic roles. For example, in Bantu culture (which encompasses many different ethnic groups), the story goes that God sent the chameleon to tell humans that they would never die. But the chameleon was slow and preoccupied with finding succulent plants to eat, so the lizard rushed ahead, hoping to please God, but garbled the divine message, saying that they *would* die, and so death was brought into the world, and lizards and chameleons are to this day both considered animals of ill-fortune.

In Asia, the religions of Buddhism and Taoism are so different from Druidism that there are few, if any, obvious connections, apart from one glaringly obvious one, namely the doctrine of *karma*. From a Sanskrit term originally meaning work, action or deed, *karma* as a spiritual or philosophical term has come to mean the mechanism by which an individual's thoughts and actions (the cause) directly influence the outcome of those thoughts and actions (the effect). Although that definition is relatively simple, whole books have been written about *karma* and its significance in relation to spiritual thinking. (The old joke is: My *karma* just ran over your dogma.) It relates strongly to Druidism for two reasons: firstly, because Druids ancient and Druids modern (mostly) believe in a real life which we experience both before we are born and after we are dead, and *karma* is similarly founded on a belief in an individual's progression through a single existence made from many lives, sometimes through many life forms, animal as well as human; secondly, because Druidism, again both ancient and modern, places great emphasis on individual moral responsibility, on the idea that we "reap what we sow" and that every thought and action, from the trivial to the grand, has consequences somewhere further along the line of time.

Hindu *karma* differs in several respects from Buddhist *karma*, and the Hindu pantheon has a vast multitude of Gods and Goddesses, which increases its general appeal for polytheistic Druids. Again, there are far too many Gods, Goddesses, incarnations and avatars to list in detail here, and they will almost certainly be less familiar to most readers than the classical or Northern Gods, but here are some of the most widely recognized Hindu deities: Brahma the Creator, Vishnu the Preserver and Siva or Shiva the Destroyer (frequently depicted with many arms and one foot raised) are the three most powerful Gods, some commentators describing them as the equivalent of the Christian Holy Trinity, with Saivists (devotees of Shiva) arguing that Brahma and Vishnu are actually lesser beings, since Shiva created them from within himself; Devi, the Great Mother Goddess, who is also called Parvati as Shiva's wife or Lakshmi as Vishnu's wife; Rama, the seventh avatar of Vishnu and hero of the great Hindu epic the Ramayana; Krishna, the eighth incarnation of Vishnu and the God of love and compassion, very widely revered, usually depicted as blue-skinned; Ganesh, son of Shiva and Parvati, depicted as an elephant, God of wisdom; Saraswati, wife of Brahma, Goddess of music and the arts; Hanuman, the monkey God and 11th incarnation of Shiva.

The Face of God: Monotheism, Duotheism and Polytheism

The three main patriarchal religions, Christianity, Islam and Judaism, insist that there is only one God, and that to worship other Gods is sinful and idolatrous. The ancient Celts believed in many Gods, as is confirmed by archaeological evidence, place names, comments by classical Roman historians, and references in the Celtic vernacular mythology, despite the fact that it was Christian scribes who first wrote those tales and poems down. For modern Druids, there are four logical choices, humanism, monotheism, duotheism and polytheism, and each of them is followed by at least some individuals or groups. Many modern Druids, while recognizing that far more complex explanations of the ordering of the Universe are now discussed in both science and religion, maintain the ancient Druidic tradition of "the three worlds"—Land or Earth, where spirits and humans live, Sky, where the Gods live, and Water or Sea, which is the home of the ancestors.

For those who reject any idea of spirits or a supernatural God or Gods, modern Druidism still offers a coherent philosophical approach to life, including a sound basis for moral and ethical decision-making. This could be called the humanist Druidic approach. Respect and responsibility, which figure largely in Druidic thinking, are universal virtues. Respect for our planet, for the creatures that inhabit it, for the natural world and all its environments, and for each other as humans, makes sense, whether you believe in a deity or not. Modern Druidism is also committed to world peace, and many of its teachings about relationships and communities are really just common sense writ large. Confucianism, founded on the teachings of Confucius or Kung Fu Tze in 6th-century BCE China, also contains a great deal of social and ethical philosophy, and in that respect is similar to modern Druidism. In our increasingly secular age, many people are not only positively convinced by scientific and empirical methodology and thinking, they are also negatively suspicious of religion in general, of what they might call superstition and self-delusion. Modern Druidism says to them, "That's okay—we're not forcing you to swallow any dogma," but at the same time it offers a positive and assertive world view and a coherent moral philosophy which emerges from that view.

Most modern Druids, however, live out their Druidism as a spiritual and religious path, as well as a philosophical one. Those who believe in one God are called monotheists. For monotheist modern Druids, the deity is either God, or the Goddess. The patriarchal religions have so greatly influenced our western culture that most people think of God as male (even if they no longer believe in God!) so to think of God as the Goddess, as Our Lady instead of Our Lord, or as Our Mother as opposed to "Our Father which art in Heaven," may be difficult for many people. It may be intuitive on a personal and emotional level, but still counter-cultural on a community level. Nevertheless, many modern Druids, following their inclination to be independent, quirky if necessary, and free-thinking, have avoided the traditional androcentric and patriarchal image of God as a venerable old man with a white beard, and have wholeheartedly reverted to the Goddess. Without any hard and fast statistical evidence to support it, my feeling is that most modern Druids are polytheists who give allegiance to many Gods and Goddesses, but give their supreme allegiance to the Goddess, modeled on the Great Mother Goddess of ancient millennia (although, in fairness, I should point out that not all modern Druids accept the idea of a Great Mother Goddess or Earth Mother, seeing that as essentially a Wiccan concept). Some have no difficulty in describing themselves as simultaneously monotheists and polytheists. (We can be very flexible.) Morgan McFarland wrote to Margot Adler:

> I consider myself a polytheist, as in the statement Isis makes in *The Golden Ass* when she says, "From me come all Gods and Goddesses who exist." So that I see myself as monotheistic in believing in the Goddess, the Creatrix, the Female Principle, but at the same time acknowledging that other Gods and Goddesses do exist through her as manifestations of her, facets of the whole.[14]

To avoid conflict over the what-gender-is-God issue, many modern Druidic groups (and notably the influential Order of Bards, Ovates and Druids) often use the neutral term Spirit or Great Spirit, and such consideration for the sensitivities of others is typical of the modern Druidic ethos. It also has the added advantage of echoing modern Native American practice, in which tribal names for God like Gitchi Manitou (Anishinabe nation), Wakanda (Omaha nation) or Wakan Tanka (Sioux nation) are often substituted by a general invocation, "O Great Spirit…"

Belief in two Gods is called duotheism. As mentioned earlier, it is the fundamental basis of Wicca, the two Gods being the male God and the female Goddess. Those modern Druids who are also Wiccan, or who absorb parts of Wicca into their belief and practice, could be called duotheists.

The Gods, Goddesses, heroes and heroines of polytheistic Celtic Druidism are legion, and their relationships can sometimes appear even more complex and confusing than the almost countless variants, reincarnations and avatars of the Hindu pantheon. We shall explore the Celtic pantheon in more detail in Chapter 3.

Life After Death, the Otherworld, the Afterworld, Reincarnation

Classical Druidism included belief in a life beyond this mortal life, although the Celtic versions of the afterlife and the Otherworld differ in many ways from both the classical visions of Hades, the River Styx, the Elysian Fields and so on, and the later Christian and Islamic visions of Heaven and Paradise.

The Celtic vernacular legend of the Assembly of the Wondrous Head tells the tale of the Welsh giant, king and God, Brân, also called Bendigeidfran or Brân Fendigaidd, literally "Blessed Crow" or "Blessed Raven"). Mortally wounded in battle (Gods can die in Celtic mythology), he orders his men to strike off his head. Reluctantly, they obey his command and are astonished to discover that the head remains alive and alert. The head commands them that under no circumstance may any of them look towards Cornwall. For seven years (which appears to them to be a blissful eternity) they travel with Brân's head, enjoying the God's company, until one of them forgets the order and inadvertently turns his gaze towards Cornwall. The God's head immediately begins to decay. He orders his followers to carry him swiftly to London and to bury the head on the White Hill where the Tower of London now stands, since Britain can never be successfully invaded while Brân remains on guard there. As we have seen, Brân's name means "crow" or "raven," which explains why there have been and will always be ravens (and official raven keepers, called "Raven Masters") at the Tower of London, and why their presence is so significant.

Caesar tells us that Gaulish warriors agreed that if they were killed in battle they would settle any small outstanding debts in the next life. He took that as evidence of how the Celts' deep and literal belief in a real and personal life after death made it easy for them to be fearsome and extraordinarily courageous warriors.

But there is also evidence from the vernacular texts that death was never taken lightly or casually. In the Irish tales, Muichertach, King of Ireland, "casts out" his family to take in the mysterious, unbearably beautiful Goddess Sín (pronounced *sheen* and meaning "Storm"—she is a personification of Death). Muichertach seats her at his right hand. After she has performed several miracles and magical feats for him, he innocently utters her name, which she has forbidden him to do. His *geis* or fate descends on him and he dies, drowned in a barrel of wine while his burning palace crashes about his head. The vernacular tales frequently mention omens of inevitable death, and Celtic folklore makes much of dogs howling, trees blossoming out of season, cocks crowing at midnight, and so on. In the Irish stories, sometimes collectively referred to as "death tales," the great hero or God tends to die not in his bed, but in battle, and at a time of flux or uncertainty: Cú Roí, Crimthann, Cú Chulainn and Conaire all die at Samhain, the autumn festival in the Celtic year, while Ailill and Flann die at Beltan, the spring festival.[15]

The belief in metempsychosis, or the "transmigration of souls," appears also to have been literal. This idea, closely related to the eastern concept of *karma*, mentioned earlier, and frequently also associated with the Greek philosopher Pythagoras, has been garbled by western tradition into the notion that weak or sinful humans are punished by returning to life as a "lesser" animal, as described in Shakespeare's *Twelfth Night*:

> CLOWN: What is the opinion of Pythagoras concerning wildfowl?
>
> MALVOLIO: That the soul of our grandam might haply inhabit a bird.
>
> CLOWN: What thinkest thou of his opinion?
>
> MALVOLIO: I think nobly of the soul, and no way approve his opinion.

Pythagoras lived on the Greek island of Samos, later moving to Croton in southern Italy, and flourished about 530 BCE. Clement of Alexandria, writing in the first century CE, claimed that Pythagoras learned the doctrine of metempsychosis *from* the Druids (rather than introducing it *to* the Druids), specifically from one "Abaris the Hyperborean," signifying Abaris who lived beyond Boreas, the North Wind, i.e., someone from the furthest northern reaches of the world. If Clement's account is true, Abaris is the earliest named Druid in history, and he probably came from Britain.

Most (but not all) modern Druidic organizations specifically mention reincarnation or life after death in their literature. However, if we return to consideration of the concept of *anam* which we discussed earlier in this chapter, it is obvious that the enthusiastic Druidic animist conception of what life means and signifies almost automatically leads to a similar conception of what death means: it is not an end, but a passage to a new beginning. After our physical death, every atom, every particle, every sub-particle of our body transforms itself and goes on somewhere else, to be part of something else, but retains its own *anam*, and our identity as an individual, our complete *anam*, also continues to live, change, experience, act and move forward within the Universe or the many universes.

For the ancient Druids, there was both an Otherworld (or Underworld) and an Afterworld. The Otherworld was a place of transition, called Annwn (pronounced approximately *an-oon*) or Annwfn in the Welsh vernacular texts. Creatures from Annwn are easily recognized by their white skin or fur and the red in their eyes and on the tips of their ears. In Druidism, white and red (not black) are the colors of death. But Annwn is not a place of punishment, or even a terrifying place—it is just another place, although magical— Ellen Evert Hopman describes it as "a place of feasting, competitions and magical pigs that are eaten and each day come magically back to life."[16]

In *Pwyll Prince of Dyfed*, one of the tales from the Welsh mediaeval stories known collectively as the *Mabinogi* or *Mabinogion*, Pwyll (pronounced approximately *pwilth*) is hunting with his dogs in the forest when another pack of dogs approaches:

... Of all the hounds he had seen in the world, he had seen no dogs the same colour as these. The colour that was on them was a brilliant shining white, and their ears red; and as the exceeding whiteness of the dogs glittered, so glittered the exceeding redness of their ears.[17]

The hounds belong to Arawn, the king of Annwn. Pwyll drives them away from the stag they have caught and allows his own pack to finish off the stag, which Arawn not unreasonably takes as an insult. In recompense for the insult, Arawn asks Pwyll to look after the kingdom of Annwn for him for a year, since he has to go off and fight a battle with someone else and needs a caretaker king. Arawn shape-shifts Pwyll into his own likeness (shape-shifting was a skill practiced by Druids as well as Gods). Pwyll spends "a year and a day" ruling Annwn in Arawn's place, while Arawn, in the form of Pwyll, rules Pwyll's kingdom of Dyfed and brings fertility and prosperity to the kingdom. Pwyll rises admirably to the challenge of ruling Annwn wisely, including having the decency to avoid having sex with Arawn's queen despite spending every night for a year in the same bed with her. After the end of the year, when they have changed back into their own bodies and semblances, Pwyll takes on the honorific title of Pen Annwn ("Chief of the Otherworld"), and returns to long and successful rule over Dyfed.

The traditional Celtic Paradise or Afterworld is Afalon (pronounced *a-va-lon*), Ynys Afallach, Ynys Afallon, Avalon, or Avallen, all meaning literally Isle of Apple Trees or Apple Orchard, where it is always summer and harvest time, there is no pain or suffering, and the lowly and humble can speak with and enjoy the company of kings and queens, heroes and Gods. Tennyson calls it:

> ... the island-valley of Avilion,
> Where falls not hail, or rain, or any snow,
> Nor ever wind blows loudly ...[18]

The Sumerians, Greeks, Etruscans and Romans all had much darker and gloomier notions of the Afterworld, which contrasted greatly with the bright Celtic vision. Even the Christian Heaven offered later seemed rather quiet and dull by comparison with the active joys and pleasures of Afalon, where food and drink and music and dance and merrymaking await in abundance. Rather like the Valhalla of the Northern tradition, Afalon was seen as especially welcoming for warriors who died in battle. The name first appears in writing as *Insula Avallonis* ("The Island of Avalon") in Geoffrey of Monmouth's *Historia Regorum Britanniae* ("History of the Kings of Britain"), published in 1132, but it is clear that Geoffrey took the name from a much older oral tradition, keeping the pronunciation but changing the spelling of the original Welsh *Afalon* (*afal*, pronounced *a-val*, is the Welsh for "apple"). The apple was one of the sacred Druidic trees, as we shall discuss later. In English

Arthurian legend, Afalon is the island to which King Arthur was taken after receiving a mortal blow in his final battle at Camlann. Because Arthur is reputed to have been buried there, the English town of Glastonbury is closely associated with Afalon. (Many other places, within England and beyond, also claim to be Arthur's burial sites.) Glastonbury Tor, a conspicuous mound and sacred site just outside the town, stands above a flood plain, which in mediaeval times frequently made it genuinely an island. The old Celtic name for Glastonbury is Ynys Wedrenn (*un-iss-wed-ren*), literally "Isle of Glass," the root of the later "Glaston-" or "Glass Town" -bury or burg, i.e., Glaston-bury.

In classical Druidic descriptions of such Afterworld places, there are repeated allusions to the notion of an *anam* or identity that is maintained outside or beyond mortal life. A cooked salmon is brought in for a feast, but no matter how much it is eaten, it remains whole, and still alive. A cauldron provides endless food and cannot be emptied, as long as those eating from it are people of courage and honor. Birds, other animals and humans all converse and understand each other perfectly.

Modern Druids probably perceive Afalon or the Afterworld in as many richly diverse and variegated ways as they perceive this one we live in, and are probably just as flexible and accommodating towards views different from their own. Although their visions may not be identical, what they will mostly have in common is an optimism and an expectation that life continues, either in some new form as in *karma*, or in some other dimension or form as yet not clearly known to us.

2. Moral Philosophy

For modern Druids, morality and ethics are of central importance. Erynn Rowan Laurie, a poet and author on Druidism explains why:

> Ethics are important. Not as the "Wiccan rede," which has no basis in Celtic tradition, but ethics based on the Brehon laws and the practices of the early Celtic peoples. Some of these ideas need to be modified to fit into modern society, but I think that the Gaulish injunction to worship the Gods, to do no evil, and to exercise strength is crucial, as is the Celtic dedication to the truth and a strong sense of ethics about what is right and what is wrong. The Celts were not an "anything goes" kind of people. They had a very complex body of laws governing what was appropriate and what was not. Celtic Pagans need both a strong sense of personal responsibility and a code of personal and social ethics in order to carry the Celtic spirit forward.[1]

(The "Wiccan rede" says, "An (if) it harm none, do as thou wilt," or, in more colloquial modern English, "Do what you like, as long as nobody gets hurt." The Brehon laws are a long and elaborate set of mostly civil laws written in Ireland in the early Middle Ages.)

Fír Fer

Fír fer or *fíre fer* is another Irish Gaelic expression. It is the current motto of *Ollscoil na hÉireann*, the National University of Ireland, where it is translated as "Manhood's Truth," which is the literal translation. It has been used to describe one of three fundamental moral principles in Druidism, and in that context "fair play," "fair dealing" or even "courage to do the right thing on principle" might be more accurate equivalents. The word *fíre* means "truthfulness," "sincerity," "genuineness" or "fidelity." The nature of *fír fer* is simple, and easily explained and understood, but its ultimate impact on the whole of western culture has been profound and longlasting.

If five warriors come in from one side of a battlefield, and one enemy warrior comes in from the other side, a fight between them is not a fair fight, and is not honorable. One against one is fair, or five against five, but one against five is not. That seems an extremely simple and obvious moral principle to us now, but before the Druids it was scarcely thought of. More fool (or more's the pity) for the single warrior was the original moral stance, and there are plenty of people who to this day will revert to that jungle law in a heartbeat and have nothing but contempt for those who are weak enough to think differently. But for Druids, ancient and modern, adherence to moral principle is far more important than any tactical or material advantage.

Another very well known example of *fír fer* is expressed in the old saying, "My word is my bond." In the warrior culture of ancient Celtic tribal society, this simple but extremely powerful moral principle had many practical effects and consequences. Captured prisoners, for example, could be released through ransom or exchange, and, once made, those contracts were absolutely inviolable by both sides. In the west, this deeply-seated respect for truth and honor manifested itself in the parole system in common use all the way up to the Napoleonic wars, in which prisoners would swear solemnly not to try to escape, and their captors would no longer place them behind bars or under physical restraint, but would accept their word of honor. (*Parole* is French for "word.") In the 1840s, this military parole was extended into civilian life by Alexander Maconochie, a Scottish naval captain who was in charge of the British convict colonies in Norfolk Island, Australia. He began offering early conditional release to prisoners who showed signs of rehabilitation and responsibility, and parole is now an established judicial rehabilitation procedure throughout the world.

The idea of *fír fer* transferred itself, over the course of many centuries, into the chivalric code, which applied originally only to the *chevaliers* or mounted and heavily-armored knights of the mediaeval courts, but which spread widely, mostly under Norman-French influence, across the whole of Europe. From there it became absorbed into Christian clerical and ecclesiastical thinking, and ultimately into the general moral fabric of western civilization.

In the original context of a highly stratified Celtic tribal society, *fír fer* offered extremely valuable protections. For example, it meant that the fine payable for a crime by a poor man could be less than the fine paid by a rich man for the same offence, even though the crimes were identical; the punishment would have a proportional impact on each perpetrator, and *fír fer* would thus be preserved.

It also offered protections for women and children. Women had equal status to men in many aspects of early Celtic tribal life. Celtic tribes, even large and powerful ones, were often ruled by women rather than by men, a practice which was extremely unusual in the classical ancient world. Male dominance over women was established very early in Europe, perhaps as early as 2500 BCE, and certainly well before the emergence of classical Greek civilization. In classical ancient Europe, there were only two groups for whom women held status equal or at least very similar to that of men: the tiny group of the followers of Pythagoras, who believed that women were as capable mathematicians as men, and Celtic tribal society, in which women could inherit property, could rule as queens, could become Druids, and where matrilinear descent and authority were as valid as patrilinear. Simple though the concept of *fír fer* was, it runs right through early Celtic culture in general and the Irish mediaeval Brehon laws in particular.

Fír fer applies to this day in sport as it once did in battle. The Cornish have a saying *"Gwari teg yw gwari hweg"* ("Fair play is fine play"), and "Fair play, now" is still a very common Welsh expression of justification. For modern Druids, it still describes a natural justice which is born of practicality and common sense, and sticks to an ethical principle, but which is capable of generating huge practical advantages in terms of human relationships and civic stability.

The Fitness of Things

The second of the three broad moral principles is the fitness of things, which is illustrated most frequently in the vernacular stories and myths. As the name suggests, thoughts and deeds should be fit and be appropriate to the given circumstances. An old saying which comes close to defining it is, "The punishment should fit the crime."

In the Welsh tale *Branwen, Daughter of Lyr*, again from the *Mabinogi*, the hero Matholwch, whose fine horses have been maimed and ruined, is offered in compensation a sound horse for every one maimed, with a staff of silver "as thick as his little finger" and "a plate of gold as broad as his face," as appropriate and sufficient recompense for the insult and suffering afforded him. What is significant about these compensations is that they far exceed the monetary value of the maimed horses. They take into account the insult, the anxiety, the grief and distress which Matholwch has had to endure. Suffering has a value, which needs to be taken into account if true justice is to prevail. As a moral concept, this is surprisingly modern, especially since it is derived from such an ancient source. In the Middle Ages, it would have been unthinkable, and even the Christian Victorians would have struggled with the concept that the overall balance of the fitness of things was more important than simple monetary or material restoration.

It is the natural world that provides the model for such balance. The tribal Druids were the judges of the ancient Celtic world, and they gave judgment even against kings, because their religious authority was derived from the immense, unstoppable and natural authority of life itself. Every *tuath* has its rights, springing from its *anam* or aliveness and its inclusion in the aliveness of all things.

A modern version of the fitness of things is restorative justice, which tries to bring together perpetrators and victims of crime in a positive way, to allow the perpetrators to fully understand the impact of their wrongdoing and the victims to explain what restoration or compensation would be most effective in helping them to recover from their distress. It is used both in legal courts and in many schools, where it supports or replaces traditional disciplinary protocols and procedures. For modern Druids, restoring harmony after conflict or crime is always best done through communication, and restorative justice is a worthy descendant of the ancient Druidic principle of the fitness of things.

True and Correct Utterance, y gwir yn erbyn ar byd

The third and actually most important of the three main principles of Druidic moral philosophy is the pre-eminence of truth. Telling the truth, speaking with true and correct utterance, is more important than anything else. There is an ancient Welsh expression which encapsulates the principle: *Y gwir yn erbyn ar byd* (pronounced approximately *uh-gweer-un-ayr-bin-ar-beed*), which means, "Truth against the world." An ancient Irish Triad expresses the same notion: "Three things from which never to be moved: one's Gods, one's oaths and the truth."

Anne Ross gives an example from the vernacular tales of the awesome power of truthful utterance:

> One story tells of a legendary king of Ireland, Lugaid mac Con, who ruled for seven years, from Tara. He took Cormac son of Art into his house as his foster-son. On one occasion, sheep trespassed on his land and ate the Queen's woad. Lugaid said the sheep were then forfeit because they had trespassed. Although Cormac was only a small boy at the time he disagreed with this verdict: he said the shearing of the sheep, not their seizure, was a suitable compensation for the shearing of the woad. As the woad would grow again on the plant, so would the wool grow on the sheep. "That is the true judgment," said all, "and it is the son of the true Prince who has given it." Immediately the side of the house in which the false judgment had been given fell down the slope and became known as "The Crooked Mound of Tara." After that, Lugaid was king in Tara for a year, "and no grass grew, no leaves, and there was no grain." After that, he was dethroned by his people for he was a "false prince."[2]

Disagreements about truth have brought down palaces figuratively as well as literally. Not only is there no set dogma or orthodox theology for modern Druidism, nor any prescribed universal liturgy or ritual texts or protocols, many modern Druids go to great lengths to avoid acceptance of any such dogmas or protocols. There are naturally many potential conflicts in such a situation, and, as we shall see in Chapters 7 and 8, there have been some actual conflicts too as modern Druidism has grown and continued to define and extend itself. The road to Hell (which Druids don't actually believe in, but I digress) is paved with good intentions, and it is often the best of intentions that have created the worst of conflicts. Somebody gets a wonderful new idea, wants to spread the good news far and wide, and in the blink of an eye a passionate, sincere, well-intentioned initiative has somehow turned into Party A muscling Party B into a direction where Party B doesn't want to go. Fortunately, the disparate nature of modern Druidism as a whole has historically provided a very useful safety valve. Whenever disagreements have become too large, individuals have tended to simply follow the new path by themselves, or switch to another group or organization, or even start a new group or organization. Lack of overall structure and authority can be a blessing.

Nevertheless, truth is an insurmountable and unavoidable moral necessity for modern Druids, just as it was for the original Druids. That question itself (i.e., is modern Druidism really a direct descendant of Iron Age Druidism or actually something quite different?) continues to be debated, but thoughtfulness, love, respect and responsibility have generally prevailed on that and other questions. At the most fundamental level, the Druidic imperative towards truth is the absolute opposite of dogma, because experience teaches us over and over again that each of us lives in a separate, individual, conceptual prison and we experience the whole universe only through our own individual prison window. We must always speak truth as best we can, but that does not mean being dogmatic.

Awen, Creativity and Courage

Awen is a very old Welsh word, found also in Cornish and Breton, which originally meant inspiration, particularly poetic inspiration; it has since come to have a much wider meaning in modern Druidism. It first appeared in writing as long ago as the 8th century, in the form *aguen*, in a Latin text by the Welsh historian Nennius or Nyniau: *"Tunc talhaern tat aguen in poemate claret"* ("Talhaern the father of the muse was then renowned in poetry"). It appears in 1194 in the form *Awenyddion* (pronounced approximately *ah-wen-uth-ee-on*, meaning "people inspired") used by Giraldus Cambrensis to describe certain people who made prophecies in his time:

> There are certain persons in Cambria, whom you will find nowhere else, called *Awenyddion*, or people inspired; when consulted upon any doubtful event, they roar out violently, are rendered beside themselves, and become, as it were, possessed by a spirit.

They do not deliver the answer to what is required in a connected manner; but the person who skillfully observes them, will find after many preambles, and many nugatory and incoherent, though ornamented speeches, the desired explanation conveyed in some turn or word; they are then roused from their ecstasy, as from a deep sleep, and, as it were, by violence compelled to return to their proper senses. After having answered the question they do not recover till violently shaken by other people; nor can they remember the replies they have given.[3]

For modern Druids, *awen* is not only poetic inspiration or divinatory dreaming, it also means much more generally the creative principle and divine as well as artistic inspiration. Surrender to the Muse, or to God, the Goddess, or all the Gods and Goddesses, can sometimes be a challenging, even frightening experience, so *awen* has taken on yet another connotation, which is courage, specifically the courage to go out on a limb and expose yourself to ridicule, disappointment or failure in search of either an artistic or a spiritual goal.

This word that has such a depth of meaning in modern Druidism also has a visual symbol. It consists of three vertical lines, which spread slightly apart from each other as they descend, like three shafts of sunshine beaming out from beneath a cloud, thus: /|\. The symbol has been used for decades by the Welsh, Cornish and Bretons in a variety of contexts and organizations, and by many Druid groups—it is perhaps the most universally recognized Druidic symbol of all. The visual representation is also simply called the *Awen* (usually with a capital A). The *Awen* is used in the revived *gorseddau* or Bardic assemblies. It typically appears on the headpieces or hoods of the Bardic and Druidic robes. In its simplest form, it represents poetic inspiration, creativity. For those modern Bards and Druids who are also Christians, it is perhaps also symbolic of the Holy Trinity. Anciently, and more generally, the term *awen* means not just inspiration, it also means or implies a sacred connectivity with all things, an expression of the basic Druidic concept of the entire universe, both animate and inanimate, being charged with the presence of the deity, with universal purpose. It symbolizes not just creativity, but also spiritual awareness.

The Awen

Some groups use "*awen*" as an invocation or chant, usually spoken or sung three times, three being one of many numbers with magical or numerological significance in Druidism, and especially associated with utterances of great importance, as it is in other cultures and religions, too (think, for example, of Peter denying Christ three times, with the cock crowing each time). The Welsh, Cornish and Breton *gorseddau* or assemblies begin with a triple call from the Archdruid or Grand Bard: "Once I ask, is there peace? Twice I ask, is there peace? Three times I ask, is there peace?" In practical terms, it's the equivalent of asking, "Do you really want to do this?" but it also matches the three rays of the *Awen* itself, and its ritual power is enhanced because it connects with the very ancient Celtic practice of grouping names, events, invocations and other utterances in groups of three or triads.

There is no doubt about the ancient origin and provenance of the word *awen*, nor about the divine inspiration which it originally signified, but it came into prominent use by modern Druids only after Iolo Morganwg reintroduced it during the Romantic Revival. Morganwg was a notorious forger (see Chapter 6), and several modern Druid groups and organizations will have nothing to do with him or his texts, or his rituals, or his vocabulary, so the *awen* is not universally accepted.

So, why have I included artistic creativity in a list of Druidic moral principles? Art doesn't have anything to do with morals, does it? In the Druidic world view, again both ancient and modern, yes, it does. *Awen* is not just about getting a good idea for a poem or picture, or writing a pretty song. It is about surrendering oneself to the divine purpose, about contributing to the furtherance of life and spirit, about bringing new things into being, and, what's more, new things of beauty and purpose and goodness. Traditional Celtic visual art is very distinctive, and one of the characteristics which identifies it so clearly is a remarkable fluidity and interchangeability of line and form, which visually parallels the fundamental belief in the active diversity and creativity of God or the Goddess in the living universe: a geometrical pattern shape-shifts into leaves, or a dog, or a cat, or a tree, or, conversely, a face or a hand or a whole human or zoomorphic figure becomes a geometrical figure, a trefoil, a diamond, a spiral, or a loop, with lines weaving under and over each other. Traditional Celtic music often has a simple underlying rhythmical structure, with 6/8 being a popular time signature, but improvisation and embellishment, especially within modal scales, have always been and continue to be characteristically Celtic. Instruments are usually simple: the drum, especially the circular drum known by the Irish name *bodhrán* (pronounced approximately *bo-rawn*, with the emphasis on the second syllable), simple flutes or penny whistles, guitars, the harp or *clàrsach*, bagpipes. There are very formal performances and competitions, such as those of the Welsh *Eisteddfod* or Cornish *Esedhvos*, but there are also countless informal gatherings and sessions where people get together to sing and play, usually known by the Scottish Gàidhlig word *cèilidh* (pronounced approximately *kay-lee*), or Irish *céilí,* which can also describe a simple get-together for a blether or chat over a cup of tea or dram of whisky, or any informal social gathering. The Welsh equivalent is *twmpath* and the Cornish is *troyll.*

Respect and Responsibility

Thomas Lickona is a developmental psychologist and emeritus professor of education at the State University of New York (SUNY). He has written several impressive books about moral education, but his work, complex and detailed as it is, reduces essentially to this simple idea: there is a common core of moral belief in the west, to which people of all religions and none can subscribe, and at its very simplest it can be expressed in just two words, respect and responsibility. Lickona is a Catholic, not a Druid, but the terms respect and responsibility are also powerful and significant in modern Druidism.

We respect Creation, in all its diversity, and (for most of us) the divinity that engendered and continues to develop that Creation. We respect the living spirit in all things, so we respect our planet and all of its wonderful natural environments and ecologies. We take responsibility for stewardship of our Earth, our Gaia. We respect the right of all beings to what the United States Declaration of Independence so simply and eloquently calls "life, liberty and the pursuit of happiness." We respect human rights, and accept responsibility for implementing and maintaining them. Although these vary from country to country and culture to culture, and are articulated and revised by a number of intergovernmental and international as well as national organizations, for modern Druids they certainly include the following, all of which were included in the seminal United Nations Universal Declaration of Human Rights promulgated in 1948, following the horrors of the Second World War: the right to life, liberty and security; freedom from slavery; freedom from torture, or cruel and degrading punishment; equal recognition before and equal protection from the law; freedom from arbitrary arrest, detention or exile; the right to be deemed innocent until proven guilty; freedom from arbitrary interference with privacy, family, home or correspondence; freedom of movement and residence; the right to seek asylum from persecution; the right to a nationality; the right to marry and found a family; the right to own property and not be arbitrarily deprived of it; freedom of thought, conscience and religion; the right to peaceful assembly; the right of access to government and equal access to public services; the right to work and free choice of employment; the right to rest, leisure and holidays; the right to education, and access to the arts and culture.

Love, Living in the World, Relationships

Not surprisingly, most modern Druids—including even those who think of themselves as followers of Druidic philosophy rather than religion—have such a deep and intense respect for all living things that the word reverence can be substituted for respect. If reverence is a passive noun (grammatically impossible, but stick with me), love is its active cognate. Despite many differences in other areas, here Druidism is at one with Christianity, Judaism and Islam: love God, love God's Creation, love each other. I have already noted that some modern Druids are vegetarian or vegan, as a result of their reverence for all living things. Buddhists, Hindus and especially Jains have a doctrine called *Ahimsa*, which means literally "no injury" or "no harm," which may mean that they abstain from meat, or that they endeavor in other ways to avoid harming any other living being. Jains, for example, are known for sweeping the ground where they are about to walk so that not even an insect will be harmed or killed by them. Modern Druids may or may not practice *Ahimsa*, but in general they certainly share the same positive reverence for life and love of all living things. That also means that we love each other, and treat each other like loving family members. Ross Nichols, who had a great influence on the development of modern Druidism, and whom we shall discuss in more detail later, strongly advocated non-violence and pacifism, and his ideas have been widely shared and accepted by many in the modern Druid community.

Connectedness

So, peace and love, doing good, being respectful and taking responsibility, treating others with love and respect as if they are family: cumulatively, this sounds not that dissimilar to the injunctions of Christianity, Judaism or Islam. But there are major differences, one of the most important being the absence of sin as a major factor in Druidic morality. We simply don't believe in sin (and, therefore, grace and redemption) in the same way that Christians and others do. What we do believe in is connectedness, what some have called "the harvest," or what you reap from what you have sown.

Markale writes:

> Sin is unknown in the Druidic tradition. There is only fault when an individual fails to accomplish what he should accomplish, when he is incapable of moving beyond himself. But this idea of fault refers more to the establishment of an individual's weakness rather than the transgression of a norm classified and established beforehand. There can be no list of capital, mortal, or venal sins, not in Druidic morality. There is only that which allows one to achieve one's own destiny or the destiny of the community, and that which prevents one from achieving this end.[4]

Markale speaks from a Catholic perspective, in which the distinctions between "capital, mortal, or venal sins" have been refined over many centuries, and their redemption returns always to the office of confession and to God's grace and Christ's sacrifice. The ancient Celts had many deities, but there was no God of goodness waging a war against a God of evil. They had laws which were to be obeyed, and taboos (the Celtic word is *geis*, plural *geisa* or *gessa*) which were to be followed, but the crimes and errors were exactly that: they were crimes and errors, not sins, because there was no concept of sin until the Christian missionaries introduced it.

Was ancient Druidic society therefore amoral, meaning strictly that they had no moral code? As we have already seen, modern Wiccans express their moral code in archaic language as, "An (if) it harm none, do as thou wilt." I think the moral code of Druidism, both ancient and modern, is much more developed and consequential than that short philosophy. But, if there was no sin, what was there? What underpinned Druidic morality, which was so highly spoken of by the classical commentators, even as they simultaneously labeled the Celts as barbaric savages?

There was a profound sense of connectedness and consequence, similar to *karma* in some ways, as we have already discussed, but which was much more flexible in real application. As we have seen with *fír fer* above, it meant that there might be two different punishments for the exact same crime, depending on the circumstances, without any loss of real justice. Fitness and truth were always major considerations, but Druidic justice came not from a fixed set of rules with humankind its principal object, but rather from a fluid and often changeable observation of the natural world and universe, in which humans were part of Creation, but neither the main purpose nor even the main part of Creation. The natural, living world was the cockpit from which moral and legal judgments were made. If a fox stole a duck's egg from the nest, was that a crime? Or a sin? We can imagine how the fox might feel, and the duck, but how would God or the Goddess view such an event? The fox has a right to feed itself and its family, the duck has a right—duty, even— to protect her eggs, and those rights seem to be about equal. Sin doesn't come into it. Nature, context and intention determine everything.

But if you believe, as most Druids do, that all things are connected, that all things relate, then moral questions and dilemmas can sometimes resolve themselves in peculiar but natural ways. There is a macabre, darkly amusing story re-told in *The Little, Brown Book of Anecdotes* (editor Clifton Fadiman, Little, Brown and Company, Boston, 1985, p. 99, originally published in John Train's *True Remarkable Occurrences*), a true story, which runs as follows: Vera Czermak discovered that her husband had been unfaithful to her. In despair, she decided to end it all by jumping out of a third-floor window. She awoke the following morning in hospital, to be told that she was still alive because she had landed on a man, who broke her fall. The man, who was killed, was Mr. Czermak, her cheating husband.

A modern, general term for such events (which are far more common than you might think) is synchronicity. It was introduced as an "acausal connecting or togetherness" principle by the psychologist Carl Jung in the 1920s (Jung is also famous for his concept of the "collective subconscious," the phenomenon of people sharing common dreams and symbols), but it is a much, much older phenomenon, which Druids have known for centuries. A simpler way of describing synchronicity is "meaningful coincidences." Chance events occur, usually over a period of time, and later a meaning or purpose seems to be evident in them. For Druids, this is simply an example of connectedness. I have lost track of the number of times such connected sequences have occurred in my own life. They often confound the normal laws of time and space. Three or four times on a particular morning, I find myself thinking, for no obvious reason, about an old friend whom I haven't seen for years, then in the afternoon the phone rings—and it is that friend. I get held up by interruptions on my way to a meeting, and eventually, frustrated and annoyed, decide that I can't go—then discover later that the meeting had been postponed anyway. I once won £87.54p on the British Football Pools—and received in the very same mail delivery an electricity bill for £87.54p.

And beyond my little life, the historical synchronicities abound. Thomas Jefferson and John Adams both died within hours of each other on July 4th, 1826, the 50th anniversary of American independence (and President James Monroe died on Independence Day in 1831). In 1864, Abraham Lincoln's son, Robert Todd, was saved from falling to his death on a railway line by Edwin Booth, brother of John Wilkes Booth, who less than a year later assassinated Lincoln (and Robert Todd Lincoln was also present when President James A. Garfield was fatally shot at a railroad station). Halley's Comet revisits Earth about every 75 years, and Mark Twain, who was born on November 30th, 1835, with the comet in the sky, predicted that he would come and go as the comet came and went—he died, as he himself predicted, of a heart attack on April 21st, 1910, the day after Halley's Comet re-emerged from the far side of the Sun. A nurse called Violet Jessop was a passenger on the *Titanic*, the *Olympic* and the *Britannic*, three passenger ships which sank, and survived all three sinkings. Although it was 200 years apart, Jimi Hendrix and George Friedrich Handel lived at 23 and 25 Brook Street, in London. In 1895, there were only two automobiles in the whole of the state of Ohio—and they crashed into each other.

Seeing patterns in events, before they happen as much as after they happen, was certainly a Druidic skill. (It was actually associated with the Ovates, or the equivalent rank of *filidh* in Ireland.) The Old Irish term for this foresight or inspiration was *imbas forosnai* (pronunciation uncertain, but *eem-bas-for-aws-nay* is likely), which is spelled in a variety of ways in Cormac's Glossary and the other original sources. It means literally "illuminated in-knowing," which might be translated as "divine vision." It describes prophecy or foresight of things to come, and is connected to the *awen* of divine poetic inspiration; the ancient Bards and Druids made a distinction between poetic skill acquired through practice and the application of learned techniques, and the poetic inspiration which comes directly from the Goddess or the Gods and is divine in nature, and therefore of far greater importance. *Imbas forosnai* was one of Fionn mac Cumhaill's noted attributes. The early descriptions suggest that the Ovates and Druids who used the technique deliberately restricted their sensory input in order to achieve the inner vision: they sealed themselves in dark or silent places.

Modern Druids use augury and divination as much as ancient Druids did, although we don't offer blood sacrifices (and it is by no means certain that human sacrifice was ever practiced by ancient Druids). We observe things, particularly natural things, very closely. We notice the wind, the sky and the weather generally. We "read" the flow of a waterfall, or the pattern of the incoming tide, or the "pictures" left by the retreating tide in the sand of the beach. We listen to birdsong, since the ancient belief was that birds carry messages between people in this world, and between this world and the Otherworld. Ellen Evert Hopman tells of a particularly clear message in her experience:

> I had an owl perch on the roof above the kitchen where I was washing dishes and hoot and hoot without stopping. Finally I said out loud, "Okay, I hear you," and I knew someone had died. The owl stopped and the next morning I found out my mentor and teacher Druid Alexei Kondratiev had suddenly and tragically passed away on a sidewalk in New York.[5]

We "read" clouds, looking for meaningful shapes or patterns (sky-reading or cloud-reading is one of my favorite methods of contemplation). We take careful notice if the animals in our lives, domesticated or wild, behave in a particular or unexpected way. We seek out places of power, like springs or waterfalls, rocks, lakes, the sea, caves, or familiar trees, where we can "listen" for news of change. We "talk" with such places. We constantly seek contact with Nature, with the living world, and we constantly seek to engage with the vitality or *anam* inherent in all things.

In other words, we are always alert to the numinous and the divine, believing that those qualities are always present in all things. Like William Blake in his *Auguries of Innocence*, we are eager ...

> ... To see a World in a Grain of Sand
> And Heaven in a Wild Flower,
> Hold Infinity in the palm of your hand
> And Eternity in an Hour.

It just so happens (actually, it doesn't—it's the same synchronicity which I described above) that (at the time of writing these words) I took the day off writing yesterday and, with my wife and step-daughter, visited the ancient Yew of Fortingall on the north shore of Scotland's Loch Tay, a tree I know and love, and have conversed with on many occasions. This tree is acknowledged to be over five thousand years old. I believe (having asked the Yew herself) that the tree was seeded not long after the retreat of the last Ice Age, and may be as much as nine thousand years old. As soon as we parked and got out of the car, a pair of wagtails came flying right up into our faces, whistling and chattering and fluttering their wings in great excitement. "What are they saying?" my wife asked. "Just that we're here," I answered. "It seems somebody was expecting us, and these guys are supposed to let them know." The wagtails flew off, still chattering with excitement, and we made our visit to the Yew, which was as satisfying and useful as always, and a revelation to my step-daughter, who had never visited Fortingall before. For modern Druids, moral behavior arises from and is sustained by this profound sense of community and fellowship with the natural world and all that is in it, and a conviction that this natural world is connected in turn to an infinite reality beyond.

3. Ancient Celtic Druidism

The God and Goddess

Because humans, like almost all other animals, fall basically into two genders, male and female, the deity is commonly perceived either as God, a male, or the Goddess, a female. (We have only comparatively recently become more aware that gender and sexual orientation are, in fact, often more complicated than simply a question of masculinity and femininity.) From archaeological evidence, both in northern Europe and in the Mediterranean region (the Minoan culture on Crete, for example), we know that the very earliest European religions were gynocentric, or Goddess-oriented. They were gradually replaced by androcentric, or male-God religions, beginning in Macedonia, then spreading through Greek influence and the expansion of the Greek Empire across the rest of Europe. The themes and stereotypes of early Celtic mythology appear closely related to many very early religious and mythological patterns across the whole of Europe, dating back as far as 6500 BCE or even earlier. The male God usurped the female Goddess, but the Goddess survives in a wide variety of aspects, and the God and Goddess appear, particularly in animal or totemic form, in a remarkably consistent pattern over millennia. The Goddess is a snake, several kinds of bird, a horse, a doe, a sow, a bee or a bear. The God is a bull, a stag, an eagle, a ram, a mushroom, or simply a phallus.[1]

In early Celtic iconography, the Goddess is Madron or Modron (simply "the Mother") and her son, lover or husband is Mabon or Maponus ("the Son"). In Britain, as elsewhere in Europe, the Mother also appears in triplicate as the *Matrones*. Ellen Evert Hopman describes the ancient Goddess trio of virgin, mother and crone as a Mediterranean rather than Celtic iconography: "Maiden, Mother and Crone is a Mediterranean idea. In a Celtic context the *Matronae* are three women of the same age. Ditto the triple Brighid, the Morrigan, Banbha, Fodhla and Eriu, etc."[2] In early cultures of the Mediterranean, the male God, totemized typically as a bull or phallus, came to hold equivalent status to the Goddess, and, after Mycenean culture had penetrated Greece, even to usurp her. In the Orphic mystery, the worshipper ate raw bull flesh. Bull worship features abundantly in the plays of Euripides, especially *The Bacchae*, which was performed after his death in 405 BCE. Eventually, the triumph of the God over the Goddess became permanently ossified in the patriarchal religions, Judaism, Christianity and Islam. The Sun, which originally represented the Goddess, became a masculine God, while the Moon, originally male, became associated with Goddesses. (Interestingly, early English Paganism stuck to the original designations: in Old English, *se mona*, "the Moon," is a masculine noun, while *seo sunne*, "the Sun," is a feminine noun.)

In the Celtic Druidic tradition, that conquest of the Goddess by the God never took place. In classical Druidism, it is the Goddess who lives forever, unchanging, while her sons become lovers and husbands and fathers and then die, to be replaced by other sons and lovers and husbands and fathers. The annual mythical cycle, which is embedded in the reality of the agricultural cycle, repeats that pattern endlessly, as we shall discuss in more detail in Chapter 10. The Goddess, who is the land, the people, the unchanging eternal territory, the *tuath*, is wooed, ploughed, impregnated by the son or lover, the Sun-God, the Belinus or Beli Mawr of Beltan (the May festival). After the harvest has been gathered, there follows the *nasadh* or commemoration at Lughnasadh (the August festival) instituted by the father God, Lugh, the God of the waning year, in honor of his foster-mother, the Goddess Tailtiu. Through the old age and death of Samhain (the November festival) and midwinter, the Father God dies to be re-born as the Son (and Sun) God, and the ageless and eternal Mother Goddess becomes at Imbolc or Oimelg (the February festival) once again the maiden, the mistress, the lover, the bride, the pregnant queen, the giver of milk, and through her the new Mabon or Bel or Son-God appears in the spring, and the cycle continues to repeat itself. (There is a very faint trace of this ancient mother-centered Goddess in the classical pantheon, in the person of the Goddess Anna Perenna, who renewed her youth each month.) The king of any given territory represented the male God, while the territory itself was the Goddess. The king was "wedded" to the land, and its fertility and prosperity depended on a successful and fruitful congress between them.

Classical Accounts

Herm describes the Celts as "the people who came out of the darkness,"[3] meaning, more prosaically, that we really don't know very much about the beginnings of Celtic history. Did precursors of the Celts help to tame the horse on the plains and steppes of central Europe around 3,000 BCE? Perhaps,

perhaps not. The Celts were renowned horsemen from earliest times, and the cult of the horse–Goddess Epona appears very early in Celtic mythology, but there is no definitive place or event which allows us to say, "Here is where the Celts began."

We do know that Celtic culture is very old, almost certainly many centuries, or perhaps even millennia, earlier than the first archaeological evidence, which dates from about 700 BCE, in what is now known as the Hallstatt period, after the region near Salzburg in Austria, where evidence was found of the substitution of iron for bronze in weapons and tools. The distinctive La Tène period, characterized by extraordinarily complex and beautiful decoration on artifacts, began about 500 BCE. The distinctiveness of this archaeological evidence encourages the use of the word Celtic to describe and define it, and Celtic art style (although it shares some characteristics with early Nordic and Germanic art), with its elaborate knotwork and zoomorphics, is still a very clear identifier to this day. The La Tène period, with its highly distinctive sophistication in art style, was flourishing in central Europe at about the same time the Persian Achaemenid Empire was occupying Thrace and Macedonia, the Etruscans still ruled where Rome was yet to come, and the first Greek proto-historians Hecateus and Ion of Chios were not yet born.[4]

Strabo, Tacitus and Diodorus Siculus all describe the typical personal appearance of the Celts. Strabo writes:

> Their hair is not only naturally blond, but they also use artificial means to increase this natural quality of color, for they continually wash their hair with lime-wash and draw it from the forehead to the crown and to the nape of the neck, with the result that their appearance resembles that of Satyrs or of Pans, for the hair is so thickened by this treatment that it differs in no way from a horse's mane.[5]

The description of lime-washing, plus hair dyeing, plus a more general preoccupation with hair as a main attribute of beauty or handsomeness, are all recapitulated in the vernacular texts. Of course, the Germanic tribes could be (and were) also described as big and blond. Tacitus, possibly the most reliable of the classical Roman historians, takes some care to try to distinguish between Celts and Teutons. Add the well-attested Celt-Iberian type, recognized by the Romans in, for example, the tribe of the Silures in what is now South Wales, who were small and swarthy, and the distinctive early Irish type with dark or black hair but blue eyes, whose DNA is still clearly traceable to this day, and we can see immediately that physical typology is actually of very limited use in describing or defining the Celts. The Celtic identity is not racial: it is cultural and historical, primarily based on distinctive language.

The archetype of the Celtic hero is a warrior, powerful, rich, splendidly dressed, armed and accoutered. Here is the portrait, from the Welsh *Mabinogi*, of Culhwch journeying to seek adventures at Arthur's court:

Off went the boy on a steed with light-grey head four winters old, with well-knit fork, shell-hoofed, and a gold tubular bridle-bit in its mouth. And under him a precious gold saddle, and in his hand two whetted spears of silver. A battle-axe in his hand, the fore-arm's length of a full-grown man from ridge to edge. It would draw blood from the wind; it would be swifter than the swiftest dew-drop from the stalk to the ground, when the dew would be heaviest in the month of June. A gold-hilted sword on his thigh, and the blade of it gold, and a gold-chased buckler upon him, with the hue of heaven's light-ning therein, and an ivory boss therein. And two greyhounds, white-breasted, brindled, in front of him, with a collar of red gold about the neck of either, from shoulder swell to ear.[6]

The hegemony of warfare is a significant characteristic of early Celtic societies. Although most if not all early societies also placed great emphasis on war and weapons, the Celtic warrior culture features strongly in classical descriptions, in archaeology, and in the vernacular literature. Strabo wrote:

The whole race, which is called Celtic or Galatic, is madly fond of war, high-spirited and quick to battle, but otherwise straightforward and not of evil character. And so when they are stirred up they assemble in their bands for battle, quite openly and with-out forethought; so that they are easily handled by those who desire to outwit them. For at any time or place, and on whatever pretext you stir them up, you will have them ready to face danger, even if they have nothing on their side but their own strength and courage.[7]

Tacitus describes different Celtic physical characteristics and comments on their attitude in war:

Who the first inhabitants of Britain were, whether natives or immigrants, is open to question: one must remember we are dealing with barbarians. But their physical char-acteristics vary, and the variation is suggestive. The reddish hair and large limbs of the Caledonians proclaim a German origin; the swarthy faces of the Silures, the tendency of their hair to curl, and the fact that Spain lies opposite, all lead one to suppose that Spaniards crossed in ancient times and occupied that part of the country.... On the whole, however, it seems likely that Gauls settled in the island lying so close to their shores.... Their strength is in their infantry. Some tribes also fight from chariots. The nobleman drives, his dependents fight in his defense. Once they owed obedience to kings; now they are distracted between the warring factions of rival chiefs. Indeed, nothing has helped us more in fighting against their very powerful nations than their inability to cooperate. It is but seldom that two or three states unite to repel a common danger; thus, fighting in separate groups, all are conquered.[8]

Women in Early Celtic Society, Female Druids

As I observed in Chapter 2, the attested attributes of women in Celtic tribal society are markedly different from those of the women of Rome, or indeed of any classical European culture. Ammianus Marcellinus tells us that Celtic women fought in battle as well as men, and Dio Cassius describes

Queen Boudicca of the Iceni as "huge of frame and terrifying of aspect and with a harsh voice." Tacitus gives us a detailed portrait of Cartimandua, the powerful Queen of the Brigantes. Tacitus and Dio Cassius also comment on the fact that Boudicca was a woman commander, with Tacitus explicitly stating, "the Britons make no distinction of sex in their leaders." Plutarch, writing in the second century CE, tells us that Celtic women of about 400 BCE took part in public affairs as mediators (or diplomats, a specifically Druidic role).

Celtic women, especially those of high status, were often warriors, literally taking arms on the field of battle. Many of the lavishly-provided graves of the sixth and fifth centuries BCE in southern Germany and eastern Gaul (now France) are for women leaders, not men. These graves, for example at Vix in Burgundy, and at Hohmichele, Klein Aspergle and Reinheim in Germany, are close to seats of tribal power. There are Iron Age female graves in Britain, too, including Wetwang Slack in Yorkshire, where the skeleton of a high-status woman was found with a mirror and a bronze box, with other warriors buried beside her. Archaeological evidence (for example, curse tablets or inscriptions, even some personal letters) shows us that women in Britain and Gaul owned property and held a wide range of public and professional positions, including merchant, wine-seller, chemist and doctor. It is also clear that women could be, and were, Druids. The Roman historian Lampridius, writing in the third century CE, describes how Emperor Alexander Severus was given a warning by a female Druid: "As he was on his way, a Druidess cried out to him in the Gallic tongue, 'Go forward, but hope not for victory, nor put trust in thy soldiers.'" Vopiscus, also writing in the third century, describes similar prophetic utterance by a female Druid, this one predicting to Diocletian that he would one day become emperor. Vopiscus also mentions Aurelian consulting "the Gaulish Druidesses." All the early written commentary on Celtic women comes either from Romans or Christians, so the point of view is always androcentric, yet even so a picture emerges of Celtic women who enjoy rights in rank, occupation, marriage, inheritance and the ability to engage in public life far above those of women in Mediterranean and other early European cultures. These classical descriptions are confirmed in the later vernacular Irish and Welsh texts, especially the law tracts, although by this time Christian androcentricity and misogyny have also begun to become apparent.

This fundamental and highly unusual attitude towards gender roles had practical consequences in Celtic society. The unchanging basic social unit was the tribe, associated with a specific geographical territory, or *tuath*, which was sacred. Women as well as men exercised political and military power. Druids, who were also both male and female, belonged to the highest ranks of the Celtic aristocracy, but were able to move freely between kingdoms if they chose, and were therefore able to act as mediators, diplomats and judges at the highest level, in addition to their functions as priests. The impact of Roman occupation on the kingdoms was significant, but the status of women was not entirely altered or eradicated, and—especially in the highlands and the wild lands—the status and function of Druids remained, I believe, also relatively unchanged.

Modern Druidism, therefore, has the unusual advantage among religions of being able to claim a long historical precedent for gender equality and treating women with appropriate respect. We also oppose discrimination on the grounds of race, ethnicity, skin color, religion, sexual orientation, or age.

The Vernacular Texts

There are two main streams or sources of material in native, vernacular Celtic languages: the Welsh and the Irish. Stories from one tradition often have very close equivalents in the other. Our main difficulty is that the early Celts had an oral tradition. Although a few things were written down—we have some inscriptions, for example, which show that the ancient Druids used Greek and Latin, plus a secret writing system called Ogham—everything else was spoken and memorized.

There are some very early Irish texts. *Audacht Morainn* ("The Testament of Morrand") dates from about 700 CE. The Brehon laws are contained in a great number of separate tracts, which date from the 8th century. An example is the *Uraicecht na Riar* ("Primer of Stipulations"), which gives information about the craft of poetry and the qualifications and experience required to achieve specific levels of status. *Bechbretha* ("Bee-Judgments") and *Coibes Uisci Thairdne* ("Kinship of Conducted Water") are two tracts believed to have been written by the same author which present legal information about relatively new animal husbandry practices to Irish law from elsewhere in Europe.

Apart from early classical accounts, it was only from the 11th century onwards that we have any sustained writing in Britain about the Celts in general or Druids in particular. The vernacular tales, in which early Celtic mythology and religious thinking are revealed in detail, were written down by mediaeval Christian monks, most of them centuries after they were first created and circulated.

Among the earliest pieces in the vernacular literature is a 12th-century manuscript of a text written probably in the 9th or 10th century, although it describes events of the 7th century, a long elegiac poem commemorating the warriors of the Gododdin who died at Catraeth (possibly modern Catterick in Yorkshire, England) resisting the incursions of the Germanic-English tribes of Angles, Saxons, Jutes and others into northern Britain. The language of the text is Brythonic, which (to simplify matters) can be called Old Welsh, even though the geographical area in which it originates is now the Scottish Borders and Northumberland—this is where the people of the Gododdin lived.

A short and obscure Welsh poem of uncertain date, called *Preiddeu Annwfn* ("The Spoils of Annwfn"), found in the *Book of Taliesin*, describes Arthur (later King Arthur) and his warriors going to a magical city (the Otherworld) to fetch a magical cauldron. There may be some connection to a genuine historical event, but, if there is, nobody has yet been able to identify it.

The most important of the Welsh vernacular tales are found in a collection known as the *Mabinogi* or (now universally, but incorrectly) the *Mabinogion*. These wonderful tales, clearly springing from a much earlier oral tradition, were written down, probably by a single scribe, somewhere around 1050, although the earliest manuscripts are the *White Book of Rhydderch* (c. 1325) and the *Red Book of Hergest* (c. 1400). Many of the mythological themes that pervade later Arthurian literature are to be found in the *Mabinogi*. For example, in the Third Branch (i.e., section), the kingdom of Dyfed becomes a wasteland requiring an act of mythical or religious redemption for its restoration—a theme that recurs in many different forms in later Arthurian literature. The geographical detail of the stories is very precise and authentic—we recognize Dyfed, Harlech and North Wales immediately. There are eleven tales in all, four of them having strong similarities in style and content, which suggest that these were by a single author. Although there are occasional Christian references, presumably added by the monks who were transcribing the stories, these tales are filled with incidents and adventures which clearly belong to the early Druidic culture and tradition.

Around 1275 to 1300 in earliest manuscript, unknown authors gathered earlier mediaeval Welsh poems, subsequently called *Trioedd Ynys Prydein* ("Triads of the Island of Britain," more frequently called simply the Welsh Triads). The poems list people and events in threes, presumably originally to facilitate memorization, although I have also previously mentioned that three was one of the Druidic sacred numbers. Here is a brief example:

> Three tribal thrones of the Island of Britain:
> Arthur as Chief Prince in Mynyw (St. David's),
> and Dewi (St. David) as Chief Bishop, and Maelgwn
> Gwynedd as Chief Elder.

Twenty-four knights of Arthur are also listed in threes, beginning with three golden-tongued knights, Gwalchmai son of Llew son of Cynfarch, and Drudwas son of Tryffin, and Eliwlod son of Madog son of Uthur, and three virgin knights, Bwrt son of Bwrt King of Gascony, and Peredur son of Earl Efrog, and Galath son of Lanslod Lak, and so on.

The Irish tradition has some tales, and some Gods and heroes, who are clearly almost exact counterparts of the Welsh tales. For example, the Irish hero Fionn (or Finn) mac Cumhaill (or McCool) is the counterpart of the Welsh or Brythonic Gwynn. In both cases, the name means "white" or "fair one." Many extant English place-names, such as Wincanton and Winchester, derive from Gwynn. The hero of the Irish Ulster Cycle is Cú Chulainn (pronounced approximately *koo-hoo-lin*, with the accent on the second syllable), and the best-known story is *Táin Bó Cúailnge* (*toyn-baw-kool-nyuh*) or the Cattle Raid of Cooley, in which Queen Medb (pronounced *Mave*), a personification of the Great Goddess, invades the Cooley peninsula to steal a prize bull, whom Cú Chulainn is sworn to defend. Like the Welsh tales, these Irish stories are filled with Druidic themes and imagery.

Celtic Gods and Goddesses

Perhaps the most immediately obvious thing to be said about Celtic Gods and Goddesses in general is that there appears to be a very great number of them. The Irish scholar Proinsias MacCana refers to the "fertile chaos of the insular tradition."[9] There are whole dictionaries of Celtic Gods and Goddesses, and these obviously do not include the presumed legion of local deities who never made it into history books or never had archaeological inscriptions carved to preserve their names. Caesar introduced the names of some of these Gods to his Roman readership and correlated them to Roman deities (see below). He also added: "The Gauls claim that they are all descended from Dis Pater; they say this is the tradition handed down to them from the Druids."[10]

Dis Pater was the Roman God of the dead. Cunliffe equates him with the Irish God Donn, "the brown or dark one." The other widely accepted correlations, some based on Caesar, are: Lugh with Mercury; Taranis with Jupiter, or Jupiter Tonans, since *taran* means "thunder"; Mabon or Maponos ("the Boy" or "the Son") with Apollo, the chief sun God; Brigit ("the bright or shining one") with Minerva, Goddess of wisdom as well as of war, and with her Greek counterpart Athene; Ogmios (God of speech as well as club-carrying warrior giant) with Hercules; and Cernunnos ("the horned one," chief God of the forest and wild lands) with Pan or Silvanus. There are many Romano-British deities who have double names, particularly localized Gods and Goddesses. Generally, the Roman deity comes first in the name pairings, as in Apollo-Maponus or Mars-Belatucadrus, but occasionally the Celtic God gets top billing, even in Roman inscriptions, as, for example, in Nodens-Silvanus ("dog God of the forest").

According to the subtitle of her book, Miranda Green describes Celtic

Goddesses as "Warriors, Virgins and Mothers."[11] Andraste, in whose name Boudicca cut off the breasts of her female prisoners and stuffed them in their mouths, is the exemplar of the warrior Goddess. The warrior hero Cú Chulainn lives with the war Goddess Scáthach on the Isle of Skye for "a year and a day" to learn warfare from her, in particular the use of the Gá Bólga or Gae Bolg, the spiral-bladed spear which disembowels. Badbh, Macha and Nemhain are warrior Goddesses from the Irish myths: they are the three aspects of the triple-Goddess the Morrígan. The virgins and mothers are legion, but include Anu or Dana, Arianrhod, Arnemetia and Epona, the horse Goddess. Ériu (also a triple-Goddess) and Medb are principal Irish Goddesses. The Goddesses are sometimes important as wives and mothers, but they are also significant figures in their own right, often with their own complex mythological tales and legends.

The following paragraphs describe very briefly the main named ancient Celtic Gods, Goddesses and divine heroes and heroines, and their provenance, principal roles or characteristics. Some are attested by archaeological evidence, for example the Gods of war to whom dedicatory inscriptions were carved along Hadrian's Wall; some are attested by place names, for example famous sacred springs or wells; and many appear in the extensive Welsh and Irish vernacular literature. Unlike Gods in some other pantheons, Celtic deities lead lives which often include very personal and human experiences, including pain and death; the fact that the God dies is unimportant, because (the same as for the rest of us) death is simply a transition to another phase of life. The descriptions here are very brief, because there are so many of these deities and heroes and there is only limited space here, but many modern Druids actively worship some or all of these beings and have longstanding relationships with them. Each of them has a story or further background, which you may want to follow up further, depending on your personal interest.

Main Deities

In the Welsh or Brythonic tradition, the universal mother is Madron or Modron, and the universal son is Mabon or Maponos, the names simply meaning "mother" and "son." Bel, Beli or Beli Mawr ("Great Beli"), whose name means "brilliant" or "bright," and may be related to the Biblical name Ba'al, meaning "Lord," is both the Sun God and Son God, God of the feast of Beltan or Beltane ("Bel's Fire"), at which livestock are purified and blessed on May 1st. Arawn is the Prince of Annwn, the Otherworld. Brân or Bendigeidfran ("Blessed Brân"), son of Llyr, whose name means "crow" or "raven," is the superhuman giant who leads the Britons against the Irish to avenge insults to his sister Branwen, and whose head survives for seven years before his companions bury it at London's Tower Hill. Arianrhod, whose name means "Silver Wheel," is the daughter of Dôn and the sister of Gwydion. She first appears as the virgin aspect of the triple Goddess, but she magically gives birth to two boys (see below). Dylan, whose name means "Wave of the Sea," is a sea God, and Lleu Llaw Gyffes ("Lleu or Bright One of the Steady Hand") is a divine warrior and God associated with light, the sky and oak trees. Gwydion, Arianrhod's brother, is a divine magician (i.e., Druid as well as God) who spends three years shape-shifted into a stag, a boar and a wolf before returning to human form, and who creates for Lleu Llaw Gyffes a wife made out of flowers, Blodeuwedd. Math, son of Mathonwy and lord of Gwynedd, assists Gwydion in this magic, and is thought to have introduced pigs into Britain. Rhiannon and Epona are other great Goddesses of the British tradition. Epona, the horse Goddess, was worshipped across the whole of Europe, in North Africa, and even in Rome. Rhiannon, whose name may be derived from Rigantona, meaning "Great Queen," is similarly associated with horses. She also has three magic birds, whose singing is so sweet that it lulls the living to sleep and, conversely, raises the dead back to life. Rhiannon marries Pwyll, the king who exchanges places in the Underworld with Arawn Pen Annwn, and their son is called Pryderi, whose name literally means "Concern" or "Worry." Manawydan, son of Llyr, is the great God of the sea, the equivalent of the Irish Manannán mac Lir.

In the Irish tradition, Anu, Ana, Dana or Danu (who may originally have been two separate Goddesses), is the chief Goddess of and gives her name to the *Tuatha Dé Danann*. The Daghda or Dagda, meaning "Good God," is the father God, and male chief. Donn is the God of death. Da Derga, whose name means "Red God," red being one of the colors of death, is probably another name for Donn. The founding Goddesses of Ireland are Banbha, Fódla and Ériu (all war Goddesses), with Ériu being the source of Ireland's Gaelic name, Éire, which is also often seen in its genitive form, as in *Poblacht na hÉireann*, the Republic of Ireland. Ériu is a solar deity, married to Mac Grené, whose name means "Son of the Sun." Brigit, Brigid or Bríd, meaning "Bright," or "Shining," a powerful Goddess of childbirth, new beginnings, healing and poetry, was probably also a triple Goddess originally. She is also associated with smith-craft. Ogmios is the God of speech and eloquence, which were and remain very important attributes in the Celtic tradition. He carries a great club, like Hercules, and is sometimes depicted with a chain of silver links coming from his mouth, representing the power of correct utterance. He created the secret Ogham alphabet. Lugh, also called Lugh Lámhfhada, "Lugh of the Long Arm," is the Irish counterpart of the Welsh Lleu Llaw Gyffes; he is a warrior and master of crafts. The passing of his foster mother Tailtiu is commemorated at the *nasadh* or funeral commemoration of Lughnasa or Lughnasad on August 1st, one of the major Celtic festivals. Deirdre, whose story appears in the Ulster Cycle, is the daughter of Fedlimid, chief Bard to Conchobar, King of Ulster. She elopes with Naoise, a God who initially appears in the form of a bird, but is captured and punished by Conchobar. She escapes by killing herself, thus becoming a symbol of courage and independence of spirit.

Oenghus is the hero of another well-known mythological sequence. Known also as Mac Óc or "Son of Youth," which relates him to the Brythonic Mabon, he is the son of the Dagda and Boann, tutelary Goddess of the River Boyne—the Dagda miraculously makes the Sun stand still for nine months so that Boann's pregnancy may be kept concealed. Oenghus's richly complex stories all involve love. In the *Dream of Oenghus*, he falls in love with Caer Ibormeith ("Yew Berry," the yew being the tree of death and resurrection) before he even meets her, having seen a vision of her in a dream, and shape-shifts into a swan to release her from a powerful enchantment, which has made her also a swan. In the lovely and very Druidic story of *Midhir and Étain*, Oenghus helps Midhir find his beloved Étain, who has been shape-shifted into a butterfly and has spent a thousand years being buffeted around the world before Midhir, with Oenghus's help, is able to find her, re-born as a beautiful maiden, and rescue her.

Nuadu or Nuada is a king of the *Tuatha Dé Danann* until he loses an arm, and thus becomes ineligible to remain king because of his physical imperfection. The divine smith Dian Cécht makes a metal prosthesis for him, and he resumes his kingship as Nuadu Argat Lámh, "Nuadu of the Silver Hand." Goibhniu, Luchta and Creidhne are divine representatives of the related crafts of smith, wright and metalworker. Goibhniu's Welsh equivalent is the divine smith Gofannon. The related common Cornish surname Angove is derived from *an gov*, "the smith."

Gods and Goddesses of Healing

There are many healing deities, often associated with sacred springs or wells. In an age when there were no eye-glasses or corrective lenses, it is not surprising that many of these Gods and Goddesses were reputed to cure diseases and afflictions of the eye. Lenus, one of the most widely venerated Gods of healing, also known as Mars Lenus, had curative sanctuaries at Trier and Pommern. He was also invoked by the epithet Iovantucarus, "Protector of the Young," suggesting that sick children were brought to him for healing. His consort was the Gaulish Goddess Ancamna, who was also a healing deity. Ancamna is also associated with Smertrius, a Gaulish father-God; a large shrine and temple complex at Möhn near Trier is dedicated to them as a couple. Icovellauna, a Gaulish Goddess with dedications found at Metz and Trier, presided over a sacred healing spring. Mullo, also called Mars Mullo, who had shrines at Nantes and Rennes, was a healer of eye afflictions; his name is the Latin word for "mule," so he may also have had a connection with mules or horses. Sirona, another Gaulish Goddess frequently depicted with a husband or consort, in this case Apollo Grannus, was the deity of a healing shrine connected to thermal springs. As at Bath in England, which was dedicated to the Celtic Goddess Sulis and later rededicated by the Romans to Minerva, natural thermal springs were widely recognized as places of healing. Coventina was the Goddess of the healing spring at Carrawburgh on Hadrian's Wall. The Goddess Aveta was a mother–Goddess of fertility and plenty, as well as of healing, depicted in small clay figurines as holding either a cornucopia of harvest foods, or a small dog.

Nodens, the God frequently depicted as or called "The Dog," is a British God, who had a large healing sanctuary at Lydney Park in Gloucestershire, England dedicated to him. His name is related to the Irish God Nuadu Argat Lámh. His sanctuary, like many others, had a special sleeping chamber or dormitory called an *abaton*, where supplicants would invite the God to visit and heal them while they slept. The word is Greek, literally meaning "do not tread" and indicating any extremely wild or inaccessible place. The Abaton at the Asclepion in Epidaurus was a building where dream cures by ενκοιμεσιο (*enkoimesis*, literally "incubation") took place. This is another possible area where the ancient Greeks and the ancient Celtic Druids shared religious thinking and practice. Another deliberate Druidic sleep ritual was the *tarbhfess* or "bull dream," in which the Druid would sleep wrapped in a bull-hide to discover through dream the name of the next true king or queen of the *tuath*. "Sleeping on it" is still a perfectly valid and viable way for modern Druids to invite a particular God or Goddess to come to them, to seek an important vision, or simply to recuperate from illness.

Aveta was one of several Germanic-Celtic Goddesses of fertility and healing. Moritasgus or Apollo Moritasgus, a Gaulish God whose name means "Lots of Sea Water," had a healing sanctuary at Alesia in Burgundy that included a bathing pool, which was also common at healing centers. Surgeons' tools found at his site suggest that the supervising Druids may have conducted surgical operations as well as leading healing prayers. The depiction of the Gaulish Goddess Ianuaria with a set of pan-pipes in her sanctuary at Beire-le-Châtel suggests that music may also have been part of healing rituals. Birds and birdsong are also frequently associated with healing. Clíodna, an Irish Goddess of the Otherworld, possessed three magical birds of healing, which lulled the sick to restorative sleep with their singing, like Rhiannon's magical birds in the Welsh stories.

Water and River Deities

Apart from natural springs, water in just about every other form was also venerated or considered the home or world of the ancestors and a powerful source of spiritual energy. Every river, large and small, had its own deity, although only the names of the largest and best known have survived to us. In Britain, Sabrina was the tutelary Goddess of the River Severn; Tamesas was Goddess of the Thames; and Trisantona, whose name means "Great Thoroughfare," was Goddess of the River Trent. Condatis ("Meeting of the Waters") is the God of the River Wear in northeast England, although he was originally a Gaulish God. Verbeia is Goddess of the River Wharfe in Teesdale, and had an altar built to her at Ilkley in North Yorkshire, where she was depicted holding a large snake in each hand.

Cluta, Clutha or Cliota is the Goddess of the Scottish River Clyde, or *Abhainn Chluaidh* in Gàidhlig. In Ireland, Sinann (pronounced *shee-nan*) is the Goddess of the Shannon and Boann the Goddess of the Boyne. Boann's husband, also a water deity, is Nechtan, who was the protector of the sacred well from which the River Boyne was created when Boann broke the *geis* or taboo against approaching it and the well overflowed unstoppably. Dana or Danu of the *Tuatha Dé Danann*, although Irish, gave her name to the great River Danube, which passes through eleven European countries. Sequana is the Goddess of the River Seine in France, and the similarly-named Souconna is the Goddess of the River Saône.

I have already mentioned the Welsh sea God Manawydan ap Llyr and his Irish counterpart Manannán mac Lir. Nehalennia, who had two shrines on the North Sea, is a sea Goddess, who was worshipped by Romans as well as by Celts; she is depicted, as Poseidon and Neptune were, with dolphins, other sea creatures, and shells, but she was also very frequently pictured as an attractive young woman accompanied by a large and friendly dog, reminiscent of Nodens, which suggests that she may also have been associated with healing. Ritona or Pritona, anciently worshipped at Trier, is a Goddess of fords and water crossings, which have practical significance because they make traveling convenient, but also have spiritual significance because they are a reminder of the narrow transition space between this world and the Otherworld. The British Goddess Latis is associated with ponds, pools and bogs. Telo, who gave her name to the French town of Toulon in the Dordogne, is Goddess of the sacred spring there.

Deities of the Forest and Wild Places

The best known of all the "wild" Gods is Cernunnos, the horned God of the wild forest and wild animals, who is depicted on the famous Gundestrup cauldron, discovered in 1891 in a peat bog in Denmark, which may date from as early as the 4th century BCE. He wears horns or antlers (his name means "The Horned One"), which may also have been part of the ancient Druidic ceremonial costume. In one hand he grips a ram-headed snake. Like his later classical counterparts Pan and Silvanus, Cernunnos represents not only stags and boars and other creatures of the hunt, he is the God of all living things and wild places. He wears antlers because he is part wild creature himself. There are countless examples of shape-shifting between animal and human forms in the vernacular mythology, perhaps the best known example being Twrch Trwyth, who is a huge, ferocious boar, but who once had been a human king. Tarvostrigaranus, depicted in stone sculptures in Paris and Trier, is a bull, accompanied by three cranes (which is exactly what the name *tarvos-tri-garanus* means). The bull symbolizes the male God, and the three cranes the Triple Goddess. Arduinna, after whom the Ardennes is named, is a bear Goddess, as is also the Germanic-Celtic Goddess Artio. Cunomaglus, whose name means "Hound Lord," is a British hunter God.

Wild places have their Gods, as well as wild animals. Arnemetia and Nemetona are Goddesses of the *nemeton* or sacred grove. Taranis takes his name from *taran*, "thunder," and is associated with hilltops and mountain peaks. Alisanos is a Gaulish God, simply of rock, which, as I described in Chapter 1, can have *anam* or *anima* just as much as an animal or a plant can. Ialonus is similarly a God who represents the land, particularly cultivated land, with the *ialo* part of the name meaning "glade," similar to *nemeton*. At Lancaster in England, he was worshipped as Ialonus Contrebis, "Ialonus Who Lives Among Us." A Goddess, Ialona, was worshipped at Nímes in French Provence.

Deities of War

There are many Celtic Gods and Goddesses of war. Andraste, also known as Andate or Andarte, known to have been especially venerated by the British warrior-queen Boudicca, is mentioned by the Roman historian Dio Cassius: "While they were doing all this [massacring Roman women] in the grove of Andate [Andraste] and other sacred places, they performed sacrifices, feasted and abandoned all restraint (Andraste was their name for Victory and she enjoyed their special reverence)."[12]

The principal war Goddesses of Ireland are Badbh, Macha, and Nemhain, who collectively are the triple–Goddess the Morrígan. Badbh means "Fury" or "Violence." Macha, meaning literally "Field," was a Goddess of the land as well as of war. Nemhain means "Frenzy" or "Panic"; in the war between Ulster and Connacht, she raises such a hideous shriek that a hundred Connacht warriors die of sheer terror. Morrígan means "Great Queen" (the cognate of the Brythonic Rigantona or Rhiannon). She is often portrayed as a crow or raven, like Brân in the Welsh tales. Scáthach, the war Goddess from Skye in Scotland, teaches the warrior-hero Cú Chulainn the arts of war. As described earlier, Celtic tribal women, as well as men, frequently fought in battle. Balor, the Irish giant king of the Fomorians, had only one enormous eye, but could kill with one glance from it; when he grew old, his eyelid became so heavy that four men with pulleys and ropes had to open it for him. Mac Da Thó appears in the Ulster Cycle. He owns a giant dog and a giant pig, and is a God of the Underworld as well as a God of war.

Belatucadrus, whose name means "Fair Shining," is a war God who was widely revered in northern Britain. Cocidius, from the same region, was worshipped both as a God of war and of hunting. In one dedication from near Hadrian's Wall, he is associated with the God Vernostonus, who is the personification of the alder tree, further suggesting that Cocidius was a God of the forest and the hunt, like Cernunnos, Pan or Silvanus, as well as a God of war. Vitiris, from the same region, appears in a number of dedications, all written by men in clumsy Latin and with a wide variety of spellings, suggesting that he was a local war God who appealed particularly to the lower ranks of the Roman imperial army.

The Roman poet Lucan, writing in the first century of the Common Era, names the three principal Gaulish Gods of war as Taranis, Esus and Teutates. We have met Taranis already: he is *taran* or thunder. Esus, which is probably a title meaning "lord" or "master," requires human sacrifice, specifically (according to Lucan) victims being stabbed, then hung in trees to bleed to death (Lucan is notorious for his gory descriptions of Celts and Druids). Teutates or Toutatis is also a title, referring to a Gaulish tribe, and is found in several inscriptions; *teuta*, the Gaulish cognate of the Irish word *tuath*, which we have already met, means "tribe," "people" or "territory."

Warrior Heroes

In addition to the Gods and Goddesses of war, there are many warrior heroes, semi-divine and usually possessed of supernatural powers as well as physical strength and courage. They are found in greatest abundance in the Irish literature. Best known of them all perhaps is Cú Chulainn, hero of the Ulster tales, whom I have already mentioned. Like a God of the forest, he is closely associated with animals: on the day he was born, two foals were also born, which became his chariot horses, the Grey of Macha and the Black of Saingliu. His birth name was Sétanta, but at the age of seven he killed the ferocious guard hound of Culann the Smith, and, vowing to replace the dog's function, took the name Cú Chulainn, literally "Culann's Hound." He has magical weapons, he has extraordinary physical characteristics, but his best-known attribute is his *ríastrad* or war frenzy (Thomas Kinsella translates it as "warp spasm"), when battle rage contorts his body into that of a monster, and he is filled with such berserk fury that he cannot tell friend from foe and is deadly to anybody and anything within his reach. Dr. Bannon and the Incredible Hulk are modern counterparts.

Ferghus mac Róich is one of Cú Chulainn's foster-fathers. He is tall as a giant, has the strength of seven hundred men, and requires seven women to satisfy him sexually. At one meal he can eat seven pigs, seven deer, and seven cows and drink seven vats of ale. His magic sword can stretch to the length of a rainbow. Conall Cernach, Cú Chulainn's other foster-father, is the son of the poet Amhairghin or Amergin and of Findchóem or Fionnchaomh, sister of the Ulster king Conchobar mac Nessa. Cú Roi, meaning "Roi's Hound," is the opposite of Ferghus and Conall, an evil sorcerer and enemy of Cú Chulainn.

Fionn or Finn mac Cumhaill is the hero of another set of tales, these concerning the band of the Fianna, the elite guard of the High King of Ireland. "Fenian," a general term for the Irish (not always complimentary) derives from the names Fionn and Fianna. Fionn is reared by a Druidess, and acquires supernatural knowledge of all things by meeting the Druid Finnegas and sipping accidentally from the Cauldron of Wisdom. I wrote a poem about that incident some years ago, and it is perhaps the simplest way of retelling that story:

> Finnegas the Druid stood three feet high,
> a leprechaun, goat-shaggy, nut-brown.
> Seven years he spent, patient and sly,
> feeding hazel nuts, big as his tiny, hairy fist,
> to the Salmon, wisest creature living, who down
> in the deep, dark pool of knowledge swished
> and thrashed, bright his staring eye.
>
> Finnegas caught him with a silver hook,
> heaved his shining, weighty shimmer
> into the bubbling cauldron to cook.
>
> Came that instant, from the forest glimmer,
> a boy, hair like frost, face like a berry,
> eyes blue as robin's eggs, his smile as merry
> as a gold sun rising on a green hill in spring.
> "Tend this, lad," said little Finnegas, knowing,
> as all good Druids do, what next must come.
>
> The boy took the wooden spoon and stirred.
> A splash fell. He licked. Like a shot from a gun,
> all things past, present and future were upon him

and in him and of him and never to be undone.
"Fionn mac Cumhaill," said the broken-hearted Druid.
The little boy nodded and slowly sucked his thumb.

Oisin (pronounced approximately *aw-shin*), Fionn's son, also has a collection of tales about him, the most famous of which is quintessentially Druidic. It describes his stay in *Tír na nÓg* (*cheer-na-nawk*), the Land of the Ever Young. Oisin meets and falls in love with Niamh (pronounced *Neev*) of the Golden Hair, daughter of the sea God Manannán mac Lir, and one of the queens of *Tír na nÓg*. Oisin marries Niamh and joins her, but after some time feels the need to go back to visit his old country. Niamh solemnly warns him that he must never set foot on his own land. Initially, he follows her instructions, but, accidentally falling from his horse and touching the ground, he instantly withers into a 300-year-old man and dies.

The Triple Goddess

In the ancient Celtic tradition, all the High Gods and Goddesses were of triple aspect, or appeared in three separate identities. The number three was powerful and sacred, so the most powerful deities demonstrated their strength in their triplication. The Celtic triple-Goddesses were simply who or what they were, but times three. For example, the Iunones (literally "the Junos") were a triplet of Goddesses derived, as the name tells us, from the Roman Goddess Juno. Similarly, the *Matres Domesticae* (literally "Home Mothers") were mother-Goddesses worshipped widely in Britain, while the almost identical *Matrones Aufaniae* were venerated in the Rhineland, wearing bonnets and long robes, and carrying baskets of fruits and vegetables. There were also the *Matres Griselicae* at Gréoulx in southern Gaul, and the *Matres Nemausicae* at the healing spring and shrine complex at Nemausus, modern Nîmes in Provence.

In modern Druidism, influenced by Wicca and the Mediterranean traditions, as well as by some of the vernacular tales, the Goddess is often depicted not just as triplicate, but as triplicated in three phases: the Maiden or Virgin, young, innocent, beautiful and alluring; the Mother, bearing and raising children, bringer of fertility and fecundity; and the Crone, source of great wisdom and experience, ritual leader, and layer out of the dead. Sometimes a Goddess represents only one of the types, while others may appear in all three roles. This Virgin-Mother-Crone triple–Goddess has become part of many modern Druidic and Wiccan traditions, and even beyond—for example, Snow White, the wicked Queen and the apple-bearing Witch are loosely modeled on her.

Étain, of the Midhir and Étain story already mentioned, is an example of the Goddess as Maiden. Arianrhod, also already mentioned, is literally a virgin at the beginning of her story, with Math, Lord of Gwynedd, able to rest his feet in her lap only because she *was* a virgin. However, when Math ruthlessly tests her virginity by making her step over his magic staff or wand, she immediately miraculously gives birth to the two boys who are known later as Dylan and Lleu Llaw Gyffes. She is now the Mother or Madron. Epona, who is always depicted with horses, and whose veneration was very widespread both geographically and across time, is essentially a Virgin Goddess, although she is also depicted with *cornucopiae* like a mother Goddess, and associated with rituals for the dead, like the Crone. Epona's complexity and widespread influence reflects how important horses were in Celtic culture. Similar to Epona in some ways, Rhiannon was also associated with horses, and first appears as a wonderfully beautiful and desirable virgin when Pwyll, King of Dyfed, tries to catch up with her while she is riding, but no matter how fast his horse gallops, her horse stays ahead of him with no apparent effort, revealing her divine status. Like Snow White, and like Clíodna of the Irish tradition, Rhiannon is surrounded by little birds, who praise her in endless sweet song, and who carry messages for her.

Rosmerta, whose name means "Wheel of Plenty," is a Goddess who brings fertility and rich harvests to the world. Aericura is a German-Celtic mother Goddess and Goddess of the Underworld. Bergusia, a Gaulish Goddess of arts and crafts, consort of the God Ucuetis, is also the Mother. In this aspect, the Goddess is very frequently represented as one half of a divine couple. Nantosuelta ("Winding River") and Sucellus ("The Hammer-Wielder") are another example of the divine couple of fecundity and prosperity. Sirona was a widely venerated Gaulish Goddess, sometimes depicted alone and sometimes with her consort Apollo Grannus ("Apollo of the Sun"). Damona, whose name means "Great Cow," is a Gaulish Goddess of fertility. The Irish Goddess Queen Medb, whose name means "The Drunken One" (associated with mead wine or liquor), and who is also intimately involved in war and death, is nevertheless essentially a Mother Goddess. At the critical climax in her desperate battle with Cú Chulainn, she is forced to ask leave to withdraw from the fight for a short while, because a terrible rush of blood is upon her: it is her menstrual period, and its inclusion right at the critical juncture of this epic mythological story demonstrates, with powerful emphasis, her nature as the fertile, child-bearing Mother Goddess, bringer of life.

Fedelma, prophetess and poet, is an example of the Wise Woman or Crone. She serves at Queen Medb's court in Connacht, and offers counsel as Medb considers whether or not to invade Ulster to capture the Brown Bull of Cooley. It is Fedelma who warns Medb of the dangers, and tells her that she foresees the warriors of Connacht defeated by Cú Chulainn and drenched in blood. A classical example of the Crone is Cassandra, Princess of Troy and daughter of King Priam and Queen Hecuba, whose fateful prophecies are ignored or denied, leading to tragic consequences. The Greek Goddess Hekate, Romanized to Hecate, is a complex Goddess, but is often thought of in Neo-Paganism (especially by Wiccans) as a manifestation of the Crone. We noted earlier how the Roman emperors Alexander Severus and Diocletian were each given prophetic warnings about their reigns by female Druids, and modern Druids may think of the keeping of wisdom and the making of true prophecies as connected with or channeled through the Crone or Wise Woman.

4. Classical Druidic Roles and Responsibilities

Classical Descriptions

Caesar, writing about the Druids of Gaul, describes their main responsibilities:

> They preside over sacred things, have the charge of public and private sacrifices, and explain their religion. To them a great number of youths have recourse for the sake of acquiring instruction, and they are in great honor among them. For they generally settle all their disputes, both public and private; and if there is any transgression perpetrated, any murder committed, or any dispute about inheritance or boundaries, they decide in respect of them; they appoint rewards and penalties ...[1]

Or, to summarize, Druids were priests, teachers and judges. Caesar also tells us that the Druids in Gaul were regulated by an Archdruid, although he does not use that term:

> But one presides over all these Druids, who possesses the supreme authority among them. At his death, if any one of the other excels in dignity, the same succeeds him: but if several have equal pretensions, the president is elected by the votes of the Druids, sometimes even they contend about the supreme dignity by force of arms ...[2]

Caesar also tells us that there was an annual gathering of Druids, and that Gaulish Druidism originated in Britain, which was still the main training center for Druidism.

Cicero and Diodorus Siculus both describe divination and augury, although Diodorus's choice of words suggests that soothsaying was separate from the main Druidic functions:

> They have philosophers and theologians who are held in much honor and are called Druids: they have sooth-sayers too of great renown who tell the future by watching the flights of birds and by observation of the entrails of victims; and everyone waits upon their word.[3]

Pomponius Mela, writing in the first century CE, describes how the Druids "profess to know the size and shape of the world, the movements of the heavens and the stars, and the will of the Gods." He also says that the Druids "teach many things to the nobles of Gaul in a course of instruction lasting as long as twenty years, meeting in secret either in a cave or in secluded dales."

Pliny the Elder (23–79 CE) gives us a detailed and (at first glance) convincing description of an important Druidic ceremonial, the cutting of the sacred mistletoe:

> The Druids—for so their magicians are called—held nothing more sacred than the mistletoe and the tree that bears it, always supposing that tree to be the oak. But they choose groves formed of oaks for the sake of the tree alone, and they never perform any of their rites except in the presence of a branch of it; so that it seems probable that the priests themselves may derive their name from the Greek word for that tree. In fact, they think that everything that grows on it has been sent from heaven and is a proof that the tree was chosen by the God himself. The mistletoe, however, is found but rarely upon the oak; and when found, is gathered with due religious ceremony, if possible on the sixth day of the moon (for it is by the moon that they measure their months and years, and also their ages of thirty years). They choose this day because the moon, though not yet in the middle of her course, has already considerable influence. They call the mistletoe by a name meaning, in their language, the all-healing. Having made preparation for sacrifice and a banquet beneath the trees, they bring thither two white bulls, whose horns are bound then for the first time. Clad in a white robe, the priest ascends the tree and cuts the mistletoe with a golden sickle, and it is received by others in a white cloak. Then they kill the victims, praying that God will render this gift of his propitious to those to whom he has granted it. They believe that the mistletoe, taken in drink, imparts fecundity to barren animals, and that it is an antidote for all poisons. Such are the religious feelings that are entertained towards trifling things by many peoples.[4]

As soon as we start looking more closely at the details of Pliny's description, however, it becomes clear that there are problems. In Britain and France (Gaul, as it was) mistletoe hardly ever grows on oaks, if at all, as Pliny himself admits—the wood is too hard. It is much more likely to be found on apple or hawthorn. There is no trace of any mistletoe cult in ancient Ireland, nor is the mistletoe directly included in the sacred tree alphabet. Graves and others have assumed that the mistletoe being cut from the oak represents the ceremonial emasculation or castration of Lugh or Ludd, the archetypal father-God, because its silvery-white berries are reminiscent of drops of semen and its Latin and Greek names *viscus* and *ixias* are related to the words *vis* and *ischus*, meaning strength.[5] There are two different species of mistletoe, mistletoe proper and the loranthus, of which the eastern European loranthus is the only one which grows on oaks, and that extremely rarely. Graves suggests that the Druids may have imported loranthus specially for ceremonial purposes and grafted it onto native oaks, although that seems unlikely to have been successful on a large scale. Similarly, white bulls were sacrificed on very rare occasions at the Roman Capitol, but it is difficult to imagine that enough of them could have been found in Gaul or Britain for regular sacrifice. White robes were worn by Roman priests, while British and Gaulish Druids were far more likely to have worn furs, feathers, plaids and earth-colored or naturally dyed fabrics. A golden sickle, beautiful as it might be symbolically, would be hopeless for cutting mistletoe, since the metal is very soft and the wood is very tough: mistletoe timber, as a parasitic plant, grows extremely slowly and can end up almost as hard as iron. All told, Pliny's famous description reads like a fabrication, written for a not very discriminating popular Roman readership. Pliny also elsewhere describes a mysterious Druidic egg, which he calls an *anguinum*, which nobody has ever satisfactorily identified or explained, and of course he trots out the standard xenophobic Roman charge of cannibalism: "Therefore we cannot too highly appreciate our debt to the Romans for having put an end to this monstrous cult, whereby to murder a man was an act of the greatest devoutness, and to eat his flesh most beneficial."

Ellen Evert Hopman defends Pliny's description (the only classical description of Druidic ritual we have) and gives her reasons and explanations:

> ...Or the sickle was gold plated bronze, in honor of the Moon, maybe, and the white robes were to honor the white berries of the plant. Yes, it is rarely found on oak, which is why it was such a big deal to find it growing on one.... It turns out the mistletoe growing on oak is the most potent for cancerous tumors, used in modern times by Anthroposophical medicine doctors as "Iscador," and I think the Druids were likely aware of this. They sacrificed white oxen in thanksgiving for this truly powerful gift.[6]

Descriptions in the Vernacular Texts

The vernacular material confirms the very high status of Druids. At the court of King Conchobar, for example, no person might speak before the king, on pain of death. This was a *geis* or taboo which was inviolable. However, King Conchobar himself was under a *geis* that he might not speak before his Druid Cathbad, so whenever the king had something important to announce, he had to stand and wait until the Druid invited him to speak.

The list of ten officers which every High King of Ireland should keep about him, promulgated in Cormac's time, listed a prince (as body attendant), a *brehon* ("lawyer," to interpret the law), a Druid (to offer sacrifices, and practice divination and magic), a physician (to practice healing), a Bard (to compose satires and panegyrics), a *seancha* ("historian," to preserve the genealogies and history), a musician (to compose and perform songs and poems), and three general stewards.

Further evidence that women could function as Druids as well as men is given in a poem from The Metrical Dindsenchas of Ireland, which includes the following verse:

> Gaine daughter of pure Gumor,
> nurse of mead-loving Mide,
> surpassed all women though she was silent;
> she was learned and a seer and a chief Druid.[7]

Ellen Evert Hopman explains why the false myth that all ancient Druids were men has persisted for so long:

> Some of the blame for this misconception can be placed on the Roman historians who reported on Celtic culture, even as they decimated the Druids who were the intelligentsia. The Romans tended to ignore, downplay or overlook the true status of the women of the tribes. The next groups to document Celtic society were male Christian monks who also tended to ignore and downplay the status of Celtic women while capturing the tales and oral histories in their *scriptoria*. Finally as modern archaeology and scholarship focused on Celtic artifacts and history, scholars until very recently were almost all men, who downplayed or ignored the role of powerful women in ancient Celtic times. But the evidence was always there for those who cared to find it.[8]

In Irish, a female Druid was called a *ban-drui*, or "woman Druid." They are also found in ecclesiastical writings, for example derogatorily called "pythonesses" in one of St Patrick's canons. The enchantresses and fairy-women called *ban-tuatha* and *ban-sídhe* or *banshee* may also have been female Druids.

Druids did not usually fight in battle, although there are many tales of Druids using incantations and battle magic in the cause of war. An early Irish poem describes how the Druid Trostan of the Cruithnigh devised an antidote for a poison in which invading warriors of the Tuatha Fiodhgha had soaked all their weapons. When Druids made incantations and prayers before or during battle, they frequently did so directly in front of the foremost warriors, i.e., in the middle of the front-line fighting zone, hopping on alternate feet and turning in a slow circle, sometimes to a drum beat. The war dances of several North American Indian tribes follow exactly the same pattern. Sometimes the purpose of the incantation was to create a "Druid fence" or *airbe druad* as it was called in Ireland, or *snaidm druad* ("Druid's knot"), a kind of "force-field" which the enemy would struggle to penetrate. Although a modern sensibility may find such magical functions childish or incredible, they were very much part of what a Druid was expected to master. In tale after tale in the vernacular literature, especially in Ireland, Druidic predictions (especially maledictions) and Druidic magical incantations feature significantly in the sequence of events, especially in war.

Druids were distinguished in appearance by a tonsure, at least in Ireland, as evidenced by the fact that St Patrick disapproved of it, and probably in

Britain too. Pádraig's disapproval also implies that the Christian monk's tonsure and the Druidic tonsure were different; it has been suggested that while the Christian tonsure was a circle on the back or crown of the head, as is familiar from many images, the Druidic tonsure may have involved the shaving of the front part of the head from ear to ear. The tonsure was called *airbacc giunnae* in Irish and *norma magica* in Latin. When the two Druids Mael and Calpair, who were brothers and the tutors of King Laegaire's daughters Ethnea and Fedelma, were converted to Christianity, Patrick ordered them to shave their heads to obliterate their Druidic tonsures. The name Mael means bald (*moel* in modern Welsh, *maol* in Gàidhlig), so his Druidic name may have referred to his tonsure. In classical times, male Druids also grew long, full beards, while the fashion among laymen was to shave the cheeks and chin, leaving a full moustache.

The initial employment by Laegaire of Mael and Calpair reminds us that Druids were teachers, not only of the next generation of Druids, but also of the children of the aristocracy in general. Even Saint Columba received his first education from a Druid. Ethnea and Fedelma were sent from the royal palace to live at Cruachan in Connaught with Mael and Calpair. Laegaire also had two "chief Druids," Lucetmail and Lochru, who organized all details of Patrick's visit to Tara.

Rituals, Ceremonial and Magic

There are almost countless Romantic Revival (see Chapter 6) descriptions of ancient ritual, magical events and ceremonials, but, as we shall see, distinguishing the historical from the hysterical in these sources can be difficult, and there is no doubt that much blatant invention, like that of Iolo Morganwg, took place. Nevertheless, here are a few brief extracts from the Sacred Sites website which give us a flavor of what, according to the Revivalists, may have been ancient practices:

...Similar actions—power over the weather, the use of incantations and amulets, shapeshifting and invisibility, etc.—were, and still are in remote Celtic regions, ascribed to witches. Much of the Druidic art, however, was also supposed to be possessed by saints and clerics, both in the past and in recent times. But women remained as magicians when the Druids had disappeared, partly because of female conservatism, partly because, even in Pagan times, they had worked more or less secretly. At last the Church proscribed them and persecuted them.... Thus the Druid Cathbad covered the plain over which Deirdre was escaping with "a great-waved sea." Druids also produced blinding snowstorms, or changed day into night—feats ascribed to them even in the Lives of Saints. Or they discharge "shower-clouds of fire" on the opposing hosts, as in the case of the Druid Mag Ruith, who made a magic fire, and flying upwards towards it, turned it upon the enemy, whose Druid in vain tried to divert it. When the Druids of Cormac dried up all the waters in the land, another Druid shot an arrow, and where it fell there issued a torrent of water. The Druid Mathgen boasted of being able to throw mountains on the enemy, and frequently Druids made trees or stones appear as armed men, dismaying the opposing host in this way. They could also fill the air with the clash of battle, or with the dread cries of eldritch things. Similar powers are ascribed to other persons. The daughters of Calatin raised themselves aloft on an enchanted wind, and discovered Cúchulainn when he was hidden away by Cathbad. Later they produced a magic mist to discomfit the hero. Such mists occur frequently in the sagas, and in one of them the Tuatha Dé Danann arrived in Ireland. The priestesses of Sena could rouse sea and wind by their enchantments, and, later, Celtic witches have claimed the same power.... In folk-survivals the practice of rainmaking is connected with sacred springs, and even now in rural France processions to shrines, usually connected with a holy well, are common in time of drought. Thus people and priest go to the fountain of Baranton in procession, singing hymns, and there pray for rain. The priest then dips his foot in the water, or throws some of it on the rocks. In other cases the image of a saint is carried to a well and asperged, as divine images formerly were, or the waters are beaten or thrown into the air. Another custom was that a virgin should clean out a sacred well, and formerly she had to be nude. Nudity also forms part of an old ritual used in Gaul. In time of drought the girls of the village followed the youngest virgin in a state of nudity to seek the herb *belinuntia*. This she uprooted, and was then led to a river and there asperged by the others. In this case the asperging imitated the falling rain, and was meant to produce it automatically. While some of these rites suggest the use of magic by the folk themselves, in others the presence of the Christian priest points to the fact that, formerly, a Druid was necessary as the rain producer. In some cases the priest has inherited through long ages the rainmaking or tempest-quelling powers of the Pagan priesthood, and is often besought to exercise them.... Causing invisibility by means of a spell called *feth fiada*, which made a person unseen or hid him in a magic mist, was also used by the Druids as well as by Christian saints. S. Patrick's hymn, called *Fâed Fiada*, was sung by him when his enemies lay in wait, and caused a glamour in them. The incantation itself, *fith-fath*, is still remembered in Highland glens. In the case of S. Patrick he and his followers appeared as deer, and this power of shape shifting was wielded both by Druids and women.... By a "drink of oblivion" Druids and other persons could make one forget even the most dearly beloved. Thus Cúchulainn was made to forget Fand, and his wife Emer to forget her jealousy. This is a reminiscence of potent drinks brewed from herbs which caused hallucinations, *e.g.* that of the change of shape. In other cases they were of a narcotic nature and caused a deep sleep, an instance being the draught given by Grainne to Fionn and his men ... Druids also made a "hedge," the *airbe druad*, round an army, perhaps circumambulating it and saying spells so that the attacking force might not break through. If any one could leap this "hedge," the spell was broken, but he lost his life. This was done at the battle of Cul Dremne, at which S. Columba was present and aided the heroic leaper with his prayers.... Several of these instances have shown the use of spells, and the Druid was believed to possess powerful incantations to discomfit an enemy or to produce other magical results. A special posture was adopted—standing on one leg, with one arm outstretched and one eye closed, perhaps to concentrate the force of the spell, but the power lay mainly in the spoken words, as we have seen in discussing Celtic formulæ of prayer.... In other cases spells were used in medicine or for healing wounds. Thus the Tuatha Dé Danann told the Fomorians that they need not oppose them, because their Druids would restore the slain to life, and when Cúchulainn was wounded we hear less of medicines than of incantations used to stanch his blood. In other cases the Druid could remove barrenness by spells.... A magical sleep is often caused by music in the sagas, *e.g.*, by the harp of Dagda, or by the branch carried by visitants from Elysium. Many "fairy" lullabies for producing sleep are even now extant in Ireland and the Highlands. As music forms a part of all primitive religion, its soothing powers would easily be magnified. In orgiastic rites it caused varying emotions until the singer and dancer fell into a deep slumber, and the tales of those who joined in a fairy dance and fell asleep, awaking to find that many years had passed, are mythic extensions of the power of music in such orgiastic cults. The music of the *Filid* had similar powers to that of Dagda's harp, producing laughter, tears, and a delicious slumber, and Celtic folk-tales abound in similar instances of the magic charm of music.... A cult of stones was probably connected with the belief in the magical power of certain stones, like the Lia Fail, which shrieked aloud when Conn knocked against it. His Druids explained that the number of the shrieks equalled the number of his descendants who should be kings of Erin. This is an ætiological myth accounting for the use of this fetich-stone at coronations. Other stones, probably the object of a cult or possessing magical virtues, were used at the installation of chiefs, who stood on them and vowed to follow in the steps of their predecessors, a pair of feet being carved on the stone to represent those of the first chief.... Connected with the cult of stones are magical observances at fixed rocks or boulders, regarded probably as the abode of a spirit. These observances are in origin pre–Celtic, but were practised by the Celts. Girls slide down a stone to obtain a lover, pregnant women to obtain an easy delivery, or contact with such stones causes barren women to have children or gives vitality to the feeble. A small offering is usually left on the stone. Similar rites are practised at megalithic monuments, and here again the custom is obviously pre–Celtic in origin. In this case the spirits of the dead must have been expected to assist the purposes of the rites, or even to incarnate themselves in the children born as a result of barren women resorting to these stones. Sometimes when the purpose of the stones has been forgotten and some other legendary origin attributed to them, the custom adapts itself to the legend. In Ireland many dolmens are known, not as places of sepulture, but as "Diarmaid and Grainne's beds"—the places where these eloping lovers slept. Hence they have powers of fruitfulness and are visited by women who desire children. The rite is thus one of sympathetic magic.... Holed dolmens or naturally pierced blocks are used for the magical cure of sickness both in Brittany and Cornwall, the patient being passed through the hole. Similar rites are used with trees, a slit being often made in the trunk of a sapling, and a sickly child passed through it. The slit is then closed and bound, and if it joins together at the end of a certain time, this is a proof that the child will recover. In these rites the spirit in stone or tree was supposed to assist the process of healing, or the disease was transferred to them, or, again, there was the idea of a new birth with consequent renewed life, the act imitating the process of birth. These rites are not confined to Celtic regions, but belong to that universal use of magic in which the Celts freely participated.[9]

Bards, Ovates and Druids

A *gorsedd* (Welsh, meaning literally "great sitting") can be an important assembly, including a national assembly, or it can be an event or a place at which some very significant incident happens. For example, the throne-mound where Pwyll, God of the underworld Annwn, first sees the Goddess Rhiannon on her magic horse is called a *gorsedd*. *Gorsedd Beirdd Ynys Prydain* ("Assembly of the Bards of the Isle of Britain"), the modern Gorsedd of Wales, revived in 1792 by Iolo Morganwg, is the mother-organization of sister-*gorsed-dau* in Cornwall and in Brittany, called respectively Gorsedh and Gorsez in Cornish and Breton, where Bard is the most senior rank available, while Wales also has Ovates and Druids. These roles no longer have any real religious significance in the modern *gorseddau*, as we shall discuss further in Chapter 7.

These three ranks, or roles, Bard, Ovate (there are various alternative names) and Druid, originated in Celtic tribal Druidism. Some American groups believe the Bard-Ovate-Druid stratification to be yet another fabrication by Iolo Morganwg, and therefore prefer to observe the more widely attributed roles which tend to predominate in the Irish vernacular texts. However, Strabo explicitly separates the Druidic functions into three separate classes or roles:

> Among [the Gauls] there are generally three classes to whom special honor is paid, viz. the Bards, the Uatis and the Druids. The Bards composed and sang odes; the Uatis attended to the sacrifices and studied nature; while the Druids studied nature and moral philosophy. So confident are the people in the justice of the Druids that they refer all private and public disputes to them; and these men on many occasions have made peace between armies actually drawn up for battle.[10]

Ammianus Marcellinus also describes the same three divisions, but calls the Uatis either Euhages or Orates. (Other writers also use the terms Vates and Manteis.) Ammianus also describes one of the purposes of Bardic poetry as being "to celebrate the brave deeds of their famous men in epic verse accompanied by the sweet strains of the lyre." He calls the Druids, "men of greater talent," and says that they were "members of the intimate fellowship of the Pythagorean faith."

The time of training for a Bard was nine years, and, if Caesar is to be believed, required the learning of some 20,000 lines of verse. It was the Bards who preserved (by memory) the complex genealogies, and who celebrated the achievements of Gods, heroes, kings and other important personages in narrative poems and set eulogies. In classical Greece and Rome, such performances were often accompanied by the lyre or harp, and it is possible that the Celtic Bards also used harps, which are still highly regarded today, particularly in the Welsh and Irish musical traditions, where the Gaelic name for the instrument, the *clàrsach*, is frequently used rather than the English "harp." The Bards also composed and performed satires, love songs, riddle songs and didactic poetry with moralizing content. As well as being expected to remember and perform a huge number of set pieces, many of which had very strict metrical and lexical conventions, Bards were also required to improvise new verses, again often within strict technical limits. Individual Bards are frequently depicted as highly competitive, since the power of true or correct utterance was so highly regarded, and the ability to find the precise phrase and the sweetest or sharpest expression was greatly honored.

The 8th-century Irish text *Uriacecht na Riar* gives detailed information about Bardic training and the different grades of poets. The Irish subdivided Bards into several different classes: the *Filidhe* or *Ollamhain Re-Dan* performed martial poems and war songs, celebrated famous deeds, and often acted as heralds and recorders during battle; the *Breitheamhin* or Brehons learned and recited the laws, and were experts in legal precedent; the *Seanachidhe* were historians, genealogists and antiquarians, and every royal or aristocratic household would ensure that they had their own *Seancha*; the *Oirfidigh* were inferior Bards who made music, often known by their individual instrument, their head being called the *Ollamh le Ceól*, which could be translated as "Master of Music"—from this practice grew the later tradition of the hereditary piper in Scotland, in which generations of players from the same family were associated with and maintained by particular clans and clan chiefs.

Wales also had different divisions or types of Bard, the most senior being a *pencerdd* or chief poet and the lowliest the *clerwr* or minstrel:

> The "chief poet" (*pencerdd*), "a poet who has won in a contest for a chair," was at least equal in honor to the highest officers. He seems to correspond to the Irish *ollam* or chief *fili*. Beneath him was the poet of the household or house-troop (*bardd teulu*), who was one of the twenty-four court officers. When the *bardd teulu* took office he received from the king a harp, with which he was never to part. He sang for the troop when it went on a raid, and before it set out for battle he sang *The Monarchy of Britain*. The term *cerddorion* seems to cover yet another class of minstrels who recognized the *pencerdd* as their lord, and there are references in the laws to the lowly *croesaniaid*. In mediaeval tracts on the art of poetry, slightly different terms seem to refer to the same classes: *prydydd* "poet," *teuluwr* "poet of the household or house-troop," and *clerwr*, "minstrel."[11]

The Ovates, who are called by a variety of titles, were principally seers and prophets, and the main functionaries in many religious ceremonies. They were also scientists, to use the modern term, since they spent a great deal of their time making observations about the natural world, encompassing geography, geology, natural science, astronomy and cosmology. They also frequently practiced medicine, especially herbalism, and probably were well informed about human as well as animal anatomy.

Bard and Ovate existed as roles in their own right, and most Bards and even Ovates would have remained in those positions without progressing to the rank of Druid. All Druids, however, had to undertake initial training and then serve as Bards and as Ovates before they could become qualified as Druids.

If Caesar is to be believed (not always the case), new Druids were acknowledged and initiated by an Archdruid, at a special *gorsedd*, having trained and prepared for nineteen or twenty years. If nine years was required to become a fully-qualified Bard, presumably ten or eleven years of further training and supervision as an Ovate would be required.

The long staff or wand was the mark of a Druid's status and authority. (According to the *Uraichecht na Riar*, Irish Bards were also allowed to carry a rod of bronze, silver or gold, depending on their rank and learning.) The Druid's staff or wand was usually made of hazel or rowan, and could be bleached or painted white, or left pale after stripping the bark and then polishing the plain timber with beeswax. Similar staves and rods were also used in ancient Egypt, Greece and Rome, and in other cultures, and are still widely used ceremonially to this day. In Europe, the rod or staff later became a symbol of a king or queen's divine authority, and was replaced by a smaller and more decorative symbolic scepter. The biblical Aaron was the keeper of the tribal rod, a talisman that each of the Twelve Tribes of Israel possessed.[12] When Moses commanded that all the rods be brought and placed before the Tabernacle, Aaron's rod miraculously budded, bearing almonds. There is also a Biblical legend that Aaron's rod or staff turned into a giant serpent which swallowed up all the serpents of the Egyptian priests [Exodus, 8:10–12]. Druids' wands or staves were reputed to have similar powers, and are sometimes depicted as serpents. My own staff or wand of rowan is called *Sarf Nija*, which is Cornish for "Flying or Swimming Snake" and represents a dragon. The *caduceus*, a staff on which twin serpents are entwined, was originally the magical staff of Hermes or Mercury, representing messengers and commerce in general. It has since come to symbolize the power of healing and medicine.

Piggott neatly summarizes the main Druidic responsibilities:

> In the first place they are the repositories of the traditional lore and knowledge of the tribe, whether of the Gods, the cosmos and the other-world, or of the corpus of customary law and such practical skills as calendrical expertise. This body of knowledge was preserved in oral tradition (and probably mainly in verse form for mnemonic reasons) and continuity achieved by explicit instruction to the younger generation entering the priesthood. The Druids' second function in Gaul was the practical application of their learning in law and to the administration of justice.... Finally, the Druids supervised sacrifices and religious ceremonies in general, in which they and other functionaries (for instance *vates* or *manteis*) participated. Any divinatory powers they were believed to exercise would fall quite appropriately within their general priestly duties.[13]

Of these, the most significant Druidic role or task was giving judgment, either in matters of religion or morality, or in questions of law, or in situations requiring diplomacy and political or strategic negotiation. In the Druidic tradition, all three would be essentially the same task: finding and articulating the truth, the fitness of things, and what was *fír fer* or appropriate conduct.

Another significant Druidic task, within the responsibility for religious ceremony, would have been the establishment and maintenance of the many sacred sites, some of which would have been public and relatively well known, and some of which may well have been secret and probably difficult of access. In the context of a national British resistance to the incursions of Angles, Saxons, Jutes and others, the network of such secret locations may have had strategic significance.

Markale makes the simple observation that, until they were influenced by the Greeks or Romans, the ancient Celts never built temples.[14] The finding and dedication of every *nemeton* or *locus consecratus* or sacred grove or ceremonial site would have been the responsibility of the Druid, whose responsibility it was to hear the Gods calling, in birdsong, or in the fall of water, or even in silence. Some public sites of Druidic worship and ceremony would have been tombs of great leaders, or (especially in Ireland) places where heroes fell in battle. But the secret sites would reveal themselves in subtle ways, and be known to few, and—most importantly—would be wild, uninhabited places. When Saint Ninian built his first Christian church at the end of the fourth century in southern Scotland, what caused the greatest astonishment was that it was a house, called the *Candida Casa* ("White House"), since the ancient Celts knew that the Gods did not *live* in houses, even if they chose sometimes to visit them or were technically in them at all times. If the Gods lived anywhere, it was in the sky, or visiting with spirits in the forest. (And for much of the time when classical Druidism flourished, most of Britain was still covered by dense and impenetrable forest.) The great Druidic sanctuary and training center on Mona or Anglesey was in a forest. Lucan, in *The Pharsalia*, tells us of a Gallic sanctuary in a forest near Marseilles, and that the Druids "live in the deep woods (*nemora alta*) and withdraw from inhabited forests." Strabo tells us that the Galatians (i.e., Gaels or Celts) of Asia Minor had a council of three hundred members who met annually at a secret place called Drumeton, which seems to represent the Druidic *nemeton* or sacred grove. Nanterre in Hauts-de-Seine takes its name from the original Nemetodurum or "fortress of the *nemeton*." Finding, guarding and preserving the hidden, sacred sites would have been an important Druidic function.

Why did the Druids not use writing in their ceremonies, or in their other functions? Caesar's explanation is that their religion "did not permit them to," but he also tells us, "in almost all other matters, and in their public and private accounts, they make use of Greek letters." We know that the ancient Druids also knew Greek and Latin, as well as using Ogham on wood and stone. It is also likely that some British Druids at least in the 5th and 6th centuries of the Common Era could speak and perhaps write the languages of the invading Angles, Saxons and Jutes, which were in the process of becoming early Old English, sometimes called Anglo-Saxon: diplomatic and ambassadorial meetings and negotiations would have made it necessary, since the still Pagan invaders had not yet acquired any Latin, and presumably little or no Celtic British.

With their secret finger-alphabet, and their intense interest in letters and numbers and in the sacred tree alphabet (see Chapter 10), it seems obvious that the ancient Druids valued literacy, if only of a very specialized kind. They almost certainly guarded such arcane knowledge jealously, and, if Bardic competitiveness is anything to go by, placed great store in every facet of linguistics, in the power of language. However, as Caesar probably justifiably points out, they also placed great store in the power of memory, and clearly supported and advocated the ancient Celtic oral tradition. Their deep belief in the power of the word, of true and correct utterance, may also have worked against the notion of writing, rather than for it. In the same way that many early religions proscribed the speaking or writing of the true name of God, early Druids may have believed that writing somehow undermined or devalued the power and virtue of the word, which, spoken rather than written, could literally carry life or death, and in which the entirety of Celtic history and tradition was cradled.

Druidic Training

As we have seen, Caesar makes clear that Druidic training was lengthy and arduous, and we can assume that the final initiation into the priesthood would have been quite an affair. Much of the training and education would have been of a kind reasonably familiar to us today: it would have included aspects of the disciplines that we now call astronomy, astrology, biology, botany, chemistry, cosmology, cosmogony, geography, geology, herb lore, history, philosophy, physics and theology. But it would also have included instruction in esoteric and magical practices that lie outside modern academic territories, such as ritual invocation and communication with the Gods, including shape-shifting.

For those of a philosophical bent, shape-shifting represents a psychological state in which intense empathy between the priest and the object or creature of interest produces a highly charged association and mutual identification, a profound melding of consciousness at some level. For those to whom shape-shifting is real, in other words those who accept the shaman as a real voyager in a real landscape, it is the same but simpler: the Druid or priest or shaman *becomes* the bear, or the otter, or the tree, and gains powerful insight as a result. Druids wear the antlers of the God Cernunnos because— in the shamanistic tradition—while they wear them they not only represent or channel the God, they *are* the God.

The concept of shape-shifting is not as unfamiliar as one might think, particularly with the re-emergence of supernatural, semi-divine and even divine characters in modern games and movies. It will be familiar to those who have read T.H. White's *The Once and Future King*, published in 1958, the first story of which, *The Sword in the Stone*, had been published separately earlier, in 1938, and which appeared as a full-length Disney animation film in 1963. J.K. Rowling has acknowledged White's influence on her Harry Potter novels, and others have seen a similarity in the relationships between The Wart (White's nickname for the young Arthur) and Merlyn (White's spelling) and Harry Potter and Hogwarts headmaster Albus Dumbledore. In the Disney film, the shape-shifting sequence is a trivial piece of animated slapstick, but in the novel, The Wart undergoes several transformations during which he thinks and feels and reacts in the manner of the animal into which he has been changed. One of the most memorable of these transformations, which has probably subsequently influenced many science fiction stories either consciously or unconsciously, is when The Wart becomes an ant. White conveys the sense of loss of personal identity and its replacement with a harsh, militaristic group or colony mentality with eloquent anger and subtle precision. Getting "inside" a different or alien species is far more common in literature and film nowadays, but in White's time the creative and empathetic imagination that he demonstrated was quite exceptional. Modern Druidism has to some extent at least completed the circle from ancient Druidism, and includes an intense and sincere connection with all living things, so that even if shape-shifting is not literal or real it does at least represent something real, namely that connection and empathy with all manifestations of the life principle.

Ancient Druidic teaching would have contained a great deal of rote learning, but it would also have contained a great deal of close observation of the living world and universe: trees, plants, flowers, animals, insects, clouds, stars, the firmament. The vernacular stories confirm that interest, but the blazingly obvious evidence is Celtic art, in which whirls and trefoils and leaves and dogs and otters and circles and deer and snakes and curves all weave and flow in and out of each other in an endless cascade of movement and light. Particularly in the Ovate stage, my guess is that field study of rocks, pools, waves, tracks, animals, trees, insects and so on would have been an important part of the normal teaching and learning practice.

Much of the material, particularly the Bardic and genealogical compositions, must have been taught and learned by rote, which may have chafed the minds of the more creative. At the other end of that spectrum, much of the legal, moral and religious teaching probably required the exact opposite of a rote-learning mentality, i.e., an enquiring and open mind willing to ponder and debate deep and abstruse matters. Those who finally completed their

Druidic training would have been, therefore, a persistent, determined and generally very able minority. The rewards for graduation were considerable—we have already noted that Druids were equal or close to royalty in social status, and probably wealth, too—but twenty years of close study and hard grind would have eliminated many who were not entirely able or suited to such a demanding priesthood.

In the initiation and training of young warriors, women are often depicted as the leaders or tutors,[15] confirming the comments made earlier about the unusually high status of women in Celtic society, and their frequent appearance as warriors. We have no direct evidence that training in warfare was part of Druidic training, but sensible inference suggests that it would have been. In the Celtic tribal tradition, all children would have learned some form of self-defense, and the children of the royal households and tribal aristocracy would have been expected to learn how to use weapons and ride a horse. Training in literacy, rhetoric and perhaps mathematics, especially geometry, would have been important in Romano-British aristocratic households, but it is also quite likely, in a still relatively wild province far from Rome, that weapons training and horsemanship would have been on the syllabus for Romano-British children too.

The evidence from the vernacular tales is that children being educated generally went to live with their teachers, as Ethnea and Fedelma were sent from the royal palace to live at Cruachan in Connaught with Mael and Calpair, rather than their teachers living with or visiting them. This would be normal in a society where fostering was widespread. The picture that emerges is of the Druid not as a solo performer or itinerant lone priest, but as the head of a retinue, sometimes quite large, which might either reside with a particular king or queen, or within a particular tribal area, or just as often travel from place to place as need arose. In some of the vernacular tales, Druids even have their own troops of guards, or small armies. We know that the other Druidic functionaries, the Ovates, the Bards, the musicians, must almost certainly have formed part of the retinue, and it seems likely that there were also students among them of many ages and at many different stages in their education and development. In Celtic society, where social mobility was the norm, presumably students as well as Bards or musicians could transfer from one Druid to another, or from one court to another, by agreement.

5. Some Famous Druids in History and Legend

Amergin Glúingel

There are at least three different Amergins of importance in early Irish history and legend, from three different periods. There are also many variant spellings of the name, including Amorgin, Amorghain and Aimhirghin.

Amergin Glúingel or Amhairghin Glúingheal (meaning "of the white knees") was acknowledged in early legend to be both poet and Druid. He was one of the seven sons of Míl Espáine (from Latin *Miles Hispaniae* or "Soldier of Spain"), whose final conquest of Ireland drove the *Tuatha Dé Danann* into hiding as the Gods and fairy people of the hills and caves. It was Amergin Glúingel who named Ireland after the Goddess Ériu, in return for her granting the Milesians permission to settle. Acting as judge and ambassador (classical Druidic roles), Amergin reached an agreement with the *Tuatha Dé Danann* that the invading Milesians would retreat to a position "behind the ninth wave," a symbolic magical border, while negotiations continued. The *Tuatha Dé Danann* broke the truce by raising a storm to keep or drive the Milesians away, but Amergin sang a song of invocation to the spirit of Ireland to allow the Milesians to come ashore and take possession of the land. The invocation, now famous as *The Song of Amergin*, is powerful, beautiful and enigmatic, and has been the subject of much study. Robert Graves calls it "an ancient Celtic calendar-alphabet, found in several purposely garbled Irish and Welsh variants" and gives a restoration of the text as follows:

> I am a stag: *of seven tines,*
> I am a flood: *across a plain,*
> I am a wind: *on a deep lake,*
> I am a tear: *the Sun lets fall,*
> I am a hawk: *above the cliff,*
> I am a thorn: *beneath the nail,*
> I am a wonder: *among flowers,*

I am a wizard: *who but I*
Sets the cool head aflame with smoke?

I am a spear: *that roars for blood,*
I am a salmon: *in a pool,*
I am a lure: *from paradise,*
I am a hill: *where poets walk,*
I am a boar: *ruthless and red,*
I am a breaker: *threatening doom,*
I am a tide: *that drags to death,*
I am an infant: *who but I*
    Peeps from the unhewn dolmen arch?

I am the womb: *of every holt,*
I am the blaze: *on every hill,*
I am the queen: *of every hive,*
I am the shield: *for every head,*
I am the tomb: *of every hope.*[1]

We will revisit this poetic invocation, and its full meaning, in Chapter 10.

A second Amergin, Amergin mac Eccit, was the son of Eccet Salach, a smith in the court of King Conchobar mac Nessa in Ulster, possibly in the 3rd century CE. Until the age of fourteen, Amergin neither spoke nor washed himself. Then suddenly, after fourteen years of complete silence, he burst forth with a powerful, cryptic, Druidic-style poem, which was overheard by a servant who had been sent by the court poet Athirne to collect an axe from the smith. When Athirne heard about this event, he came with the new axe to kill the boy-poet, but Eccet Salach had cunningly made a full-sized clay replica of his son, which Athirne destroyed, thinking he had killed the boy of whom he was so afraid and jealous. Eventually the deception was revealed, Athirne was forced to pay compensation (the fitness of things) to Eccet and to take Amergin on as his apprentice, and in due course Amergin replaced Athirne as court poet. One of his later warrior exploits, which certainly seems entirely Druidic in character, was to make enormous boulders fly through the air to impede the advancing army of Connacht. His magic was countered by Cú Roi, who launched boulders of his own, and the stones from both sides smashed themselves to smithereens in the sky until Queen Medb, growing tired of the constant rain of dust and pebbles, ordered the bombardment to stop.

The third Amergin, Amergin of Magh Seòla, lived in the middle of the 6th century, and was the father of a Christian saint, but—as if often the case with early Celtic history and legends—it is not clear whether Amergin himself was Pagan or Christian. He was the chief smith of King Tighernach, and smiths were reputed to have great spiritual and magical power in the Druidic tradition. Against Tighernach's wishes, Amergin married a member of the royal household, and he and his bride were sentenced to be burned to death.

As the flames began to consume them, an extraordinarily sudden and powerful thunderstorm erupted and washed out the fire, allowing them to escape unharmed. They later had a child, who was baptized in the name Luan or Lochan. When Luan was taken, a few years later, to a monastery to be educated, one of the monks observed that the hair (*barra* in Irish) of the boy was *fionn* (white or fair), so Luan from that day became known as Fionnbharra or Finbarr, who later became Bishop and then patron saint of the city of Cork.

Bé Chuille

Bé Chuille was a sorceress or Druid of the *Tuatha Dé Danann*. She helped to defeat an evil Greek warrior and sorceress called Carman of Athens, who, with her three sons Dub ("Black"), Dother ("Evil") and Dian ("Violence"), had attempted to invade Ireland. Bé Chuille's story is told in the 12th-century *Book of Leinster*. Although Carman is the villain and Bé Chuille the heroine of the story, Carman later gained a strong following of her own. Her grief as a mother became worthy of comment and remembrance, and a commemorative festival in her name developed in Leinster and was incorporated into the larger festival of Lughnasa on the 1st of August.

Bé Chuille's name is alternatively written as Becuille or Bé Chuma, which has led to confusion with another Bechuma, Bechuma of the Fair Skin. This Bechuma is definitely a villain rather than a heroine. The wife of Eogan Inbir, she commits adultery with Gaidiar, son of the God of the sea, Manannán mac Lir, and is exiled from the *Tuatha* to live among mortal humans, where she marries Conn of the Hundred Battles, but behaves flirtatiously with Conn's son, Art. Conn's Druids warn him that Bechuma is a menace to the kingdom, and she is exiled.

Relbeo

Like Carman, Relbeo was also a Greek sorceress or female Druid. In fact, she was also a princess, daughter of the King of Greece. The presence of Greek characters in the earliest of the Celtic mythological stories adds weight to the suggestions made by several commentators from classical times onwards that there had been a significant interchange and correspondence between ancient Druids and early Greek philosophers, including Pythagoras. Relbeo, like many other heroines in the early legends, was imprisoned in a tower, having been made a concubine of King Conann. She was the mother of Fergus Lethderg, whose second name means "Red Side," and Alma One-Tooth, a warrior-hero, both of whom are of the Muintir Neimhidh, "People of Nemed" or Nemedians, one of the successive invading tribes of Ireland.

Biróg

Like Bé Chuille, Biróg was also a *ban-drui* or female Druid of the *Tuatha Dé Danann*. Balor, the one-eyed giant God of the Fomorians, had been given a prophecy that he would be killed by his own grandson, and was determined that the prophecy would not be fulfilled. He imprisoned his only daughter, Eithne, in a high tower on Tory Island, so that no man could find her. Balor later stole a magically productive cow from a man called Mac Cinnfhaelaidh (McKinley). Biróg helped Mac Cinnfhaelaidh gain his revenge by magically bringing him to Eithne in the high tower, where he seduced Balor's daughter and made her pregnant. Eithne subsequently gave birth to triplets (a common event in Druidic legends). Balor ordered a servant to murder the three infants, but the servant, having drowned two of them, unwittingly dropped the third, still alive, in the harbor. Biróg rescued the baby and brought it back to Mac Cinnfhaelaidh, who, in turn, gave it to his brother, Gavida the smith, in foster-age. In due course, the baby grew into a man (the personification of the God Lugh) and killed Balor, to fulfill the prediction.

Tadg mac Nuadat

Tadg was a Druid named in the Fenian Cycle, the stories about the Irish warrior-hero Fionn. The second part of his name means "son of Nuada," but it is not clear which Nuada is intended. In some stories, he is the son of the High King Nuada Necht, but in most of the tales his father is Nuada or Nuadu Argat Lámh, "Nuadu of the Silver Hand." His story is sad but not particularly edifying. He had a daughter Muirne, who was admired by many suitors, including Cumhal, leader of the war-band of heroes, the Fianna. Tadg turned them all away, but Cumhal seized Muirne and abducted her. With the support of the High King, Conn of the Hundred Battles, Tadg pursued Cumhal, who was killed eventually by Goll mac Morna, who took over leadership of the Fianna. Muirne was already pregnant with Cumhal's child, however. Tadg ordered her to be burned, but Conn over-ruled him and sent Muirne into exile instead, where she gave birth to Fionn. Fionn eventually grew up and replaced Goll as leader of the Fianna. Challenged by Fionn mac Cumhaill, whose aim was to avenge his father, Tadg backed down and gave Fionn his estate on the hill of Almu. The three lessons of the story, rather disappointingly, appear to be that (a) Druids have family troubles, just like anybody else, (b) Druids were wealthy enough to have estates that they could give away and (c) sometimes Druids end up having to do what other people tell them to do.

Bodhmall

Bodhmall or Bodmall also belongs to the Fenian Cycle. She was a Druid, the sister of Fionn's father Cumhall. After Goll mac Morna had killed Cumhal and taken over the leadership of the Fianna, Fionn's mother, Muirne, was fearful for her son's safety. Bodhmall and her companion Liath Luachra ("The Grey One of Luachair") took Fionn into hiding deep in the forest of Sliabh Bladhma or Slieve Bloom, where they raised him and trained him in battle craft.

Bodhmall represents two distinctive attributes of early Celtic society. Firstly, fosterage was a very powerful social custom among the aristocracy. (It was also occasionally practiced by the lower classes.) It survived until the eighteenth century in the Scottish Highlands. Sons, and sometimes daughters, of lesser nobles were sent to be raised and trained in arms by more powerful nobles. The main advantage to all parties was increased opportunity and social flexibility. The lesser family would acquire additional status and security from association with the greater noble. The greater noble would have a firmer hold on the families whose children resided with him, particularly in times of warfare or potential rebellion. Secondly, Bodhmall's and Liath Luachra's war training of Fionn, like Scáthach's training of Cú Chulainn on Skye, reminds us that Celtic women were often highly respected as warriors who were as good as if not better than many male warriors, and confirms the unusually high status of women in traditional Celtic society by comparison with almost all other early tribal societies.

Diviciacus

The earliest historical Druid attested by classical writers for whom we have a name is Diviciacus or Divitiacus, who lived in Gaul, modern France, in the 1st century BCE. He is named by Julius Caesar as a "senator" of the southern Gaulish tribe of the Aedui. The Aedui lived between the Bitruriges to their west, the territory boundary being the upper River Loire, and the Sequani to the east, that boundary being made by the River Saône, whose tutelary Goddess, as we saw in Chapter 3, was Souconna, who gave her name to both the river and the tribe. The Aedui were a powerful tribe, who allied themselves to Rome. They had replaced their earlier system of direct monarchy with a semi-republic of aristocratic senators or political judges, and Diviciacus the Druid was one of these.

The Sequani, with the help of the Arverni, defeated and largely massacred the Aedui at the Battle of Magetobriga in 63 BCE. A delegation of Aeduan senators, including Diviciacus, went to Rome to seek support from Caesar, but he was intent on using inter-tribal conflict in Gaul as an excuse for invading and conquering the whole province, so their mission was unsuccessful. Caesar briefly restored Aeduan independence in 58 BCE, but their faith in him was so low that they joined in the general Gallic resistance to his advances until finally, after Vercingetorix had been defeated at Alesia, they returned to Roman allegiance. Augustus later changed the name of their ancient capital of Bibracte to a mixed Latin-Celtic name, Augustodunum, which is the root of the modern Autun.

Diviciacus is an important figure because he represents one of the most significant roles of the ancient Druids: he was an ambassador, a political representative with power and authority. By all accounts, Caesar was greatly impressed by him, and enjoyed his company socially. We can infer from his role and responsibilities that Diviciacus spoke good Latin as well as his native Gaulish.

Cathbad

Cathbad or Cathbhadh features in the Ulster Cycle of Irish tales. He was the "Chief Druid" and in one story also the father, of King Conchobar mac Nessa. Nessa, who was the daughter of the previous king, Éochaid Sálbuide, asked Cathbad one day what the time was propitious for, knowing the Druid's gift of foretelling the future. "For begetting a king on a queen," was Cathbad's reply, and so she took him to her bed, and Conchobar was the ultimate issue.

Cathbad is famous for two other prophecies. In the first, he prophesied that whoever took arms on a certain propitious day would have a short life but would earn immortal fame. Cú Chulainn, still a child, rushed up immediately, begging to be armed. In the second, Cathbad was present at the birth of Deirdre, and prophesied the details of her tragic story, which is one of the best known of the Irish mythological tales.

Deirdre (the name is pronounced *deer-dree* in England, but the original Irish pronunciation is closer to *dare-druh*), often called Deirdre an Bhróin or Deirdre of the Sorrows, grew up, as Cathbad had prophesied, into a young woman of exceptional beauty. Cathbad had also prophesied that she would cause great bloodshed, and that Ulster's three greatest warriors would be sent into exile because of her. For these reasons, her father, the royal storyteller Fedlimid mac Daill, had tried to kill her at birth, but King Conchobar had her taken away to be raised in a secluded place by the poet and wise woman (i.e., Druid) Leabharcham (*lyaw-ar-chum*, "Crooked Book") until she grew old enough for Conchobar to marry her. One snowy day, a raven landed on the snow with its prey, and Deirdre told Leabharcham that the colors she saw there would be the colors of the man she would love: hair black as a raven's wing, skin white as snow, cheeks red as blood. Leabharcham blurted out that her description could only be of Naoise (pronounced approximately *na-ee-shuh*), a young warrior of Conchobar's court. With Leabharcham's help, Deirdre and Naoise fled to Alban or Scotland, where they lived a happy life, hunting and fishing. A furious Conchobar sent Ferghus mac Róich to bring them back. One of Conchobar's men, Éogan mac Durthacht, killed Naoise with a spear. Conchobar took Deirdre as his wife, against her will. After a year, during which Deirdre treated Conchobar with coldness and contempt, he asked her whom she hated most in the world. She replied that it was Éogan mac Durthacht, the man who had killed her beloved Naoise. Conchobar then cruelly told her that he was going to deliver her to Éogan, to be his wife. As she was being driven under escort to Éogan in a chariot, Conchobar told her that she looked like a ewe between two rams. In despair and disgust, Deirdre threw herself from the chariot and dashed her brains out against a rock.

Mogh Ruith

One of the best-known Druidic tales about battle magic is the story from Ireland which tells how the renowned blind druid Mogh Ruith or Mag Ruith, Druid at the court of King Fiacha Muilleathan of Munster, worked great magic to defeat the three Druids Cicht, Ciotha and Ciothruadh, who served the High King Cormac mac Airt. At Ciothruadh's urging, Cormac's Druids set a fire of rowan trees (one of the sacred trees most often invoked or used in battle), which Mogh Ruith countered with an even stronger Druidic fire, fed by a fireball which he made in his own hands, mixing butter with shavings from every spear in the Munster host, while chanting:

> I mix a roaring, powerful fire;
> It will clear the woods; it will blight the grass;
> An angry flame of powerful speed;
> It will rush up to the skies above.
> It will subdue the wrath of all burning wood,
> It will break a battle on the clans of Conn ...[2]

Mogh Ruith fanned the flames with a Druidic breath, which fell on the enemy as a shower of blood. The blind Druid then put on a bull-hide cloak and a bird headpiece and flew up into the air. He pursued Cormac's fleeing army and blew another Druidic breath upon them, which turned Cormac's Druids, Cicht, Ciotha and Ciothruadh, into stones.

Mogh Ruith was also renowned for his use of wheel divination, the precise mechanics of which remain unclear. One text refers to Mogh Ruith as *magus rotarum* or "magician (Druid) of wheels," while another reports that Mogh Ruith's daughter Tlachtga traveled to the East with him for Druidic training and learned how to make the *roth ramhach* or "rowing wheel," used in divination, which was also described in mediaeval texts as a flying machine or early airplane. Perhaps the device was something like a roulette wheel, with a ball falling into slots marked with significant letters or other symbols, or perhaps it had sails like a windmill which made it spin in the wind.

Tlachtga

Tlachtga, as noted above, was Mogh Ruith's daughter, and herself a Druid of great power. She traveled the world with her father. According to one legend, she was raped by Simon Magus, supposedly Mogh Ruith's spiritual mentor. (Simon himself is a very interesting figure. *Magus*, plural *Magi*, as in the Wise Men who came to Bethlehem for the birth of Jesus, means "sorcerer" or "magician," and Simon was reputedly a powerful Samaritan Pagan (he could levitate and fly) before he was converted to Christianity by Philip the Evangelist. Simon argued with Jesus's disciple Peter, and the Christian sin of simony, or bribery to obtain power or influence, is named after him.)

Tlachtga gave birth to triplets (a common occurrence in Celtic mythology, implying divine origins, as I mentioned earlier, except that these particular triplets had the unusual distinction of each coming from a different father). Tlachtga died of grief, and after her death a fortress was constructed about her grave, called the Hill of Tlachtga, which is generally assumed to be the Hill of Ward in County Meath. Much later, this was the site of a very large and popular mediaeval fair, large enough to rival the similar fair at Tailtiu or Teltown. There have been historic reported sightings of Mogh Ruith's *roth ramhach* or flying wheel at the site. The High King Ruadrí Ua Conchobair staged a massive open-air assembly there in the year 1168.

Finnchaemh

Finnchaemh was Druid to Dathi, High King of Ireland from 405 to 428 CE. At Cnoc-nan-Druad, or The Druid's Hill, in Sligo, Dathi asked Finnchaemh to foretell what would happen to him during the following year. Finnchaem read the clouds for a whole night during the feast of Samhain, and at dawn roused the king, saying, "Are you still asleep, King of Erin and of Alban?" Dathi was King of Erin (Ireland) but not yet King of Alban (Scotland), but the detailed prognostication given by Finnchaem, that Dathi would rule Scotland, as well as make incursions into Britain and Gaul, subsequently came true. When the witches in Shakespeare's *Macbeth* tell Macbeth, Thane of Glamis, that he will also become Thane of Cawdor and then King of Scotland, they are performing the same Druidic function as Finnchaem.

Ambrosius Aurelianus

Ambrosius Aurelianus was a British war leader of the 5th century, a precursor and possibly tutor of Arthur. As with the earlier Maximus or Macsen, he was also known as Emrys Wledig, i.e., "the Landed One" or "the Powerful." (Emrys, which is still a popular name in Wales, is an early Celtic adaptation of Ambrosius.) He is the only British war leader actually named by the 6th century historian, Gildas, which is an indication of his importance. Ambrosius's parents are described as "of the purple," which suggests that they were not just Romano-British aristocrats but perhaps actual members of the imperial family, in which case he would have been of very high birth indeed. However, nowhere is he accorded the title "King." According to most chronicles, he comes after Vortigern, but before Arthur, which would put his time of greatest influence between about 410 and about 475 CE. That is such a long period of time that some historians have suggested that Ambrosius Aurelianus may, in fact, have been two people, or even three: grandfather, father and son, all bearing the same name. When we look closely at the name, that possibility becomes greater.

Ambrosius is Latin. It comes from Greek αμβροσια (*ambrosia*), which most people know was the sacred food of the Gods in the classical pantheon. But *ambrosia* also meant "eternity," so the adjective or epithet *ambrosius* (Greek *ambrosios*) means "immortal," "eternal," or "divine." Aurelianus is definitely a Roman name, actually of a *gens* rather than an individual. The word *gens* can be translated as "stock" or "clan" (or *tuath*, to use the Irish word). It means a group of families connected by a common name and sometimes by common religious rites or family or tutelary Gods (*lares*) held in common. *Aurelius, aurarius, auratus* and *aureus*, which are closely related, all mean "golden" or "of gold," and could also be used as epithets. There were several well-known classical Aureliuses (or Aurelii), including Lucus Aurelius Cotta, who wrote an important early law about judicial procedures, and Sextus Aurelius Victor, a Roman historian of the 4th century CE. Marcus Aurelius Antoninus was emperor of Rome from 161 to 180—he succeeded Antoninus Pius, builder of the British Antonine Wall in 142. So Ambrosius Aurelianus appears to mean "the divine or eternal one of the tribe or *gens* Aurelius," which is clearly as much a title or description as it is a personal name. It is equally obviously a religious title, which, in the context of 5th-century Britain after the end of the Roman occupation, could either be Roman or Druidic: both are possible.

The name or title of Ambrosius would be especially fitting for a British Druid whose nobility derived from Roman or imperial family connections. The name is unequivocally Latin, but its meaning and reference are highly appropriate for one who speaks for the Gods or, in spiritual communion, represents the God, as a Druid does. As either name or title, it may have been used by several Druids, or even Archdruids. Perhaps, by usage or association, Ambrosius had come to mean a Druid, sage, wise person, priest, or representative of the "divine one" if not actually the divine one in person.

Taliesin, 6th Century CE

The poet Taliesin, who authored several praise-poems about King Urien of Rheged, who died about 590 CE, describes his Druidic initiation in language which is clearly mystical and ecstatic, even hallucinatory:

> I was first modeled into the form of a pure man in the hall of Cerridwen, who subjected me to penance. Though small within my ark and modest in my deportment, I was great. A sanctuary carried me above the surface of the earth. Whilst I was enclosed within its ribs, the sweet Awen rendered me complete; and my law, without audible language, was imparted to me by the old giantess darkly smiling in her wrath; but her claim was not regretted, when she set sail. I fled in the form of a fair grain of pure wheat; upon the edge of a covering cloth she caught me in her fangs. In appearance she was as large as a proud mare, which she also resembled: then was she swelling out, like a ship upon the waters. Into a dark receptacle she cast me. She carried me back into the sea of Dylan. It was an auspicious omen to me, when she happily suffocated me. God, the Lord, freely set me at large.[3]

This is poetic (some might just say jumbled), because it is, after all, the poet Taliesin supposedly speaking. The "old giantess" is the Goddess in the form of Cerridwen or Ceridwen ("Crooked Fair One" or "Crooked Blessed One"), who is often depicted as a sow, and the tale of the shape-shifting chase is very well known:

> Cerridwen bore a son, Morfran ("Great Crow") or Afagddu ("Black Face"), who was hideously ugly. To compensate for that, she brewed a potion in her magic cauldron, which would bring him poetic inspiration and knowledge of all things. The potion had to boil for a year and a day. She set her young servant, Gwion Bach ("The Little Fair One"—Gwion is the Welsh cognate of the Irish *fionn*, meaning "white") to tend the broth. Just as in the parallel Irish tale of Finnegas the Druid and the hero Fionn mac Cúmhaill, described earlier, the magical broth splashed onto the boy, who sucked his thumb and was instantly filled with wisdom and poetic inspiration. (Sucking a thumb is a traditional Druidic method of concentration.) Furious, Cerridwen chased Gwion, intending to punish him. Gwion shape-shifted into a hare, so Cerridwen shape-shifted into a greyhound. He changed into a fish, so she became an otter. He changed into a bird, so she became a hawk. Finally, he transformed himself into a single grain of corn. She changed herself into a hen and pecked him up. (Some perceive this series of transformations as representing a Druid or priestess instructing or tutoring a student in the art of shape-shifting, which is how T.H. White presents his version with Merlyn and the Wart in *The Once and Future King*.) Nine months later, Cerridwen gave birth to a child, who was the God Gwion transformed into the renowned mystical poet Taliesin.

The name Taliesin means "Radiant Brow." In the ancient texts he is also called Taliesin Ben Beirdd ("Chief of Bards"), and it is largely for his poetry that he is remembered, but the exceptional circumstances of his birth, at least according to the legend, are typical of a God, or at the least of someone with great spiritual power, so the speculation that he was a Druid is strongly supported. His grave (Bedd Taliesin in Welsh) is supposedly by Tre Taliesin near Llangynfelin, but the site itself is an Iron-Age burial chamber which probably houses the remains of some unknown but much earlier Celtic warrior or noble.

Bec mac Dé

Bec mac Dé was an Irish Druid, Bard and prophet, who died, according to the Irish Annals, some time shortly after the year 550. The most famous story about him is his prophecy concerning the death of a king, in the saga *Aided Diarmata*, or *The Death of Diarmait*. In the story, two Christian saints, Ciarán and Ronan, prophesied that King Diarmait would die from a roof-beam falling on him. To out-prophesy them, Bec gave a list of all the details of the death that awaited Diarmait: he would be drowned, burned, and then finally crushed by a roof-beam.

The Scottish Gàidhlig word *cabar* means a large pole, and is fairly well known as the caber of "tossing the caber," a sporting event in Highland Games athletics. It can also refer to roof-beams. The very old Gàidhlig phrase "*Fo na h-aon chabair*," literally "under the same roof-beams," means "from the same family." In the mythological tales, kings are often finally killed by a roof-beam falling on them, which may be a metaphor for being killed or replaced by another family member.

There is a persistent theme in Irish mythological stories of the ritual killing of kings by wounding, drowning and burning, the so-called "triple execution." Lindow Man, whose body was found at Lindow Moss in Cheshire in 1984, appears to have been deposited in the bog there in the 4th century BCE. His moustache was neatly trimmed and his fingernails clipped, suggesting aristocratic status. His body had been painted several different colors, and was naked apart from an armlet made of fox fur. He had been pole-axed, garroted and had his throat cut, before being kneed in the back and pushed into the pool. On forensic examination, his stomach was found to have contained several kinds of grain, possibly from a ritual bread, and mistletoe pollen, which certainly suggests a Druidic connection.[4] Craig Weatherhill emailed me about Lindow Man:

> Have you read *The Life and Death of a Druid Prince* by Anne Ross and Don Robins? It's a fascinating piece of archaeological Sherlock Holmes work to try and determine who Lindow Man might have been. They conclude that he was a young Druid, possibly

of royal blood and from Ireland, who offered himself as a sacrifice to atone for the twin disasters of the Romans savagely clearing out Druidry on Ynys Mon, and the defeat of Boudicca. They even suggest that his name might have been Louernios, from the fox-fur armlet totem that was the only thing he was wearing.[5]

Bec was meticulously precise about the details and unusual circumstances of the death awaiting Diarmait. The king would be killed by Áed Dub mac Suibni ("Black Áed, son of Sweeney"), in the house of Banbán the innkeeper; he would be wearing a shirt made of linen grown from a single flax seed; he would be drinking ale brewed from a single grain of corn; he would be eating pork from a sow that had never farrowed. Banbán offered his own daughter for the king's pleasure that night, and she innocently reveals to the king that the nightshirt which Banbán has given him was made from a single flax seed, that the ale he was drinking was brewed from a single grain of corn, and that the pork given to him by Banbán was from a sow which had never farrowed. In panic, Diarmait tried to run from the house, but Áed Dubh was waiting for him at the door, spear in hand. Diarmait ran back into the house, which Áed's men set on fire. Diarmait leaped into a vat of ale in an attempt to escape the flames, but a burning roof-beam fell on his head and killed him.

Gwenc'hlan

Like Merlin (see below), there is uncertainty about whether a real, historical Gwenc'hlan actually existed. By repute and legend, he was a powerful and influential Breton Druid and Bard of the 6th century. He first appeared in a miscellany published by Hersart de la Villemarqué in 1839 called *Barzaz Breiz* ("Bards of Brittany"). This was one of the earliest collections of traditional material in the Breton language, and represents an important development in the Romantic revival, which we shall be discussing in more detail in the next chapter. Gwenc'hlan's great work was his *Diougan Gwenc'hlan* or "Gwenc'hlan's Prophecy." According to this text, Gwenc'hlan was blinded and subsequently imprisoned as a punishment for refusing to convert to Christianity.

Another Gwenc'hlan (it is a Bardic name—the original Gwenc'hlan's personal name was Kian) wrote a poem in about 1450 which is a conversation between the poet and King Arthur, but the Breton in this poem already shows signs of French influence and the intrusion of French vocabulary.

Myrddin/Merlin

Merlin is perhaps the most easily recognized personification of a wizard in the world, and quite a few people, if asked to think about what a historical

Druid might have been like, would see or imagine a Merlin-like figure, even though the evidence for a real, historical Merlin is thin on the ground.

The legendary Merlin appears to have been put together from earlier folk traditions by Geoffrey of Monmouth in the 12th century, with other significant elements of his story added later as the whole legend developed. In the 1980s, Nikolai Tolstoy wrote a highly influential and still widely respected study, *The Quest for Merlin*, which suggested that Merlin was a real, historical figure, but that he lived in the second half of the 6th century, about a hundred years later than any possible historical Arthur.

Geoffrey had already published a series of *Prophetiae Merlini* ("Prophecies of Merlin"), while he was working on his first major success, the *Historia Regum Britanniae* or History of the Kings of Britain, which was completed in 1136. He later incorporated the Merlin material directly into the *Historia*. Even later, about 1150, he wrote a separate *Vita Merlini* ("The Life of Merlin"), capitalizing to some extent on the character's huge popularity with the reading public, but really writing for a different, smaller and more discriminating readership. He claimed in a dedicatory preface to the *Historia* that his book was a translation from "a certain very ancient book written in the British language" which had been given to him by Archdeacon Walter, but this original has never been found or identified satisfactorily. The "British language" is generally assumed to be early Welsh, but it could also be Cornish or even Breton. Merlin's original name was Myrddin, but Geoffrey changed it to Merlin (after the bird) because Myrddin or Merdinus was too close to the Latin word *merda*, meaning dung or faeces.

Merlin's first appearance is as a child. King Vortigern was attempting to build a fortress for himself in Wales to escape the Saxons (this part of the story is taken from Nennius). His masons worked on the foundations, but every day's work came to nothing, because whatever had been made during the day mysteriously vanished each night. Vortigern's Druids (often translated as "magicians," but the original Latin is *magis suis*, and the word *magus* usually denoted or implied a Druid in mediaeval texts) told him that he had to find a fatherless boy, kill him, and sprinkle the foundation stones with the sacrificial victim's blood. Vortigern's warriors found a fatherless boy in the town, which was later called Kaermerdin (Carmarthen or Myrddin's fortress), and brought him to Vortigern.

Merlin boldly asked Vortigern why he and his mother had been summoned, and Vortigern told him truthfully that the intention was to sacrifice him. "Tell your magicians to appear in front of me," said Merlin, "and I will prove that they have lied." The Druids were duly sent for, and Merlin demanded that they explain what lay beneath the foundation. They could not. Merlin told Vortigern to have his men dig in the earth, where they would find a pool. When the pool was found, Merlin further prophesied that two hollow stones would be found within it, each holding a sleeping dragon. The dragons were found, one white and one red. As soon as they emerged, they began to fight. Merlin explained that the red dragon represented the British and the white dragon the Saxons or English. The white dragon initially drove the red dragon backwards, but Merlin explained that the red dragon would recover and eventually prevail. He also predicted the triumphant intervention of "the Boar of Cornwall" (i.e., Arthur), who would come to "bring relief from these invaders, for it will trample their necks beneath its feet."

In this short section of text, a significant phrase about Merlin is included, namely *qui et Ambrosius dicebatur*, meaning "who was also called Ambrosius." It looks like a later gloss in the original manuscript, although within a few lines Merlin is again referred to as Ambrosius Merlin. As I described earlier, it is highly likely that the Ambrosius part of the name was a religious epithet or title.

Geoffrey's story goes straight from the dragons into the full prophecies of Merlin, which take up an entire section. Merlin's predictions made a significant contribution to the *Historia*'s success. One prophecy was, "The lion's whelps shall be transformed into sea fishes (*catuli leonis in equorios pisces transformabuntur)*" which seemed to allude clearly to the drowning of Henry I's son in 1120. A few lines after that prediction came another: "Woe to thee, Normandy, because the lion's brain shall be poured upon thee, and he shall be banished with shattered limbs from his native soil (*ue tibi neustria quoniam in te cerebrum leonis effundetur et dissipatis membris a natiuo solo eliminabitur)*." Henry I died in Normandy on 1st December 1135, his death triggering a civil war which was to last another twenty years before the accession of Henry II. In these troubled circumstances, Merlin's prophecies, no matter how transparently fictional in origin, took on a mystique which made him an object of fascination across much of Europe.

The next major Merlin event in Geoffrey's story is the construction of Stonehenge. We need to take a deep breath here and recognize that 12th-century notions of ancient history were very different from our own. According to Geoffrey, Stonehenge was built by Merlin, under orders from Aurelius Ambrosius (Geoffrey's version of the name Ambrosius Aurelianus), some time after the first English settlements. We know full well that Stonehenge is thousands of years older than Geoffrey's story would allow for, and we can take note of many other historical mistakes he makes: for example, Geoffrey appears to confuse Stonehenge with Avebury and gives the impression that he thinks of them as a single place.

According to Geoffrey, Aurelius duly summoned Merlin and asked him to design and construct "some novel building which would stand for ever in memory of … so many noble men who had died for their fatherland." Merlin accepted the commission, and asked Vortigern to:

> ... send for the Giants' Ring which is on Mount Killaraus in Ireland. In that place there is a stone construction which no man of this period could ever erect, unless he combined great skill and artistry. The stones are enormous and there is no one alive strong enough to move them. If they are placed in position round this site, in the way in which they are erected over there, they will stand for ever.[6]

We know now that Geoffrey's suggestions about the curative properties of the stones, and that the (or at least an) original purpose of the complex was to honor the dead, may well be true. Although Geoffrey had the stones brought from "Mount Killaraus in Ireland," we also know that the central bluestones were probably hauled some 150 miles from the Preseli Hills in what is now Pembrokeshire in Wales, which is sufficiently close to Ireland both geographically and culturally (at the time) to account for the error.

Merlin's role in helping Uther to the begetting of Arthur is even better known than the building of Stonehenge. Gorlois, Duke of Cornwall, had a wife, Igraine (Ygern or Ygerna and many other variant spellings). Uther developed a passion for Igraine and demanded that Merlin help him to consummate it. At Gorlois's fortress-palace of Tintagel in Cornwall, Merlin magically shape-shifted Uther into the semblance of Gorlois; he also changed Uther's servant, Ulfin, into a character called Jordan, and himself into a character called Britaelis. This is clearly not shape-shifting in the classical Druidic or shamanistic sense, but rather simple mediaeval magic. Geoffrey tells us that the magic was effected by the use of drugs, but does not make clear whether it was Uther or Igraine who ingested them. Uther, in the guise of Gorlois, slept with Igraine and impregnated her. Gorlois was killed in a separate battle at nearby Dimilioc. Geoffrey neatly summarizes the "happy ending":

> The King set out and made his way towards his own army, abandoning his disguise as Gorlois and becoming Utherpendragon once more. When he learned all that had happened, he mourned for the death of Gorlois; but he was happy, all the same, that Ygerna was freed from her marital obligations. He returned to Tintagel Castle, captured it and seized Ygerna at the same time, she being what he really wanted. From that day on they lived together as equals, united by their great love for each other; and they had a son and a daughter. The boy was called Arthur and the girl Anna.[7]

Merlin is mentioned only once more in Geoffrey's story, and the reference makes no sense. Much later in the *Historia*, an Angelic Voice speaks to King Cadwallader and tells him that God "does not wish the Britons to rule in Britain any more, until the moment should come which Merlin had prophesied to Arthur (*quod Merlinus Arturo prophetaverat*)." But the last time we saw Merlin, he was still disguised as Britaelis and conjuring up Uther's first love-tryst with Ygerna, so Arthur was not yet conceived, let alone born. In Geoffrey's story, Arthur and Merlin never actually meet.

The Merlin whom Geoffrey created now appears to be at least in part based on a possible historical Myrddin or Merlin of the 6th century. The story of Merlin's origin in the north, or specifically Scotland, was known to Geoffrey. *The Black Book of Carmarthen*, which is the earliest of the Welsh texts, dates from about 1250, more than a century after Geoffrey's *Historia*. It contains poems attributed to Merlin. *The Red Book of Hergest*, in which *The Dialogue Between Merlin and his Sister Gwenddydd* appears, dates from the late 14th century, or perhaps the first quarter of the 15th. However, the nucleus of the poems dates all the way back to the 6th century, soon after the Welsh language first came into existence, which makes them the oldest extant vernacular literature in Europe apart from Latin and Greek.

In one of the poems, *Yr Afallennau* ("The Apple Trees"), we find the following passage:

> Sweet apple tree which grows in a glade,
> Its peculiar power hides it from the men of Rhydderch,
> A crowd by its trunk, a host around it,
> It would be a treasure for them, brave men in their ranks.
> Now Gwenddydd loves me not and does not greet me
> I am hated by Gwasawg, the supporter of Rhydderch—
> I have killed her son and her daughter.
> Death has taken everyone, why does it not call me?
> For after Gwenndolau no lord honours me,
> Mirth delights me not, no mistress visits me,
> And in the battle of Arderydd my torque was of gold,
> Though today I am not treasured by one of the aspect of swans ...
> For ten and forty years, in the wretchedness of outlawry,
> I have been wandering with madness and madmen;
> Now I sleep not, I tremble for my lord,
> My sovereign Gwenddolau, and my fellow-countrymen.
> After enduring wickedness and grief in the Forest of Celyddon
> May I be received into bliss by the Lord of Hosts.[8]

This is Myrddin talking to an apple tree (every stanza in the poem begins with an address to the sacred tree). Despite the Christian scribe's obligatory plea to "the Lord of Hosts," there could hardly be a simpler or clearer declaration that the narrator is a Druid. The apple tree not only shelters and supports him, it gives him a cloak of invisibility which keeps him hidden from Rhydderch's men. He acknowledges that he is now a madman. It was the battle of Arderydd that drove him to madness, after his lord Gwenddolau was killed. He himself wore a torque of gold, in other words he was one of the nobles leading the battle. The swan reference may seem obscure, but in early Celtic mythology swans, who were both royal and sacred birds, are often depicted as joined by slender chains of gold, a metaphor for the ties of tribe and family, and by extension between the land of the living and the land beyond the Veil. Now he is being hunted by the men of Rhydderch, who won at Arderydd and killed Gwenddolau. His sister Gwenddydd no longer visits him, because he has killed his nephew and niece, her son and daughter.

In Geoffrey's *Vita Merlini*, the names are given as Rodarcus, Guennolous, Ganieda and Telgesinus, but in history, as in the poems, they are Rhydderch Hael, Gwenddolau, Gwenddydd and Taliesin. The reference to the killing of his sister's children is obscure, but this Myrddin's allegiances and battles are plain. Myrddin's lord Gwenddolau is Pagan, and his enemy Rhydderch is Christian. In the 12th-century *Life of St Kentigern*, Glasgow's patron saint is a close friend and associate of King Rederech, i.e., Rhydderch Hael ("the Generous"). Rhydderch led a military expedition from the north against Gwynedd in North Wales. He fought against the English heathen kingdom of Bernicia, and was an ally of Urien of Rheged. He fought with Áedán mac Gabráin, King of Dál Ríada.

Gwenddydd was not only Merlin's sister, she was his *twin* sister. "The other one" in Welsh is *yr un arall* (pronounced very approximately *ur-een-ar-athl*) or *llall* (*thlathl*) for short, so it would not be impossible for Llallwg or its diminutive Llallwgan or Llallawgan to be a nickname referring to the other of a pair of twins. Llallwgan (pronounced approximately *thla-thloo-gan*) and Laloecen or Lailoken are reasonably similar in sound. In the original text, Gwenddydd uses the nickname Llallawg to refer to her brother, so it seems at least a possibility that Llallwgan is the origin of Lailoken.

In the *Life of St Kentigern*, King Rhydderch maintains at his court, presumably out of charity, a madman called Laloecen, whose madness and grief arose from the saint's death. Other sources name this person as Lailoken, whom the saint met as a naked and hairy wild man in the forest, who told him that he had been driven mad by a terrible battle and a voice from the sky holding him responsible for all the slaughter. He makes some prophecies, and then foretells his own strange triple death, in which he is first stoned and beaten by shepherds and then slips down a bank of the Tweed where he is impaled on a stake and simultaneously drowns. The prophecy is fulfilled, the madman dying exactly as he has foretold.

It appears that Laloecen or Lailoken and the Myrddin or Merlin of the *Yr Afallennau* poem are the same person, and very likely a genuinely historical figure. The 16th-century chronicler Elis Gruffydd called this figure Merlin Wyllt ("Merlin the Wild").

It is hardly a great leap of the imagination to suggest that Myrddin or Merlin was a Druid. In almost every version and variant of the legends in which he appears, Merlin deals with the supernatural in one form or another. He is mage, magus, wizard, prophet, seer, manipulator, trickster, conjuror and wise man. Add priest, judge, lawyer, diplomat, politician and possibly linguist and you reach an almost complete descriptive definition of a Druid.

The Lailoken tales explicitly connect Lailoken and Merlin. One says,

"He was known as Lailoken, and some say he was Merlyn, who was an extra-ordinary prophet of the British," while another says, clearly meaning Lailoken, "Pierced by a stake, suffering by stone and water, Merlin is said to have met a triple death (*Merlinus triplicem fertur ississe necem*)."

As the real, historical Druids and real Merlin faded away into the stuff of legend, the original power and influence of Druidism was replaced by glamourie, conjuring and magical tricks, and finally by science. But it was as much Merlin's prophecies as anything else that rocketed *Historia Regum Britanniae* to national and international fame. Geoffrey was either cunning or lucky in apparently predicting Henry I's death in Normandy. It was a piece of colossal, unbelievable luck (or divine intention) that William Caxton's publication of Sir Thomas Malory's *Morte Darthur* in 1485 was followed just three weeks later by the death of Richard III and the accession of Henry Tudor, who could now claim that he represented the restoration of the hegemony of the Red Dragon.

6. The Romantic Revival

Freemasonry and Druidism

Modern Druidism, generally called Druidry in Britain, began in Britain in the 18th century as a cultural movement, growing into a philosophical, religious and spiritual movement later in the 19th century. The revival of interest in ancient Druidism was based as much on cultural, political and national enthusiasm as on knowledge, and is now generally known as the Romantic or Romanticist Revival. Some modern Druids claim, or attempt to claim, direct and continuous descent from the ancient Druidic traditions, but, while it is obviously true that ancient and modern Druidism are closely connected, most modern Druids accept that the connections are often diffuse and vague, and that the comparative ignorance of the 18th- and 19th-century revivalists led to a great deal of speculation, invention and serious errors in understanding, which modern Druidism should and does reject. The precise nature of the correspondence between ancient and modern Druidism remains an important subject of debate among contemporary Druids and Druid organizations.

In the late 18th century, the first modern Druids looked to Freemasonry as their organizational model. Freemasonry, which was and still is a powerful and influential international fellowship, was also founded on ancient traditions, theirs dating back to the medieval trade guilds of the 14th and 15th centuries. Originally, being a Freemason or Mason was open only to men, and only white men, and only white men who believed in a supreme being. Arguments and schisms have developed over the centuries as international Freemasonry has wrestled with gender and racial equality, and the disapproval of some organized religions, in particular the Catholic Church. Those differences have resolved themselves into two broad types of modern Freemasonry: while Regular Freemasonry still insists on Christian holy scripture, belief in a supreme being, and no admission for women, Continental Freemasonry is now the term applied to those Lodges which do not accept some or all of those restrictions. But early Freemasonry shared with early revived Druidism a general optimism and sense of beneficent human purpose, a delight in fellowship, accompanied by enough ritual and mysticism to provide interest without overtly challenging most personal religious beliefs (predominantly if not exclusively Christian) or non-belief, plus a loosely confederated assortment of different groups, all of which to some extent might be said to describe some aspects of the organization of modern Druidism.

In part, the earlier idea of the "noble savage" fed into the Druidic Revival. Often attributed to Jean-Jacques Rousseau, who never actually used that term, the idea is much older. It appears very clearly in Thomas Hobbes's *Leviathan* of 1561, where he famously describes human existence as "solitary, poore, nasty, brutish, and short," praises the native American Indians, and introduces the term "State of Nature," which has subsequently been used to describe a wide range of natural, ecological and environmental conditions worthy of positive regard. For the self-styled Druids of the early revival, the Iron-Age Celts and their Druids were worthy of praise and emulation *because* they were savages, not *despite* their savagery.

John Aubrey (1626–1697)

John Aubrey, who never called himself a Druid, and who was considered a very minor and insignificant eccentric in his own lifetime, might be considered the "father" of modern Druidism. He wrote a collection of amusing biographical sketches called *Brief Lives*, published in the 1690s, which delivered descriptions of such worthies as Francis Bacon, Robert Boyle, Thomas Browne, John Dee, Sir Walter Raleigh, Edmund Halley, Ben Jonson, Thomas Hobbes, and William Shakespeare in an informal, entertaining, nod-and-a-wink style, peppered with anecdotes. The book was an immediate success, and a dramatic version of it by Patrick Garland, which first appeared in 1969 starring Roy Dotrice, was very successful and is still highly regarded. From that publication onwards, Aubrey was a minor celebrity, but generally thought of as an eccentric gossip and hack.

But Aubrey's interests ranged very widely, and they included archaeology, which in his day was a fairly unscientific science. He visited and described Avebury (the first modern writer to do so) and Stonehenge, among other monuments. There are post-holes at Stonehenge now named the Aubrey Holes in his honor (although they are not actually the same holes which he originally described). He wrote about folklore and traditional beliefs. He started several large writing or research projects but left them uncompleted, and to this day much of his work is either unpublished or only partially published. His observations of Stonehenge were only part of an intended definitive history of the English county of Wiltshire, in which Stonehenge stands, but which he never finished. His personal life and finances were chaotic, and he characteristically died on the road, aged 71, of an apoplectic fit, which he suffered while traveling in June of 1697.

John Aubrey

Despite the fact that they attracted very little interest in his own time, Aubrey's combined descriptions of Stonehenge and Avebury, crude though they are by comparison with all the detailed and researched descriptions that are available to us now, along with his descriptions of ancient British folklore and religious customs and beliefs, were the apple seeds from which the trees of the Druidic Romantic Revival grew, and modern Druids admire and respect his important early contributions.

William Stukeley (1687–1765)

Stukeley was a Church of England minister, a Fellow of the Royal Society, a qualified doctor and Fellow of the Royal College of Physicians, and a Freemason. He was also a pioneer archaeological investigator, particularly of Avebury and Stonehenge (which he believed had been built by ancient patriarchs of a religion akin to Christianity), and obsessively interested in ancient Druidism (which he perceived as that religion), from which combination he is frequently described as one of the main founders of modern Druidism. He was a friend of Isaac Newton (who, despite his immense fame and historical importance, was a strange and difficult man, with very few friends at all), and one of Newton's earliest biographers. (The unsubstantiated story that Newton understood gravity instantly when he saw an apple falling first appeared in Stukeley's biographical memoir.)

Stukeley wrote detailed descriptions of Avebury and Stonehenge, which were published in 1740 and 1743. In collaboration with the respected astronomer Edmund Halley, he developed what is perhaps the earliest theory of an astronomical alignment for Stonehenge. The details of his conclusions were wrong, and quite spectacularly wrong—he assumed a northerly orientation of the monument to Polaris, the Pole Star, and from that assumption then calculated that Stonehenge was built in 460 BCE, which is about three thousand years later than the probable date of original construction—but the new and main idea of an astronomical and calendrical alignment was correct in principle, and a very significant insight in its day.

William Stukeley (Welcome Images)

The 1740 and 1743 publications about Avebury and Stonehenge were intended to be part of a much larger historical study, which Stukeley never actually completed. They contain his idea that humankind followed an original, patriarchal religion from earliest times (we now know that it was almost certainly matriarchal in most cultures), but that "Old Religion" had been replaced by idol-worship. Stukeley had no difficulty in reconciling his obvious and profound commitment to Christianity with his admittedly limited vision of a monotheistic, patriarchal Druidism. His enthusiasm earned him the nickname or epithet of "Archdruid," even though that precise role, or indeed any Druidic ceremonials or institutions, had not yet been reconstructed at the time of Stukeley's death in 1765.

Iolo Morganwg (1747–1826)

Iolo Morganwg is the assumed Druidic name of Edward Williams from Glamorgan in Wales. (Morgannwg is the Welsh name for Glamorgan.) He was a stonemason originally, but began collecting old manuscripts as a hobby, then moved on to writing poetry. At the age of 26 he moved to London, where he was introduced by the antiquary Owen Jones to expatriate Welsh writers and societies, including the Gwyneddigion Society and the Cymreigyddion Society. He was impressed by them, but they were equally impressed by him, and his obvious enthusiasm for (and pretended knowledge of) ancient Welsh manuscripts. Four years later, he returned to Wales to take up farming, at which he was not very successful. He began creating forged manuscripts to support his theory of a continuous and unbroken Druidic tradition from before the Roman occupation of Britain. He was a frequent user of the alcoholic tincture of opium known as laudanum, which some say accounts for the obvious lapses in integrity which were undoubtedly part of his character. Nonetheless, whatever reservations remain about his integrity, there is no doubt that Iolo Morganwg made an extremely significant contribution to the Romantic Revival, and his influence remains powerful to this day, not least in

Iolo Morganwg (courtesy Rhondda Cyron Taf Libraries)

the only prayer which is common to many modern Druidic groups or organizations, particularly in Britain (see below).

In 1789 Morganwg published *Barddoniaeth Dafydd ab Gwilym,* supposedly poems by the 14th-century Welsh Bard Dafydd ap Gwilym, but, as we now know, including a number of allegedly recently-discovered poems which were, in fact, by Morganwg himself. Regardless of (and, at the time, ignorant of) the additional forgeries, the reading public bought the book and approved it. On the back of that success, Morganwg returned to London, where he organized and conducted a revival of the ancient Welsh assembly of Druids, Ovates and Bards known as a *gorsedd,* which, as we observed earlier, literally means "great sitting." The revived *Gorsedd,* which he led as a public ceremony on Primrose Hill in London on Midsummer's Day of 1792, was highly successful, and attracted a great deal of public interest. Morganwg claimed that the rituals, invocations, prayer texts and ceremonial protocols he used in that ceremony were all from ancient Druidism, but it is now obvious that some, if not most or all, of the material was created by Morganwg himself. Two years later, he published some of his own poetry, and again this was well received.

A prayer from that original *Gorsedd* remains in the Welsh, Cornish and Breton ceremonials to this day, and is also found in the ritual texts of many other Druid groups. I give it below in both Welsh and English. Different groups and individuals use the prayer with slight textual variations, for example "Spirit" or "Goddess" in place of "God."

Llyma weddi'r orsedd	The Gorsedd Prayer
Dyro Dduw Dy nawdd;	Grant, O God, Thy protection;
Ag yn nawdd, nerth;	And in protection, strength;
Ag yn nerth, deall;	And in strength, understanding;
Ag yn neall, gwybod;	And in understanding, knowledge;
Ag yn gwybod, gwybod y	And in knowledge, the knowledge of
cyfiawn;	justice;
Ag yn gwybod y cyfiawn,	And in the knowledge of justice,
ei garu;	the love of it;
Ag o garu, caru pob hanfod;	And from love, the love of all creation;
Ag o garu pob hanfod, caru Duw;	And from love of creation, love of God;
Duw a phob daioni.	God and all goodness.

It is a simple, beautiful, powerful and moving prayer. I have spoken it many times myself (in Cornish) at the Cornish Gorsedh, with other groups, and even privately by myself. But it was written by Iolo Morganwg, not by any ancient Druid, and it is Morganwg's dishonesty in presenting his forgeries and claiming them to be authentic ancient Druidic material which still rankles to this day—to many modern Druids, especially those who follow a scholarly, reconstructivist approach, Morganwg is pure poison. Understandably, falsehood like his, no matter how eloquent or moving, lends credence to the claim that all modern Druidism is just "made up" stuff, although that is patently not true either, as only a little research soon reveals.

Morganwg left his writings and manuscripts in an untidy jumble at the time of his death in 1826, and it was his son, Taliesin ab Iolo, who collected them in 26 volumes, a selection of which was published in 1848. Had Morganwg's forgeries been obvious, or philosophically or religiously unacceptable, or of low literary quality, it would be easy to dismiss them entirely, because they are false, and truth above all things (*y gwir yn erbyn ar byd*, "truth against the world") is such a fundamental Druidic moral concept that blatant forgery, especially of religious thoughts, is clearly a serious and shocking wrongdoing, and completely unforgivable for many modern Druids. Because the ancient Druidic tradition was oral rather than written, it is now virtually impossible to ascertain what material, if any, from Morganwg's vast collection is of genuine provenance: certainly not all of it, and perhaps, regrettably, none of it. His supporters, mostly British and from the *Gorsedd* tradition, claim that it doesn't matter: the strongest material is so imbued with spirit, so inspiring and powerful, so beautifully articulate, that we should simply accept it and use it. Certainly the continuing success and growth of the Welsh, Cornish and Breton *gorseddau* owe an incalculable debt of gratitude to Iolo Morganwg for having the vision and energy to bring about that first revived *Gorsedd* on

Primrose Hill in 1789. His detractors, mostly American, say that it absolutely does matter: we should forget about trying to make dubious or even blatantly made-up connections with the Iron Age, and concentrate instead on creating a truthful, valid and useful modern religion or philosophy for our own times, based on genuine ancient sources only and using our own hearts and minds, not forging or pretending connections that don't actually exist and never did. Ellen Evert Hopman summarizes the disdain for Iolo Morganwg very crisply: "Celtic-oriented Druids avoid him like the plague. We do not use his prayers and we do not use his writings. We prefer to stick to actual historic Celtic material wherever possible. It's only the British Orders that honor or are fascinated with this person."[1]

In fact, the pro-Morganwg and anti–Morganwg factions—indeed, the pro– and anti–Revivalist factions more generally—are not so simply or equally divided between the UK and the USA. Philip Carr-Gomm points out that the Ancient Order of Druids in America (AODA), one of the larger groups in the USA, is happy to include Iolo Morganwg material in their archives, and that the UK-based Order of Bards, Ovates and Druids (OBOD) is certainly very well aware of the complaints and concerns about Morganwg's falsehoods and perfectly understands the American Reconstructionist approach.[2]

Godfrey Higgins (1772–1833)

Godfrey Higgins, born in Yorkshire, England, a landowner, magistrate and well-known social reformer, is almost the exact opposite of Iolo Morganwg. He was undoubtedly a truthful, thoughtful and utterly sincere man, but many of his Druidic ideas and theories are now recognized as either doubtful or simply wrong, based on enthusiastic errors and misunderstandings.

The 19th century saw a number of Christian theologians trying to assimilate and connect Biblical mythology and traditions with the rapidly increasing awareness of other religious cultures. For the most part, their approach was to identify Christian themes with a hypothesized earlier, universal paternalistic religion (see Stukeley above), and they made many guesses and assumptions, most of which have not stood the test of time. Higgins was certain that the lost continent of Atlantis was the source of all the early religions which subsequently came into the world, including Druidism. Nowadays, there are very few people who believe that the religion of the ancient Druids came from Atlantis, or from the far side of the Moon, for that matter.

Nevertheless, Higgins was sincere and energetic in pursuing his theories. He expounded and expanded them in a series of publications over several

years. *Horae Sabbaticae* (1826) was a progressive but otherwise fairly traditional discussion of the Sabbath and sabbatarianism. *The Celtic Druids*, published between 1827 and 1829, made (or tried to find) connections between
early Druidism, early eastern religions, and ancient worship sites like Stonehenge and Carnac. Higgins now postulated that Druidism came from India
in its earliest form. He completed his intended *magnum opus, Anacalypsis*,
in 1833, just before his death at the age of 71, but it was not published until
1836, in a limited edition of 200 copies. In it, Higgins argues that the Biblical
Abraham was, in fact, the God Brahma of Hinduism, that both the Druids
and the Jews originated in India, and that there was a worldwide but secret
pantheist religion which understood all these truths, but could not speak
them openly for fear that they would be corrupted by an untrustworthy Christian establishment. He believed that the Greek deities were all black, and that
God Himself was black, because man, in the form of the black Jews of Ethi-
opia, had made God in their image, and then claimed the reverse, that it was
God who had made *them* in *His* image.

Despite what appears to us now to be the strangeness of many of Higgins's ideas, he was highly respected by his contemporaries. He was a Fellow
of the Society of Antiquaries. His social reform campaigning was strenuous,
sincere and effective. He uncovered and campaigned against the widespread
abuse and mistreatment of the mentally ill, many of whom were simply locked
away and horribly neglected in dreadful asylums. He campaigned against the
exploitation of child labor in factories. Most modern Druids would summarize Higgins as sincere but misguided.

William Price (1800–1893)

The name William Price is so common that Wikipedia has 36 entries
for its disambiguation. Nevertheless, our William Price was a singularly
uncommon and distinctive figure. The 19th-century lithograph of him, heavily bearded, wearing a Druidic uniform and sword and a fox-fur hat, and carrying a lunula in his left hand and a flaming torch in his right, has been
reproduced widely in books about Druidism. He lived to be 92, and was quite
a character.

He was born to a working-class, Welsh-speaking family in Monmouth-
shire. In his childhood and adolescence, Price showed signs of mental illness,
although he was never formally diagnosed. He would swim fully clothed,
because people had complained about him swimming naked in full view. He
cut bark from trees and burned it, muttering incantations. He attacked neighbors, firing a gun at one of them.

In 1820 he went to London to complete medical studies and qualify as a doctor, eventually becoming a member of the Royal College of Surgeons, before returning to his homeland. His first interests were political, rather than religious. He was a strong Welsh nationalist, and an ardent supporter of Chartism, the British working-class national protest movement that began in 1838 with the publication of a Charter demanding greater democracy, specifically universal suffrage without property qualification for all males aged 21 and over. Although Chartism continued into the 1850s, government suppression in 1839 led Price to flee to France, disguised as a woman, to escape possible prosecution. In France, he became convinced that he had a divine mission to liberate Wales from English hegemony. He returned to Wales and enthusiastically allied himself to the Celtic Druidic Welsh revival movement begun by Iolo Morganwg.

In 1834, still a young man of 33, Price gave a speech on Welsh heritage at the Welsh national *Eisteddfod*. The speech was widely acclaimed by many, including the wealthy and influential Lady Charlotte Guest, who first published the full collection of the *Mabinogi* in Welsh. (It was Lady Guest who made the grammatical mistake of calling the collection the *Mabinogion*, which is a double plural, like "childrens" in English.) Price rapidly became a leading figure in the nationalist revival. He joined a Druidic group, which met and conducted ceremonies regularly at *Y Maen Chwyf* ("the rocking stone") in Pontypridd. He gave Welsh lessons every Sunday, defending the language against the relentless onslaught of English.

Later, he declared himself first as a Druid, and then as the Archdruid (although nobody had nominated or elected him). His Druidism was highly individualistic, often improvised from his own inspiration. He began wearing Druidic clothing of his own design, usually made of emerald green cloth. He carried a trident, as well as a lunula. His wizard-like beard and long hair were unusual, even for the generally whiskered male society of the 19th century. He declared marriage to be immoral because it enslaved women, and practiced his preaching by entering into an unmarried relationship (again, considered profoundly immoral and shocking at the time) with Ann Morgan, who bore him a daughter. He baptized the baby himself at Y Maen Chwyf, naming her Gwenhiolan Iarlles Morganwg ("Gwenhiolan, Countess of Glamorgan"). He later made her a Bard, at a public *eisteddfod* for which nobody turned up, apart from Price and his daughter.

Price came to the attention of the authorities by practicing what he preached, in a case that achieved considerable notoriety at the time. Gwenhiolan eventually returned to her mother, and a more conventional life. At the remarkable age of 81, Price then created fresh scandal by beginning a new relationship with Gwenllian Llewelyn, a 21-year-old farmer's daughter. She bore him a son, whom he defiantly named Iesu Grist ("Jesus Christ"), but the baby boy died in 1844 at the age of five months. Following his belief that human burial polluted the Earth, Price himself attempted to cremate the baby's body. He was arrested before the body had been consumed by the flames. The police confiscated the little, singed corpse and put Price on trial. He argued successfully that, although the Christian establishment might find his actions repugnant or morally wrong, there was no actual law against what he had done. He was acquitted, and subsequently completed the cremation. (The case led to the implementation of the Cremation Act of 1902.) Gwenllian subsequently gave birth to another boy, also called Iesu Grist and considered by Price to be the realization of the Second Coming, and, in 1886, a daughter whom they named Penelopen.

When Price himself died in 1893, at the age of 92, he was cremated on a two-ton pile of coal, according to his wishes, and 20,000 onlookers attended the event. Nowadays, of course, cremation is an established procedure, but in Price's time it was considered profoundly immoral, primitive, barbaric and shocking. It specifically defied the Christian claim that we are resurrected in the body as well as in spirit after death, and was therefore widely condemned as blasphemous. After Price's death, Gwenllian married a road inspector, became a Christian, and had Iesu Grist re-baptized as Nicholas. Nicholas led an uneventful life, and did not bring Armageddon or the End Times to the world.

Some of Price's Druidic thinking would be described by most people today as plain madness. He had frequently carried live snakes around in his pockets as a boy, and as an old Druid he formulated a theory that the whole universe was created by God the Father from a snake's egg (which may be crazy, but is not dissimilar to some other early Creation myths). He claimed that the ancient Greeks were, in fact, Welsh, and that Homer had been born near Caerphili. But Price's challenging ideas and behavior, which were generally considered mere lunacy and wicked foolishness by 19th-century society, sprang from an intensity of conviction which had a profound impact on his followers, and which in turn created a huge general interest in Druidism as well as in Welsh and Celtic identity, and which still resonates to this day. He was an eloquent and courageous man, even if he was mad, who lived out his beliefs with conviction. Although his truth was impossibly strange to his contemporaries, and still strange in many parts to us as well, it was the truth for him, and he respected it sufficiently to risk ridicule and imprisonment in its name.

The Influence of the Romantic Revival

The Romantic Revival had many positive effects. It rescued and preserved a great deal of genuine early material from ancient Celtic culture. It contributed enormously to a general growth in archaeology, both professional and amateur, which continues to this day. It began a stout and vigorous support of Celtic identity and Celtic language, again still very much alive in our own time, despite constant pressure from English as a language and Anglo-centricity as a cultural force. It encouraged co-operation and a sense of shared identity between all the Celtic nations (Ireland, Scotland, Isle of Man, Wales, Cornwall, Brittany, Galicia and Asturias), which still exists through the Celtic Congress, the international annual *Festival des Cornemuses* in L'Orient, and a host of other cultural, artistic, musical and sports events. It encouraged access to and interest in ancient Celtic culture, including Druidism. It created the Welsh, Cornish and Breton *gorseddau* and *eisteddfodau* (see next chapter), which, with their Goidelic counterparts, such as the *Mòd Nàiseanta Rìoghal* or Royal National Mod of Scotland, play an essential role in the continuing support and development of all aspects of Celtic culture.

But the Romantic Revival also had negative effects. The strong desire to find a direct link between paternalistic, monotheistic Christianity and free-thinking, polytheistic Druidism was doomed to failure, even though, paradoxically, there are many Druids today who also describe themselves as Christian; they have achieved that Christo-Druid synthesis by resisting dogma and allowing flexibility into their thinking, which the leaders of the Romantic Revival (many of them ordained Christian clerics) were unable to do, generating a great deal of nonsense during their intellectual and spiritual struggle to square the circle. The deliberate lies and inventions of the Romantic Revival made it very easy for the academic and intellectual world (and particularly the various ecumenical religious groups) to dismiss Druidism, ancient and modern, as insubstantial and untrustworthy, an attitude which unfortunately is still very prevalent to this day.

7. Some Modern Groups and Organizations

We have already seen that there were two different elements at play in the Romantic Revival: first, a scholarly interest in ancient religion and possible ancient precursors of Christianity, and, second, a cultural and political Celtic nationalism. From the first came what is often called fraternal Druidism, a generally benevolent movement, modeling its structure on Freemasonry, which sought to do good works and support charitable causes while offering a friendly fellowship, but staying free of politics, religion and other disputatious areas. From the second came cultural Druidism, which was conversely very interested in politics, strongly supportive of maintaining Celtic language and culture, and energetic in support of the arts, particularly the ancient Celtic arts of poetry and music. The Welsh, Cornish and Breton *gorseddau* and *eisteddfodau* (see below) were born of this second tradition.

The spirituality in both was initially similar: it was essentially Christian, although the religious element was generally tacit, not active. The meeting hall would have a Bible on the table, but religious discussion, like political discussion, was discouraged, and the Bible would sit unopened. It was not really until the 20th century that a third kind of Druidism began to emerge, partly through individual enthusiasts like George Watson MacGregor-Reid (see Chapter 8), but also through a general loosening of the dead-handle Victorian influence that had pervaded Britain for so many decades. It took *fin-de-siècle* artistic daring, Edwardian social unrest, and a shocking World War to shake and stir that Christian passivity. There had been plenty of speculative religious thinking in the 19th century, for example in Theosophy, Rosicrucianism and the Order of the Golden Dawn, but Druidism—the Pagan religion of ancient savages—needed a larger and more general loosening of public thought to emerge from its obscure hiding places.

In the 1940s and 1950s, two British individuals, whom we shall consider in more detail in the next chapter, finally shook Paganism and Druidism free:

they were Gerald Gardner and Ross Nichols, who vastly influenced—some would say shaped—the Wicca and modern Druidism we know today. However, before we look in more detail at individual influences, we need to recapitulate the origins and current status of some modern Druidic groups and organizations.

Gorseddau, Eisteddfodau

Whatever reservations we may have today about some of the leading lights of the Romantic Revival, or about the correctness or incorrectness of their thinking, there is no doubt that modern Druidism could not have come into existence without them. The modern Welsh, Cornish and Breton *gorseddau* and *eisteddfodau*, which owe their existence to Iolo Morganwg and others, are not actually truly Druidic nor even religious organizations, even though their public ceremonies include ritual text and prayers, the best known being the Gorsedd Prayer given above. The Cornish *Gorsedh* has only one rank, that of Bard, and is very careful to avoid political or religious controversy. All three *gorseddau* almost fall outside the remit of this book, since they are really neither philosophical nor religious in nature, but they are, nevertheless, derived largely from the same roots as modern Druidism, and remain very active and effective in protecting and defending Brythonic Celtic culture.

Each of the modern, revived *gorseddau* meets annually in a public ceremony, conducted respectively in Welsh, Cornish or Breton. There are no equivalent assemblies in Scotland, Ireland or the Isle of Man. The ceremonies must be conducted in the open air, in public rather than in secret: as *Gorsedh Kernow*, or the Cornish Gorsedh, expresses it, *adherag an howl, lagas an jydh* ("before the Sun, the eye of day"). This was an important feature of the original revived Welsh Gorsedd, which in turn was probably a feature of the ancient *gorseddau*, as explained by Meyryg of Glamorgan:

> A Gorsedd of the Bards of the Isle of Britain must be held in a conspicuous place, in full view of hearing of country and aristocracy, and in the face of the sun and in the eye of light; it being unlawful to hold such meetings under cover, at night, or under any circumstances other than while the sun shall be visible in the sky.[1]

Gorsedd Cymru, or more properly *Gorsedd Beirdh Ynys Prydain* ("Gorsedd of the Bards of the Isle of Britain"), the original Welsh Gorsedd, was instituted, as we have seen, by Iolo Morganwg in 1792. Gorsedd traditions have developed considerably over the years. The three ranks of membership were: firstly, Bards, in blue robes; secondly, Ovates, in green robes; and, thirdly, Druids, in white robes. The supreme authority of the Gorsedd is the Archdruid, whose robes are gold in color. Nowadays, the Gorsedd places less emphasis on rank (it allows all *Gorseddygion* to call themselves "Druid," for example), using the different colored robes to indicate sphere of interest or achievement rather than rank. The Breton *Gorsez* now uses the same system, but in Cornwall all members are Bards and wear blue robes, the leader being known as the *Bardh Meur* or Grand Bard. All three *gorseddau* follow very similar ceremonial sequences, including the opening call for peace. In Welsh, the Archdruid asks the assembly three times, "*A oes heddwch?*" while the Cornish Grand Bard asks "*Eus kres?*" both meaning "Is there peace?" and the members shout either "*Heddwch!*" or "*Kres!*" three times in response, to ensure that there is peace among all before the ceremonies begin. The rituals are closed with the same invocation of peace and harmony.

Gorsedh Kernow, the Cornish Gorsedh, which has about 450 to 500 living Bards at any given time, most in Cornwall, but some of them in England or elsewhere in Europe, or in far-flung Canada, America, Australia or New Zealand, was instituted in 1928 at the ancient stone circle of Boscawen-an-Un, led by Henry Jenner, whose Bardic name was Gwas Myghal or "Servant of (the Archangel) Michael." Jenner and twelve others had been initiated by the Archdruid of Wales. The stated aim of the Gorsedh is, "to maintain the national Celtic spirit of Cornwall." I myself was made a Bard of *Gorsedh Kernow* in 1978, the Gorsedh's Golden Jubilee year, and still consider it the greatest honor awarded to me in a long and eventful life. *Gorsedh Kernow* has subsequently established an *Esedhvos*, the Cornish equivalent of the Welsh *Eisteddfod*, which is a festival of art, writing, music and crafts, and a celebration of Celtic national spirit and identity. There are similar cultural festivals in the Goidelic Celtic nations, Scotland, Ireland and the Isle of Man, as well as in Galicia and Asturias.

Gorsez Vreizh, the Breton Gorsedd, was established earlier than *Gorsedh Kernow* (the Breton Bardic Association received official proclamation from the Welsh Gorsedd in 1908), but the process of its formation was much more protracted and complicated. *Gorsez Vreizh* still receives Welsh and Cornish delegations at its annual public ceremony. However, in 1936 a splinter group who wanted the Breton *Gorsez* to be much less anodyne and Christianized, and much more Pagan and religiously Druidic, finally established themselves as a new and separate modern Druid organization, which is still active today. It was originally called *Kredenn Geltiek* ("Celtic Creed"), then became *Kredenn Geltiek Hellvedel* ("Celtic Creed of the World"), and is now very different in character and purpose from the traditional *Gorsez*. Michel-Gerald Boutet of Quebec, whose Druidic name is Boutios, is a member of *Kredenn Geltiek Hollvedel* and of *Druuidica Comardia Eriutalamonos*, a Canadian branch of the Breton *Comardia Druidiacta Armorica* (CDA). In his words, the new group was formed because, "the other Meso-Druidical groups of the time were all pseudo–Pagan, Masonic and Christian-based "Grail religion" type groups."[2]

Ancient Order of Druids

This organization, which calls itself "the parent and founding order of the modern Druidic Societies," was inaugurated (it says "revived") on the 29th of November 1781, so it was born directly out of the Romantic Revival. It describes its object as being, "to preserve and practice the main principles attributed to the early Druids, particularly those of justice, benevolence and friendship." It also claims to have "adapted itself to modern conditions," although in many aspects it remains very close to the original Freemasonry model which so many early Druidic organizations followed. Its membership in England is restricted to men only (members are "brothers"), it has several oaths of secrecy, and it has a hierarchical system of promotion and advancement. It states categorically, "Ours is not a religious organization—in fact any discussion on religion or politics is forbidden within the lodge rooms." (Many of these early benevolent societies and fraternities were not trying to be censorious or prescriptive; rather, they were simply anxious to avoid the political and religious quarrels which were not only frequent but also often violent in the 18th century—the AOD describes its first members as "gentlemen of a quiet frame of mind.") It has many lodges (a Masonry word) in England, as well as in the rest of the world, notably Australia, Denmark, Finland, Germany, Iceland, Norway, Sweden, Switzerland, the USA and Canada, and is involved in many charitable enterprises. Some lodges began admitting women and children in the 19th century. In 1913, the various international lodges and organizations amalgamated under the motto "Unity, Peace and Concord."

The Druid Order

The Ancient Druid Order, also called the Druid Order or *An Druidh Uileach Braithreachas* ("The Universal Brotherhood of Druids," a name devised by John Aubrey) say that they can trace their origins to centuries before the Romantic Revival, and they are certainly much more clearly a religious and philosophical organization. They claim to trace their beginning back to the Pheryllt, a group of mediaeval alchemists who were "guardians of the Druid mysteries of Ceridwen at Cor Emrys on the Penmaen ridge of Snowdon."[3] They founded a Druidic grove in Oxford before the University was established there, and were persecuted in 1166 by the Bishop of Oxford, who ordered that their documents and paraphernalia should be burned. The Mount Haemus Grove was re-established in Oxford in 1245, incorporating in its belief system a mixture of Christianity, Gnosticism and Druidism, and the Druid Order succeeded it in 1717. They list their Chief Druids (they do not use the term Archdruid) chronologically as follows, and the list shows both the longevity and continuity of the organization and the quality of their leadership (we have already met and discussed some of these people): John Toland 1717–1722; William Stukeley 1722–1765; Edward Finch Hatton 1765–1771; David Samway 1771–1799; William Blake (the poet and mystic) 1799–1827; Godfrey Higgins 1827–1833; William Carpenter 1833–1874; Edward Vaughan Kenealy 1874–1880; Gerald Massey 1880–1906; John Barry O'Callaghan 1906–1909; George Watson MacGregor-Reid 1909–1946; Robert MacGregor-Reid 1946–1964; Thomas Lackenby Maughan 1964–1976; Christopher Sullivan 1976–1981; David Loxley –the present Chief, since 1981.

(It is worth remarking that these are all men. The first British organization to be led by a woman appears to have been the Cornish Gorsedh: Ann Trevenen Jenkin was the first woman to be elected Grand Bard of *Gorsedh Kernow*, from 1997 to 2000; her husband, Richard Jenkin, had been Grand Bard before her from 1972 to 1976. Since then, there have been three other women Grand Bards: Vanessa Beaman, Bardic name Gwenenen, 2003 to 2006; Maureen or Mo Fuller, Bardic name Steren Mor, 2009 to 2012; and Elizabeth M. Carne, Bardic name Melennek, from 2015 to the present.)

The flexible spirit of the Druid Order (and, in fact, of modern Druidism in general) is admirably captured in the text of a speech given by Dr. T.L. Maughan to the College of Psychic Studies in 1967:

> I don't know how many of you know what a Druid is, but if you do not you can take comfort from the fact that there are many who wear the white robe who still don't know either. To me, the Druid is a kind of caretaker. They look after the things worthwhile until somebody wants them. They do not propagate, they do not sell, they do not form groups, they just look after. If you destroy the world and have to start again, it will be a Druid that comes out of his corner to tell you when to sow and when to reap. If you have learned that sufficiently so that you have time to spare they will teach you to follow up with arts and crafts, and when your civilisation is once more developed they will go on to the sciences and religion. That's Druidry. And when you enter into persecution and feudal wars they just vanish again. We are a religious body but we do not have a religion. It is all one to us whether we have a Hindu, a Muslim, a Buddhist, Shintoist or a shaman—we take them from there. We do not believe in conversion. Conversion is equivalent to asking you to get from this [upstairs] room to the street without going down the stairs. It is not practical. If you want to get to the street, you first rise from your seat, walk from your seat to the door; it is no use telling you how to manoeuvre in the street until you get there. So if we have a Hindu or a Muslim we take them within their own faith and enlarge them in their own right as a human being until they outgrow their faith, if they outgrow it. And should they outgrow their faith to which they were born they will find the next step immediately in front of them just as you will when you reach the door—the next step takes you out to what is the other side of it. That is our method.[4]

The method may be too warm and fuzzy for many modern Druids, and "we do not have a religion" flies directly in the face of what many of us believe, but the flexibility and pragmatic kindliness are part and parcel of modern Druidism, and remain very valuable, I believe. The Druid Order is based in London and holds regular meetings, as well as conducting public ceremonials.

Spiritual Environmentalism

By the 1960s and 1970s, the increasing concerns about destruction of our planet's resources and our often selfish and wasteful attitudes towards the environment took an unusual turn. While, for some, environmentalism remained simply a political issue, others began to connect it to ideas that could not be called anything other than religious. Arnold Toynbee wrote a highly influential article, which appeared in 1972 in the *International Journal of Environmental Studies*, which stops short of openly advocating a religious solution, but certainly points clearly in that direction:

> In popular pre–Christian Greek religion, divinity was inherent in all natural phenomena, including those that man had tamed and domesticated. Divinity was present in springs and rivers and the sea; in trees, both the wild oak and the cultivated olive-tree; in corn and vines; in mountains; in earthquakes and lightning and thunder. The Godhead was diffused throughout the phenomena. It was plural, not singular; a pantheon, not a unique almighty super-human person. When the Graeco-Roman World was converted to Christianity, the divinity was drained out of nature and was concentrated in one unique transcendent God.... The plight in which post–Industrial-Revolution man has now landed himself is one more demonstration that man is not the master of his environment—not even when supposedly armed with a warrant, issued by a supposedly unique and omnipotent God with a human-like personality, delegating to man plenipotentiary powers. Nature is now demonstrating to us that she does not recognize the validity of this alleged warrant, and she is warning us that, if man insists on trying to execute it, he will commit this outrage on nature at his peril.[5]

So now a new dimension was added to the various formulae for creating Druidic groups or organizations: spiritual environmentalism, which, over time, has become the clearest single identifier of Druidism. We love and protect the Earth because it is good husbandry, good economics, common sense, etc. But we also love and protect the Earth because the Earth is sacred, the Earth is our Mother. Every modern Druid group has some variant of that simple philosophy somewhere in its vitals.

Reformed Druids of North America

Carleton College in Northfield, Minnesota, was originally founded as a liberal arts college by the Congregational Church. Although it had become nondenominational by the early 1960s, it still required students to attend religious worship on Sundays, either at the college's own services or at a recognized church of their own choosing. In 1963, as a humorous protest against this requirement, a group of students jokingly created the Reformed Druids of North America, which they claimed they would attend, thus meeting the college requirement. They required members to drink whisky as part of "church" ritual, in protest of the college's ban on alcohol.

The original basic tenets of Reformed Druidism were written in a mock, pseudo–Biblical style to continue the joke:

1. The object of the search for religious truth, which is a universal and a never-ending search, may be found through the Earth-Mother; which is Nature; but this is one way, one way among many.
2. And great is the importance, which is of a spiritual importance of Nature, which is the Earth-Mother; for it is one of the objects of Creation, and with it do people live, yea, even as they do struggle through life are they come face-to-face with it.

These were later abbreviated to:

1. Nature is good!
2. Nature is good![6]

Ironically (or perhaps because the Goddess was enjoying and participating in the joke), when the college finally admitted defeat and rescinded the requirement for church attendance in 1964, the Reformed Druids of North America not only continued to function, it actually increased its membership and activities, and has been active ever since.

Here is how the original members, still continuing the mock–Biblical style, described the abolition of the regulations at Carleton:

1. Now it came to pass that in those last days a decree went out from the authorities;
2. And they did declare to be abolished the regulations, which had been placed upon the worship of those at Carleton.
3. And behold, a great rejoicing did go up from all the land for the wonders which had come to pass.
4. And all the earth did burst forth into song in the hour of salvation.
5. And in the time of exaltation, the fulfillment of their hopes, the Druids did sing the praises of the Earth-Mother.[7]

What began as a protest and anti–Establishment joke became a *bona fide* religious organization. Today it claims to have more than 40 groves throughout the USA and Canada, with the Carleton Grove as the Mother Grove, approximately 400 grove members, approximately 4,000 Druids and approximately 100 Priests and Priestesses.

The original members were anything but Neo-Pagan: they were Christians, Jews, agnostics, or atheists, the only original commonality between them being the sense of outrage at being required to attend a weekly religious service.

Very quickly, however, they discovered another important core belief, one we have already identified, and one which remains at the heart of RDNA as it does for every other Druid group or organization: the love of Nature, and a profound sense of respect and responsibility for the natural world and all living things. From that simple beginning, RDNA expanded and developed into a large and complex religious organization. It has an extended system of initiation and advancement. It has produced a vast collection of literature. In common with many other organizations, it has incrementally altered or ridded itself of gender discrimination over the years, to allow women to take as full a part in its activities as men, including, for example, being Archdruids: Marta Peck was elected as the first woman Archdruid of Carleton Grove as early as 1968.

Ár nDraíocht Féin

Ár nDraíocht Féin (pronounced approximately *arn-ree-ocht-fayn*, Irish Gaelic for "our own Druidism," although many members also simply use the same initials ADF to represent the English phrase A Druid Fellowship) is a long-standing American organization, formed originally from schism within the Reformed Druids of North America, which describes itself as "a Pagan church based on ancient Indo-European traditions expressed through public worship, study, and fellowship."[8] It was founded in 1983 by Isaac Bonewits (see Chapter 8) and has grown into one of the largest Druid organizations in the USA and the world. It asks for membership subscriptions, but has a Compassionate Membership Fund so that members who fall on hard times can continue as members without having to pay. Probably more than any other Druid organization or group, ADF has focused on ritual over many years, and has produced an extensive body of ritual text and liturgy, an example of which you will find in Chapter 11. All of this material (there is a lot of it, and it's all good) is available on the ADF website, https://www.ADF.org. ADF give detailed guidance on ritual and liturgy, including this simple explanation of why we get involved in rituals at all:

> The most consistent and personal result of sincere participation in ritual is the creation or strengthening of the patterns of our spiritual cosmos in the souls of individual worshippers. We need not enter into a discussion of whether this pattern exists innately in all people or whether we must create it there through our work. In either case the pattern will be strengthened and deepened by repeated meditation and ritual enactment.[9]

ADF (as it is very commonly known, since Ár nDraíocht Féin is something of a mouthful) is a very large organization, with many Groves (local congregations), Guilds (specific skill groups), Kins (groups with a particular cultural focus), SIGs (special interest groups) and SNGs (social networking groups). At the time of writing there are 73 ADF Groves, most in 43 states of the USA, with others in Britain, Germany, Brazil, Canada and Australia.

The Henge of Keltria

The Henge of Keltria, also a very large American organization, was founded in 1987 and works with both groups and individuals to provide information, networking and training. It has chartered groves in Atlanta, Georgia, and Syracuse, New York, and Keltrian Study Groups in Durango Colorado, Sanford, Florida, Columbia, Michigan, Santa Fe, New Mexico, Binghamton, New York, and Raleigh, North Carolina.

The organization's cofounders were Tony Taylor, his wife Sable, Ellen Evert Hopman and two others. Tony Taylor explains how the new group came into being:

> At the Pagan Spirit Gathering in 1986, four or five of us, after careful consideration created a list of concerns regarding Ár nDraíocht Féin. That list was taped on Isaac Bonewits' van door. It was meant to be humorous in a way, mimicking Martin Luther and the Ninety-Five Theses that he nailed to the Wittenberg church door. At the same time there was a serious side. It outlined thirteen concerns numbered 1–12… 95, which we felt were important enough to be addressed by Isaac and the ADF leadership. In our estimation a number of these issues warranted immediate attention. During the course of the following year, none of the identified concerns were adequately addressed, so Pat [or Sable, Tony's wife] and I decided to leave ADF and found our own organization. Our studies had convinced us that Druidism was a Celtic phenomenon while ADF embraced Druidism encompassing the entire Indo-European world. Though other Indo-Europeans performed similar practices, they didn't have an organized priest class referred to as Druids, therefore, Keltria would be specifically Celtic in its focus.[10]

The Henge of Keltria is structured around what it calls nine "hallmarks" or indicators of its priorities:

1. We celebrate the Gods and Goddesses of ancient Ireland. This is accomplished through our rituals and sensing their inspiration in our lives.
2. We revere the Spirits of Nature. This is also achieved through ritual and awareness of their messages received as we move through our daily routines.
3. We honor our Ancestors. As with our Gods, Goddesses and Nature Spirits, our Ancestors provide us with guidance and encouragement. *You do not have to be of any specific ancestry or heritage to practice Keltrian Druidry. We welcome people of all backgrounds.*
4. We respect all life and do no harm without deliberation or regard. It is wrong to kill or maim without reason, regard and necessity. We place the responsibility of choice firmly in the hands of the individual.
5. The virtue of an action is judged by the action itself, the intention behind the

action and its outcome. An individual determines their own ethics based on self-respect and consideration of others.

6. Justice is sought through restorative measures. Justice is best served not by reward or punishment, freedom or confinement, but in the efforts toward restoring the health of broken relationships.

7. We gain knowledge and develop wisdom by learning what we can and teaching what we are able. Our purpose in life is to grow and evolve in wisdom.

8. We encourage people to follow their own paths. We do not have the one, right, only true way. The Henge of Keltria provides a framework for self-exploration and choice.

9. We endorse the growth and evolution of the Henge of Keltria and the membership. The Henge of Keltria is prepared to accept new, proven scholarship even if it alters core practices. We recognize the importance of an individual's evolution and provide guidance when requested.[11]

Keltria encourages individuals to explore by themselves, but requires the novice to attach themselves to a mentor after the initial six-month to twelve-month period. They use Twitter, Facebook, Skype and all the other apparatus of modern communication to facilitate these interactions, as well encouraging beginners to find face-to-face groups in their vicinity if they can.

The Order of WhiteOak

The Order of WhiteOak (written White Oak, WhiteOak or Whiteoak) is an American Celtic Reconstructionist order, which, as the name suggests, looks back to the Celtic historical past for its substance and identity. Ellen Evert Hopman explains how and why the group began:

I founded the original White Oak on-line mailing list in 1996 at a time when pedophile scandals and other unfortunate behaviors were rocking the Druid community, because I was upset that the perpetrators were still calling themselves "Druids," an ancient title of respect and scholarship which I did not feel they were entitled to. After a full year of discussing "What a Druid is and is not," about fifty experienced Druids created the study program and list of basic Druid books and beliefs. Our focus was on the oldest manuscripts and Celtic texts we could get our hands on because we felt that these 7th-century documents, written down by Christian monks but from the far older Pagan oral tradition, were the closest thing to actual Druid teachings we still had. We studied the *Audacht Morainn*, the *Brehon Laws*, the *Uraicecht na Riar* and other such texts for their ethical teachings. We also mined the *Rig Veda*, the *Upanishads* and other Vedic writings because we understood that Hinduism was the eastern end and the Celtic religion the western end of a vast Indo-European continuum of ideas and ritual practices. But the major focus was and still is ancient Celtic tradition, history and culture. We eventually morphed into The Order of White Oak at Winter Solstice of 1997 when twelve of us underwent our self-initiations. Some of the original twelve went on to teach Druidism and to serve as officers within the Order. I was Co-Chief of White Oak for five years, along with English Druid Craig Melia. I am now Archdruid of Tribe of the Oak (www.tribeoftheoak.com), an international teaching Grove for those desiring deeper study and initiation into White Oak Druidism, with a particular focus on 7th-century Irish wisdom texts.[12]

In description of the White Oak Order, I give below its full Statement of Belief, taken from the website www.whiteoakdruids.org, which I think is a good example of how different Druidic groups and organizations establish their own identities and priorities, while remaining open to dialog with all other groups and traditions:

> The Order of WhiteOak is a modern Druidic order which bases its beliefs and practices on what we know of the original faith and practices of the Pagan Celts. We use historical research and poetic inspiration to build a viable tradition. Our source material for this research includes such names as Miranda Green, Alwyn and Brinley Rees, and Barry Cunliffe.
>
> Based on our studies of works by those and other authors, we believe that the ancient Druids were philosophers, lawyers, healers, judges, lorekeepers, and poets as well as ritual leaders and teachers. Thus, we strive to achieve similar skills in these modern times.
>
> We also draw upon the writings of the Celts, such as the *Audacht Morainn* and the Brehon Laws. From those, we learn that the Celts respected the virtues of justice, impartiality, conscientiousness, firmness, generosity, hospitality, honor, stability, beneficence, capability, honesty, eloquence, steadiness, truth in judgment, and mercy.
>
> We seek to uphold these virtues in our daily lives. Some of us have found value in studying other Indo-European traditions in the search for understanding, such as the Vedic texts of the Hindus, while others turn more inward in the quest to fill the gaps in the records.
>
> We do not believe we are inheritors of the priesthood of Atlantis. We do not believe that Druidry was the sole province of men, as our studies have shown us that women were Druids both in the insular areas as well as on the continent. We do not derive our traditions from medieval romances about Arthur and Merlin. We are not Wiccans or Witches of any sort, as witchcraft and Druidry have been separate though coexistent paths throughout their mutual histories. We do not believe we are the only true Druids.
>
> We do not seek to control all Celtic Pagans as a dogmatic priesthood. We do not even hold all of our members to one interpretation of the ways of the Celts, as not even they worshiped identically to each other across the multitude of tribes and centuries.[13]

Order of Bards, Ovates and Druids (OBOD)

The Order of Bards, Ovates and Druids, commonly called OBOD because it's shorter and easier, began life in Britain but now has a world-wide membership and sphere of influence. It describes its purpose very simply:

> The Order of Bards, Ovates & Druids works with Druidry as a spiritual way and practice that speaks to three of our greatest yearnings: to be fully creative in our lives, to commune deeply with the world of Nature, and to gain access to a source of profound wisdom.[14]

OBOD has a complex and sophisticated structural organization which also somehow manages to keep relationships on a straightforward, friendly and very accessible level. Most of the OBOD members I have met speak very enthusiastically about their membership and the broadening of their social interactions as well as their spiritual experiences and horizons. OBOD also has a very extensive library of well-written and well-researched Druidic lore, tradition and history. This is partly because Philip Carr-Gomm, the current Chief Druid of OBOD (see Chapter 8) is a published author who has written extensively about Druidism (he calls it Druidry), and he has brought a lot of his own research and of other knowledgeable writers into the OBOD domain.

Through the Oak Tree Press, OBOD publishes a graded course in Druidry, which can be taken either as an individual or in a group. I said very early in this book that most modern Druids are free-thinking, free-wheeling, independent-minded types who don't like rules and rigid structure, and while I may or may not be entirely right about that, I also have to acknowledge that one of the things OBOD members have told me is that they like the very supportive structure of the OBOD course; they find it practical, experience-based and straightforward to follow. It progresses in three grades: Bard, Ovate and Druid, each with its own initiation. Here is OBOD's description of the first grade, the Bardic course:

> The aim of the Bardic course is to help your life flourish and blossom—to help your Soul express itself fully in the world. It does this by helping you discover the sources of your creative power, so that their gifts can flow fully in your life. In addition, it teaches the fundamental skills and techniques of Druid spirituality: the use of ritual, of sacred space, of the circle, the directions and elements. During the first year you are taught thirteen rituals in addition to the eight Druid seasonal ceremonies. These rituals help to attune you to the natural world, to the rhythms of the earth and moon, the sun and stars. And as they do this, they help you to access your Deep Self, your Soul—that part of you which feels at one with all life.[15]

Council of British Druid Orders (COBDO)

The Council of British Druid Orders was formed in 1989, with founding member Rollo Maughfling (a fellow Cornishman) still playing an active role in its leadership to this day. The Council represents a number of Druid groups collectively: the Glastonbury Order of Druids (GOD); Druids of the New Aeon; the Order of Wandering Peace Poets; the Dolmen Grove; the Iolo Morganwg Fellowship (IMF); the Cumbria Druid Order; the Insular Order of Druids; the Universal Order of Druids; the Bardic Order Group; the Druidic Order of Tamaris; the Phoenix Order of Druids; and the Avebury Group. At any given time, the number of groups may change. It also maintains contact with individual Associates, academics, and representatives of other Pagan groups. The Council was formed after confrontations with English Heritage at the site of Stonehenge in 1988, when a four-mile exclusion zone was established to keep Druids and others out of a site which, by any standards, is the most obvious place for Druid congregation, celebration and prayer in the whole of Britain, if not the world. Discussions, sometimes heated, took place between COBDO and English Heritage from 1995 onwards and finally, in 2000, permission was granted for free and open access to the stones for the Midsummer dawn ceremony. Access has been maintained annually since then. The Council functions "to bring heads and representatives of Druid groups and Orders together."

Rollo Maughfling, Archdruid of the Glastonbury Order of Druids, identifies potential divisions between different kinds of Druid that reappear with some frequency, and are still not resolved: they have been there since the Romantic Revival. On one hand are Druids who believe firmly in knowledge obtained through diligent research, and on the other are Druids who trust their intuition and inspiration first and foremost. In certain contexts, this can become almost a class conflict. Maughfling, who has been intensively involved in the never-ending troubles surrounding access to Stonehenge, describes how these differences presented themselves for him some years ago:

> On Summer Solstice 1988 we went to Stonehenge because we felt very strongly that the spirit was at Stonehenge. There was a somewhat old fashioned Druid Order that used to work there. Because of the Stonehenge festival and various things that had been going on, unfortunately, this great divide came between us and an old fashioned Druid Order which was only answerable to itself and did not want to discuss any of its business, least of all with people who looked like hippies and travelers, scruffy looking but not necessarily unintelligent at all.... In fact this was the trouble. They couldn't quite understand it. The whole traveler thing that happened in this country was that suddenly a whole lot of people were thrown headlong into the intuitive side of Druidry and Wicca. What you learn when you actually live in the hedgerows, in nature, all day long and all night long under the stars, with the birds and the animals and the rest of it.... So these people were slowly becoming instinctively and intuitively very knowledgeable. And these Druids would talk to them and treat them as if they were nobody because they hadn't read so and so's book or something.[16]

The Druid Network

A significant recent milestone in the evolution of modern Druid organizations was the achievement by The Druid Network (TDN) of official charitable status in Britain in 2010. After a four-year fight, TDN was the first Druid group in Britain ever to be accepted by the Charity Commissioners and entered onto the Register of Charities, a move which, in TDN's words, "establishes Druidry as a bone fide religion under English Charity Law, and gives

Druidry equal status with other qualifying religions." Phil Ryder, Chair of Trustees for The Druid Network, had overall responsibility for making the application. He said: "It was a long and at times frustrating process, exacerbated by the fact that the Charity Commissioners had no understanding of our beliefs and practices, and examined us on every aspect of them. Their final decision document runs to 21 pages, showing the extent to which we were questioned in order to finally get the recognition we have long argued for." Emma Restall Orr, who founded The Druid Network in February of 2003, commented: "The Charity Commission now has a much greater understanding of Pagan, animist, and polytheist religions, so other groups from these minority religions—provided they meet the financial and public benefit criteria for registration as charities—should find registering a much shorter process than the pioneering one we have been through."[17]

8. Some Modern Druids

It would be impossible to describe in full the individuals and personal interactions which collectively produced the modern Druidic revival, but certain key players made contributions that significantly influenced or changed the direction of the movement. There has never been an overarching or even dominant organization for modern Druidism, and it seems unlikely that there ever will be, since its strength (and, some would argue, its weakness) is its diverse, eclectic, and free-wheeling nature. Independent thinking and a general anti-authoritarian approach are now deeply embedded characteristics of modern Druidism, and unlikely to change. We now look briefly at some of the individuals who helped to create modern Druidism.

Gerald Massey (1828–1907)

Massey was first and foremost a poet, but his wide-ranging interest in philosophy and religion made him, for a short while at least, an influential figure in the early development of modern Druidism. He was born into a desperately poor family in Hertfordshire, England, and began hard physical labor while still a child. He was self-educated, and showed great self-determination and independence of thought from an early age. He was attracted to Christian socialism, and was strongly influenced by Charles Kingsley, whose novel *The Water Babies* (1863), about the privations and suffering of a child chimney-sweep, is still one of the most powerful and memorable calls for social reform. Kingsley in turn was friendly with Charles Darwin and other luminaries of the new science, so Massey progressed at a great pace from his very humble beginnings into a powerful and influential intellectual circle of friends. He became fascinated by Egypt. Dr. Birch, the Curator of the British Museum, befriended Massey and encouraged him to explore the museum's huge treasury of Egyptian and Assyrian artifacts. Massey taught himself how to read hieroglyphics. He published his first volume of poems in 1850, still aged only twenty-two, and they were sufficiently well received to attract the interest and approval of Lord Tennyson, the Poet Laureate.

Like Godfrey Higgins (see Chapter 6), Massey believed that Christianity had its origins in the East. While Higgins had also (at different times) suggested India or Atlantis, both men saw connections with Egypt. Massey specifically identified Jesus with the Egyptian god Horus in his book *The Natural Genesis* (1883). Among other things, he noted that Horus had been born of a virgin on the 25th of December, had raised the dead back to life, was crucified, and was resurrected three days later:

> Christian ignorance notwithstanding, the Gnostic Jesus is the Egyptian Horus who was continued by the various sects of gnostics under both the names of Horus and of Jesus. In the gnostic iconography of the Roman Catacombs child–Horus reappears as the mummy-babe who wears the solar disc. The royal Horus is represented in the cloak of royalty, and the phallic emblem found there witnesses to Jesus being Horus of the resurrection.[1]

Not surprisingly, the Christian establishment was not very impressed by Massey's theories. Darwin and Kingsley had already become enemies of the Catholic Church, and Massey's name was simply added to the list. He was subjected to a series of attacks in print, and occasionally in sermons. Academic critics pointed out that December 25th as Christ's birth date does not appear anywhere in the New Testament (it was not actually proposed until the 3rd century CE), and therefore that Massey's knowledge of simple history and Christian holy writ was inadequate. They cited other egregious errors in basic historical accuracy. With his impoverished childhood background and self-education, it was an accusation that Massey could not easily shake off. Nevertheless, Massey had developed great strength of character from his privations, and made his friends well in adult life. He advocated Druidism from a similar standpoint to Stukeley, Higgins and others, trying to make a connection with Christianity (or a presumed pre–Christian monotheism), and still driven by the ideas of Christian socialism and general social reform which Kingsley and other friends also supported.

Jean le Fustec (1855–1910)

Le Fustec was born in Restrenen (spelled Restrenenn in Breton) in Brittany, which to this day is a center for the continuing support of the Breton language, largely because of the nationalist influence of Le Fustec and his close companion, Erwan Berthou (see below). Through the language support group *Ya d'ar brezhoneg*, a language plan was devised for Restrenen in 2004, and by 2008, 34.5 percent of its primary-school children were being educated bilingually in French and Breton, counter to the general trend of decline in

Breton speaking over the past several decades.[2] It was Le Fustec and Berthou who persuaded the Welsh Gorsedd to institute a Breton equivalent. Le Fustec was the first Archdruid of *Gorsez Vreizh*, from 1901 to 1903, after which he was succeeded by Berthou. Le Fustec's Bardic name was Yann ab Gwilherm (John son of William), and his Druidic name was Lemenik, which means "vital" or "filled with life."

Le Fustec and Berthou together published in 1906 a collection of mystic, Druidical poems called *Eur to gir of rear Varzed* or, in French, *Triades des druides de Bretagne* ("Triads of the Druids of Brittany"), a Breton translation of one of Iolo Morganwg's "discovered" manuscripts, but the poems were later identified as one of Morganwg's skillful forgeries.

Erwan Berthou (1861–1933)

Berthou, Le Fustec's friend and close collaborator, succeeded Le Fustec as Archdruid of the Breton *Gorsez* in 1903, and held that position until his death in 1933. He also was a poet and Bard, using the names Alc'Houeder Treger and Erwanig. His Druidic (or Archdruidic) name was Kaledvoulc'h, which is derived from the Welsh name Caledfwlch (pronounced approximately *ka-led-voolkh*, meaning "Hard Handle"—it is the original form of the name of King Arthur's sword, Excalibur). Berthou and Le Fustec worked together on the text and lit-urgy of the Breton *Gorsez*, but Berthou's influence was the greater because of the greater length of his service as the *Gorsez* grew and developed. Ber-thou had served in the French Navy, visiting China, Africa and the Caribbean, and he was a qualified and experienced engineer, so he brought a very diverse and eclectic experience to his role as champion of the Breton national cause, and he was very highly respected, in-ternationally as well as in Brit-tany. His Druidic thinking, which is mystical, poetic and very modern in many ways, was best expressed in *Sous le*

Erwan Berthou

chêne des druides ("Under the oak of the druids"), published in 1931, two years before his death. Where the poet Gerald Massey had begun his life in desperate poverty but dragged himself out of it, Erwan Berthou began life comfortably but found himself in desperate financial straits towards the end of his life. He had taken over his parents' farm in Pleubian in 1918, but (rather like Robert Burns in an earlier era) he was a poet, not a farmer, and he struggled. His wife suffered a mental breakdown because of the stress, and the Breton national movement collected funds to support Berthou during the last years of his life. He is still remembered with great respect and affection.

Paul Ladmirault (1877–1944)

Ladmirault was a Breton composer and Druid, inducted in 1908. His Druidic name was Oriav, which means "Gull." He was prolific and widely respected in the musical world. He was also obsessed by Celtic mythological themes, which provided the inspiration for almost everything he wrote. Like most composers, he also wrote some Christian religious music, notably a mass for voice, organ and orchestra called *Tantum Ergo*, but most of his work was inspired by Pagan legends and themes. Claude Debussy praised Ladmirault's "fine dreamy musicality," finding fault only in his diffidence and unwillingness to be bolder or more challenging. At the personal level, Ladmirault was quiet and self-effacing to a fault, although his nationalist political opinions were quite the opposite: he subscribed to the Breton fascist magazine *Breiz da Zont* ("Brittany of the Future"), which was openly anti–Semitic and in 1931 published an article supporting Hitler.

Ladmirault was a child prodigy. He composed a sonata for violin and piano at the age of eight. When he was fifteen, he wrote a three-act opera, *Gilles de Retz*. He studied at the Paris Conservatoire under Antoine Taudou, André Gedalge and Gabriel Fauré. From 1902 until 1921 he worked on an opera called *Myrdhin* (Merlin), which he finally completed, but which has never been performed. His ballet *La Prêtesse de Korydwenn* ("The Priestess of Ceridwenn") was first performed at the Paris Opéra on the 17th of December 1926. In 1928, he wrote an article for the Celticist magazine *Kornog*, in which he expounded a nationalist argument that Breton music should stick to its Breton roots rather than follow German, Italian and (especially) French influences, but in the same article he curiously deprecated Breton folk music, claiming that it was far inferior to the folk music of Scotland and Ireland. Agree or disagree with him, it was politically a very clumsy statement for a Breton Druid to make, and, whatever people may now think of his music and his creative genius, he is remembered mostly for his political naïveté and fascist sympathies.

François Taldir-Jaffrennou (1879–1956)

Taldir-Jaffrennou was also a significant and influential member of the Breton nationalist movement. Taldir, meaning "Hard Brow," was his Druidic name. Along with twenty-one other Bretons, he was received into the Welsh Gorsedd in 1899, taking the Bardic name Taldir ab Hernin ("son of Hernin," the name of a Breton saint). He later translated the Welsh national anthem *Hen Wlad Fy Nhadau* (literally "Old Land of My Fathers") into Breton. To this day, the Welsh, Cornish and Breton national anthems are all sung to the same tune, written in 1856 by James James of Pontypridd in Glamorgan. The Cornish title is *Bro Goth Agan Tasow* and Taldir-Jaffrennou's version is entitled *Bro Gozh Ma Zadoù*. The Welsh original and its literal English translation begin as follows:

> *Mae hen wlad fy nhadau yn annwyl i mi,*
> *Gwlad beirdd a chantorion, enwogion o fri;*
> *Ei gwrol ryfelwyr, gwladgarwyr tra mad,*
> *Dros ryddid collasant eu gwaed.*
>
> (Chorus) *Gwlad, gwlad, pleidiol wyf i'm gwlad.*
> *Tra môr yn fur i'r bur hoff bau,*
> *O bydded i'r hen iaith barhau.*

> The old land of my fathers is dear to me,
> Land of bards and singers, famous men of renown;
> Her brave warriors, very splendid patriots,
> For freedom shed their blood.
>
> (Chorus) Nation [or country], Nation, I am faithful to my Nation.
> While the sea [is] a wall to the pure, most loved land,
> O may the old language [i.e., Welsh] endure.

Taldir-Jaffrennou wrote for the Breton newspaper *La Resistance* in Morlaix from 1898 to 1899, then for *L'Ouest-Éclair* in Rennes. With Le Fustec and Berthou (see above), he created the *Gorsez Vreizh* in 1901. He subsequently created, published or wrote for a number of Breton nationalist publications, including *Ar Vro* ("The Nation"), *Ar Bobl* ("The People"), *La Bretagne Libertaire* ("Libertarian Brittany") and *An Oaled* ("The Foyer" or "The Atrium"). He succeeded Berthou and served a long term as Archdruid of the *Gorsez*, from 1933 to 1955, a year before his death in 1956.

Taldir-Jaffrennou perceived himself as a moderate, resisting what he saw as the more extremist views of some of his fellow Breton nationalists. His training as a lawyer had made him thoughtful and cautious in his political expression. He was pro–British and anti–German in the late 1930s before the outbreak of the Second World War, and was greatly concerned at what he saw as the dangerous intrusion of fascism into the Breton national movement. Nevertheless, in 1944, he was arrested by the French resistance on charges of collaboration with the Germans. He was acquitted, but then re-arrested. It was only after appeals to Charles de Gaulle and interventions by Britain and Israel that Taldir-Jaffrennou was finally pardoned. Not surprisingly, he was greatly embittered by these experiences. He is remembered as perhaps one of the clearest examples of cultural Druidism, where nationalist politics and linguistic and cultural identity are dominant elements.

Morvan Marchal (1900–1963)

Maurice Marchal, known as Morvan, was another Druid heavily involved in Breton nationalist politics. He studied architecture, but he was also a poet, painter and illustrator. In 1923 he designed the black-and-white flag which is still Brittany's national flag. (The Cornish and Breton flags are the only national flags in the world whose only colors are black and white.) Like Taldir-Jaffrennou, he was caught up in the great schism of the 1930s. When the fascist Breton National Party was set up in 1931, Marchal joined the Breton Federalist League in opposition to the fascists. They were opposed to many things: fascism; the Catholic Church; reactionary thinking; "puerile" anti–French bias; capitalism; and racism.

Marchal was swept up in the confused and confusing post-war recriminations which dogged Breton and French politics in the 1940s. Marchal left Brittany to live in Paris, where he died in poverty and obscurity in 1963. He is remembered for the Breton flag, but also as a founder member and first Archdruid of *Kredenn Geltiek Hollvedel* ("World Celtic Creed"), which, as we saw earlier, separated itself from the original *Gorsez Vreizh* in 1936 and has subsequently followed a much more explicitly Pagan Druidic path.

George Watson MacGregor-Reid (?–1964)

We saw in Chapter 7 that George Watson MacGregor-Reid was Archdruid of the Druid Order from 1946 until 1964. There are some other facts about his life that can be verified, but Reid was an extraordinary man in every way, who re-invented himself several times and openly mixed fiction with reality as he did so, making it difficult to keep fact and fiction separate. Dr. Adam Stout, whose excellent biographical portrait of Reid was the Fifth Mount Haemus Lecture for the Order of Bards, Ovates and Druids, described Reid as "eccentric, acerbic, always unique," … "bombastic and impatient, quarrelsome, wonderfully conceited" and "still one of the most inspirationally different characters I've ever come across."[3] It was Reid who, amongst other achievements, decisively put modern Druidism outside the Establishment (in Britain, at least), if not openly opposed to it, and more specifically fired the first salvos in the long battle for access to Stonehenge, which continues to this day.

Nobody knows where, or even in what year, Reid was born. He said himself that he was born George Watson Reid on February 22, 1850, at Dunvegan on the Isle of Skye. Registration of births did not begin in Scotland until 1855, so there is no official record. Reid later made several variations of his birth year, without convincing explanation. The Scottish registry recorded the birth of a George Watson Reid at Anderston in Lanarkshire in 1862, but nobody knows whether this was the child who eventually became the Archdruid. Reid's childhood was miserable, by all accounts, principally because his mother died while he was still very young. At the age of nine, he joined his uncle as a fisherman (fisherboy, we should say), and when the uncle died in 1874 George joined the Navy (aged either 12 or 24, depending which birth year you favor). He served for twelve years, and saw battle at sea in the Mediterranean. In 1886 he joined the Merchant Navy, and in 1887 joined the Coast Seamen's Union in San Francisco. By 1888 he was back in Scotland, working as a docker in Glasgow, and giving regular open-air, socialist lectures for the Social Democratic Federation. By all accounts, he was an impressive speaker, using his bulky physique, powerful voice and passionate style of rhetoric to great effect. He was commissioned as a delegate by the National Amalgamated Sailors' and Firemen's Union, but after some friction, including his being arrested and fined in 1889, he returned to America, where he worked as an organizer in the Atlantic ports on behalf of the NASFU.

Things went well to begin with. He persuaded a group of New York dockers to form the grandly titled International Brotherhood of Dockside Laborers, but they later accused him of stealing money from the Union's funds, and he found himself on the run again. He was expelled from the Union, but what happened next remains unclear. From references he made in later years, where he used the word "wounded" (the claim was literally of physical wounds, although his critics later interpreted the word to mean psychological distress), it's clear that this was a very difficult time for him. He later claimed that during the difficult early 1890s he had been a ship's doctor, had traveled to China and become a Buddhist, had "tramped as a beggar through Tibet," and had stood (in 1892) as a People's Party candidate in the election for the 10th Congressional District of New York (although the People's Party was not created until 1901). In 1893, a London company published Reid's pamphlet *The Natural Basis of Civilization*, which suggests that he may have been back in England by then. Between 1893 and 1906 he married and had a son, Robert, and began to acquire a reputation as a healer, or more precisely a practitioner of natural or homeopathic medicine. Orthodox doctors denigrated Reid and his methods, one of them calling him a "dangerous dreamer." At some point, he took upon himself the additional surname of MacGregor, becoming George Watson MacGregor-Reid. The name MacGregor had been proscribed after the failure of the 1745 Jacobite rebellion. MacGregors, no longer able to use that name, called themselves many other names, including Campbell (the clan enemy, deliberately encouraging confusion), Orr (from the—or of Gregor), and King, since the Gregor clan motto was "'S Rioghal mo Dhream" ("Royal is my Race"). The taking of the name by MacGregor-Reid, as he now was, simultaneously proclaimed his Scottishness, his tribal allegiance, and his defiance of the Establishment. The name was also assumed by some prominent members of the magical order the Golden Dawn, including the famous (or infamous) English occultist and ceremonial magician, Aleister Crowley. At the same time, MacGregor-Reid was exploring a wide range of esoteric and religious systems, including Buddhism, Bahà'i, the Golden Dawn, and others. He was, of course, not alone in looking to the East and to other cultures for inspiration.

But it was in Celtic Druidism that he found most clearly what he was looking for. It must have resonated with the MacGregor in him. He began making connections with other religions and cultures, which others continue to explore to this day. In 1912, MacGregor-Reid founded the Church of the Universal Bond, which promoted socialism, anti-imperialism, revolution, and sun worship. In addition to all his other esoteric research, he also initially flirted with Zoroastrianism, the ancient Iranian or Persian religion in which the prophet Zoroaster or Zarathustra proclaimed the coming victory of the "Wise Lord," Ahura Mazda. Zoroastrianism was a Messianic religion, with a vision of Heaven and Hell, and free will in humans, so it has some features in common with Christianity, although it entered recorded history about 500 BCE, and may possibly be as much as 2,000 years older than Christianity. But MacGregor-Reid began to perceive universality as more important than any single doctrine or religion, and he began to promote Druidism as the best way to move towards universality. This was an important development in the early history of modern Druidism, which remains to this day a very diverse and eclectic movement.

Beginning in 1912, Reid organized gatherings or *gorseddau* of the Church of the Universal Bond at Stonehenge, at which new Druidic rituals were introduced. On the 29th of June 1912 the local newspaper, the Salisbury Journal, carried the headline: "Sun-worship at Stonehenge."[4] The then-owner of the land on which Stonehenge stood, Sir Edmund Antrobus, was neither pleased nor impressed by the fledgling Druid assembly. Nor was he the only one. Archaeologists, who knew even in those days that Stonehenge and similar stone circles and alignments pre-date historical Celtic Druidism by thousands of years, were extremely concerned at this appropriation of the most important archaeological site in the whole of Britain, and were very concerned to protect it from people whom they considered to be well-meaning but mis-guided religious fanatics. In essence, that remains the same argument about Stonehenge as the one that persists to this day. The arguments began just before the Midsummer solstice of 1913, when Antrobus declared emphatically that he would allow "no political or religious meetings" on his land, effectively telling the tiny, newly-formed Druid group that they could not conduct a Midsummer ceremony at the stones, as they had done the year before. MacGregor-Reid, typically, ignored and defied Antrobus, conducting and leading a Druidic ritual in the heart of Stonehenge, and telling all authorities who tried to prevent him that he was acting "as the direct successor of the Chief Druids who have been."

At the 1914 solstice, MacGregor-Reid confused matters somewhat by conducting what was essentially a Zoroastrian, rather than Druidic, ceremony. It made no difference to Antrobus. He called the police in, and MacGregor-Reid and the handful of other celebrants present were forcibly removed from the Stonehenge site. Antrobus died in February of 1915, and there was no attempt at conducting any ceremony at the 1915 Midsummer solstice, although one of the Druidic followers was arrested for standing in a prohibited area. Public opinion began to mobilize against the Druids. They were called a "brawling party of cranks" and "suburban dervishes." Following Antrobus's death, the land was bought at auction by Cecil Chubb in October of 1915, and for the next three years, despite the public condemnation which they had attracted, Chubb allowed the Druids to conduct their Midsummer ritual in peace. In 1918, Chubb gave Stonehenge to the nation, a generous action which the Druids initially approved. But things went sour again very quickly. The original caretaker, with whom MacGregor-Reid had had vehement argu-ments, was retained, and the public admission charge was not only retained, but increased. For the modern Druids who have used and continue to use Stonehenge for ceremonial purposes, these and other restrictions on access have been nothing less than a violation of their human rights, in particular their right to worship freely. For non-believers, including some archaeolo-gists, there is no demonstrable connection between the site and modern Neo-Pagans or Druids; they should pay their entrance fees and stick to the foot-paths like everybody else. At the time of writing (2017), there is an active proposal to divert the main road which passes Stonehenge, the A303, into a tunnel passing *beneath* the monument. Hardly surprisingly, while planners have quietly approved this plan as a sensible solution to problems of access and traffic-flow, Druids, other Neo-Pagans and supporters have howled in indignation at the incalculable sacrilege and potential damage proposed to one of the most important religious sites in the entire world. It is an issue which is not likely to go away quickly.

In 1924, the Office of Works gave permission for MacGregor-Reid to scatter the ashes of cremated former members of the Church of the Universal Bond at Stonehenge. There were immediate protests from the Royal Archaeological Institute, the Wiltshire Archaeological Society, the Society of Antiquaries and others. Eventually, in 1932, the Church grew tired of the battles and moved its rituals from Stonehenge to a nearby site, Normanton Gorse, which would not attract the same levels of contention and controversy. (Druidic ceremonials did return to Stonehenge in the 1950s, to the continuing dismay of many archaeologists, but MacGregor-Reid had died in 1946, his precise age still a matter of dispute.)

Throughout the 1910s, 1920s, 1930s and the Second World War, MacGregor-Reid was a larger-than-life character, both in the advancement of Druidism and in local and national politics. Like Higgins before him (see Chapter 6), MacGregor saw social reorganization, politics and religious awareness as inseparably related and connected, and he launched into all of them with extraordinary vigor and conviction. As a socialist, he was intimately involved in the political processes that led to the foundation of the British Labour Party in 1918. As a social reformer, he was constantly arguing for better and fairer work and living conditions for ordinary people, and was a thorn in the side of the political Establishment. As a leader of the growing modern Druid movement, he experimented widely (some would say wildly), but always with a deep and growing conviction, and with such charisma and energy that he carried modern Druidism forward positively and significantly.

Gerald Gardner (1884–1964) and Ross Nichols (1902–1975)

I have put these two men together because, while Gardner is identified as the founding father of Wicca and Nichols as one of the founding fathers of modern Druidism, they were both initiated as Druids, they knew each other well, and they spent a great deal of time together in discussion, making it sometimes difficult to separate out which of them was primarily responsible for some of the important innovations which they introduced. It is interesting to note that originally they were also both ordained Christian ministers.

Philip Carr-Gomm, who was later one of Nichols's pupils, describes how Gardner and Nichols met, and what they felt they had in common:

Nichols, a teacher, was a vegetarian and pacifist, and was fascinated by the mythology of Britain. He loved the procession of the seasons through the year, and had published poetry before the war filled with seasonal imagery. Gardner, a retired civil servant, had spent most of his life abroad in Malaya. He was also intrigued by mythology—he was a member of the Folklore Society and had studied indigenous spiritualities in Malaya— and he was a member of the Ancient Order of Druids.... When Nichols and Gardner met at the Naturist resort of Spielplatz in the 1930s they were already convinced of the dangers of sexual repression. Nichols wrote that Christianity's attitude towards sexuality effectively made it evil, thereby stunting human development. He studied the work of Freud who pioneered an understanding of the importance of sexuality and of the dangers of its repression, and he also read the works of Jung, who was fascinated by alchemy and its understanding of the deeper, sacred nature of sexuality as a vehicle for human spiritual growth and creativity.[5]

The two men later took slightly different stances on how this shared respect for unrepressed sexuality should be reflected in ceremonies and rituals. Nichols had read a great deal about Jainism, a pacifist, non-violent and vegetarian religion from India, which used the term *Digambara*, meaning "clothed in the quarters of the sky" or "sky-clad" (or naked) and the term *Shvetambara*, which means "white-clothed" or "white-robed." Carr-Gomm explains how Nichols and Gardner used these concepts:

> Both Nichols and Gardner were convinced of the benefits of Naturism, and had found that freeing oneself of clothes in a natural setting also frees one's mind and spirit. While Gardner took the bold step of introducing a spirituality which took this sense of freedom into its acts of worship, decreeing that Wicca should be practised "skyclad," Nichols confined his Naturism to his own personal life and when meeting with Druid friends at his private woodland retreat. In his public Druidry he was "white-robed."[6]

Gardner's background was British upper-middle-class, which meant in practice that his critics (and there were many) often described him as "suburban" or "privileged," particularly when they were trying to ridicule his Naturism or more generally his promotion of a simple and natural lifestyle. After retiring from the civil service and a brief spell in Cyprus, he returned to live in England near the New Forest. He joined the Rosicrucian Order Crotona Fellowship, through whom he discovered the New Forest witch coven, into which he was initiated in 1939. He moved to London at the end of the Second World War. The Witchcraft Act of 1735, which had made it a crime to claim magical powers or to practice witchcraft, was repealed in 1945, and Gardner took advantage of the new dispensation to write extensively about witchcraft during the 1940s and 1950s. As noted earlier, he increasingly used the simpler term "craft" rather than "witchcraft," and finally introduced the name Wicca, which has now gained very wide acceptance. He founded the Bricket Wood coven in Hertfordshire, which is still active to this day, initiated several followers in the 1950s and 1960s who went on to be writers and activists in their own right, and through his writings attracted followers in the USA, Australia and elsewhere, to the extent that his particular style and type of Wicca acquired an adjective, Gardnerian, all of its own, which is still used today.

Britain is (in world terms) a fairly small place, with a climate which tends to be fairly cool and damp even in high summer, and a collective psyche which is similarly temperate: it is no longer as prudish as it was in Victorian times, but it remains generally conservative, especially about nudity. Gardner's advocacy of "sky-clad" worship was widely loathed and ridiculed: he was often simply called a "dirty old man." Gardner was married, but his wife, Donna, was not interested in witchcraft and did not take part in any rituals. Most controversial was the Great Rite, in which the spirit or manifestation of the Goddess is invoked or "drawn down" into a female priestess or witch, usually the High Priestess, with whom the male High Priest then has sexual intercourse as the temporary incarnation of the God. In many covens, this explicitly sexual rite has been replaced by a symbolic act of union, in which the High Priestess brings the athamé or ritual blade into a cup or chalice of wine held by the High Priest. In either actual or symbolic form, this ritual of high power is intended to invoke the tremendous spiritual energy of the explicitly sexual union between the God and the Goddess.

In a 1951 newspaper interview, Gardner casually claimed a doctorate in philosophy from Singapore and a doctorate in literature from Toulouse. One of his followers, Doreen Valiente, later discovered both claims to be false. She and some other Gardnerians eventually left the coven, concerned about many issues, including Gardner's blunt rejection and dismissal of tabloid criticisms, although many years after his death she still spoke of him with respect and affection, saying: "With all his faults (and who among us is faultless?), Gerald was a great person, and he did great work in bringing back the Old Religion to many people. I am glad to have known him."[7]

Ross Nichols was 18 years younger than Gardner. He was born in Norwich, England in 1902. As we have seen, they first met in the 1930s at the Naturist resort of Spielplatz ("Play Place"), which, despite the German name, was near St. Albans in Hertfordshire, England. Nichols read history at Cambridge University, and went into a mixed career of teaching, writing and social work. Like many a Druid before and since, he read widely in the works of Sigmund Freud, Carl Jung, Robert Graves and Jessie Weston, as well as diverse poets, ancient and modern. He became a dedicated socialist, pacifist, vegetarian and naturist. He had four books of his own poetry published between 1941 and 1947. In 1949, he became assistant editor of a short-lived magazine called The Occult Observer. Although his tenure was brief, two significant events arose from that post. First, a contributor, Mir Bashir, wrote an article for the magazine called *The Book of Shadows*, which Gardner later used (or stole) as the title of his compendium of traditions, core rituals, spells and Wiccan philosophy. Second, Nichols wrote his first article about Druidism for that periodical and thus began his own long and fruitful journey of exploration and exposition in what he called Druidry. Although he was building on a foundation of long standing, as we have already seen in some detail, Nichols introduced or significantly developed three important elements of

modern Druidism: a return to serious and scholarly examination of the original ancient Celtic traditions, including the Bardic craft, which finds its fullest
expression perhaps in modern Celtic Reconstructionist orders like the Order
of WhiteOak; celebration of the eight (originally four) traditional annual
Celtic festivals, with fuller understanding of their meaning and significance;
and a graded program of induction and training into Druidism, which
became in practice the main platform of the Order of Bards, Ovates and Druids, or OBOD.

Nichols wrote prolifically, but his best-known book, *The Book of Druidry*,
was not published until 1990, several years after his death in 1975. Philip
Carr-Gomm, who took over as Chief Druid of OBOD in 1988, played a major
role in gathering the original materials of Nichols's book. In the Foreword,
Carr-Gomm describes how his relationship with Nichols began:

I first met the Chief of the Order of Bards, Ovates & Druids when I was eleven or
twelve. I interviewed him for a magazine I had started. I can remember very little of
our meeting except vague images of a figure who was both warm and authoritative.
Three years later, when I had my own darkroom, my father introduced me to him again.
He invited me to photograph the ceremonies. Over the next few months, as I pho-
tographed the elaborate public rituals on Parliament Hill, in which Druids welcomed
mayors and mayoresses, Buddhists, white witches or Morris dancers to their rites, I
became more and more intrigued by these strange events which often combined deeply
mystical moments of union with Nature with the absurd—as when stray dogs or children
would be drawn into the magic circle, or when sudden gusts of wind would sweep off
head-dresses, or downpours of rain would remove any semblance of reverence from
the proceedings.

I began to visit Ross once or twice a week after school—first of all to show him the
photos I had taken, but gradually beginning a relationship in which he became the
teacher and I the student of Druid lore. Some time later, I asked to be initiated, and on
May Day in 1969 I formally entered the Order on Glastonbury Tor. For the next six
years I visited my teacher frequently, and he taught me in an apparently haphazard way.
After making me a cup of tea, or a meal, he would talk about one or other aspect of
the Order's teaching. He would draw diagrams of Stonehenge on sheets of paper that
I have kept to this day, write notes to clarify points, and hand me typed or duplicated
sheets with written expositions and discourses. It was only years later that I found all
these teachings, so apparently disparate as they had seemed at the time, formed a coherent and practical whole which spoke of an ancient heritage that had become fragmented
and lost over the last two millennia.[8]

The Book of Druidry covers a lot of ground in intense detail, and requires
slow and careful reading. It establishes the historical context of Druidism
and gives very full descriptions of ancient Druidic concepts and wisdom, but
it is unusual in also devoting a large central section to the geography of British and Irish Druidic history, which Nichols simply entitles Greater Sites of
the Britannic Islands. This extensive section covers: Avebury; Stonehenge;

Parliament Hill in London; Glastonbury; the Penmaenmawr Circles in Wales; Callanish on Lewis in the Hebrides; Iona, also in the Hebrides; the Irish centers, including Cashel, Teltown and Tara; and the Merry Maidens stone circle in Cornwall, which Nichols spells Dawns Myin but which in modern Cornish spelling is *Dons Men*, or "Dance of Stones."

The book is perhaps rather like the man, as others have described him: eclectic, somewhat rambling sometimes, but utterly sincere and filled with both knowledge and wisdom. Nichols achieved many things in the promotion of modern Druidism, but perhaps the most significant is his creation (some would say restoration) of the eight sacred festivals, which, even if only incidentally, are a perpetual annual reminder of his achievement.

Gwilherm Berthou (1908–1951)

Gwilherm Berthou (who, to the best of my knowledge, was not directly related to Erwan Berthou, who was discussed earlier) was a Breton Druid and Celtic activist, and a member of the political-cultural group *Unvaniezh Seiz Breur* ("Union of the Seven Brothers"). In the political turmoil of the 1930s in Brittany, Gwilherm Berthou was on the fascist side, in opposition to Morvan Marchal and others. He was trained as a chemical engineer, but subsequently became a pharmacist. In 1929 he formed an activist (many would say "terrorist") group to take direct action against what they perceived to be oppressive French national authority. Somewhat dramatically, he proposed the group name *Kentoc'h Mervel* ("Rather Death," i.e., better to die than submit), but this group fizzled out when Berthou's former collaborator, Célestin Lainé, formed an even more radical terrorist group, *Gwenn ha Du* ("White and Black"). Despite the apparent rift between the two groups, informants later told the authorities that Berthou, as a trained chemical engineer, had supplied the nitroglycerin for *Gwenn ha Du*'s destruction of a public statue in 1932. Berthou had worked with Morvan Marchal and other, more moderate nationalists in various previous projects, participating in the *Kredenn Geltiek* ("Celtic Creed") group, and contributing poetry and political and historical articles. He researched ancient Celtic culture (as did most others), but he also developed an interest first in Hinduism, then in Aryanism. The term Aryan, which originally was a politically neutral word describing an ethnic group in ancient Persia (modern Iran), had expanded to include practically all Indo-European cultures, but was then increasingly appropriated by fascists to mean white people from Nordic regions. Before long, under Nazi misappropriation, "Aryan" came to mean, in fascist ideology at least, "belonging to the master race." Berthou became attracted not only to Aryan mythology and culture, but also to fascist ideology, leading Marchal to disavow him and discontinue his friendship with him. Berthou's political Druidism became more extreme and idiosyncratic. He founded the periodical Ogam and was elected President of *Les Amis de la Tradition Celtique* ("Friends of the Celtic Tradition"). He predicted that the "white race" would be destroyed by the year 2018, which he called 3888, since he calculated his own personal calendar from the date of the legendary Irish Battle of Mag Tuired or *Cath Maighe Tuireadh* ("Battle of the Plain of Towers"), when the Tuatha Dé Danann took possession of Ireland from the Fir Bolg. He lived until 1951, but in post-war Brittany, former Nazi sympathizers and collaborators were given very little credence or attention.

Gwenc'hlan le Scouëzec (1929–2008)

Gwenc'hlan le Scouëzec (pronounced approximately *gwen-thlan-luh-skoo-eh-zek*), whom I met personally on four or five occasions when he attended the Cornish Gorsedh as the visiting Grand Druid of *Gorsez Breizh*, was a man of great charm and character, whose sometimes serious or even dour expression belied a very quick wit and dry sense of humor. He was born at Plouescat in Finistère, a romantically wild part of Brittany (the name literally means "end of the Earth"). His father, Maurice le Scouëzec, was a painter of some renown. Gwenc'hlan le Scouëzec studied history at the Sorbonne in Paris before doing his national military service in the French Foreign Legion in Algeria from 1951 to 1953. Between 1953 and 1957 he taught French in Crete and Athens, taking advantage of his situation to travel widely in Europe as occasion allowed, and exploring in particular ancient historical sites, especially in Greece, which fascinated him. From 1957 to 1958 he served again with the Foreign Legion, then in 1960 he switched track dramatically and began training as a doctor at the Faculty of Medicine in Paris, finally qualifying at Quimper in 1969. One of his very important "secular" achievements was the establishment of the *Skoazell Vreizh* in the 1970s, the Breton combined emergency services which still provide medical and other emergency support to the people of Brittany. (It is worth noting in passing that many Druids have made significant contributions to social reform, social care and public service, and that such service is very much a continuing part of modern Druidism.) In 1973, he participated in the "*colloque Bretagne*," the national discussion about the possibility of Breton self-government, either through devolution or complete political independence. For decades, one of the most bitter topics in Brittany was compulsory national military service. Bretons resented having their young men forcibly drafted into the French army, which they saw as an alien, occupying force. Several families refused to obey the conscription, and, as a result, their children were imprisoned. Le Scouëzec, who of course had done national service himself, as well as voluntarily taking a second stint with the Foreign Legion (which he loved), was a cool head and a calming voice in debates which often became very heated. He was elected Deputy Grand Druid of the *Gorsez* in 1979, then succeeded Per Loisel as Grand Druid in 1980. He promoted his father's art, and contributed to a variety of discussions about Druidism in general and Brittany in particular. I visited Brittany several times myself, and knew some towns and villages quite well, and, fortunately, my French was good enough to allow for some reasonable conversations at the pastry-and-saffron-cake teas

**Gwenc'hlan le Scouëzec
(raphodon | Flickr).**

which invariably followed our Gorsedh ceremonies. What I remember from my conversations with Le Scouëzec is his passionate love for his homeland, which was visceral in its strength. His religion and his region, his *anam* and his *tuath*, his soul and his land, were one and the same. His own passionate nationalism allowed him to understand and value everyone else's sense of the sacred and the numinous in their own sacred places. He loved all the Celtic nations, and was the essence of diplomacy when discussing them, but he said enough for me to know that, next to his beloved Brittany, he had a special place in his heart for Kernow (Cornwall). Or perhaps that was just subtle flattery. He was a very charming and convincing man.

Robert Lee "Skip" Ellison (1948–)

The Rev. Robert Lee Ellison, invariably known as "Skip", is a long-serving member of Ár nDraíocht Féin, who, through writing and teaching, as well as his huge volume of work for ADF, has made a significant contribution to the advancement of modern Druidism, in America and worldwide. In particular, he has done a great deal of work on developing a modern liturgy. ADF takes all of Indo-European culture as its area of provenance, so the ADF rituals include not only Celtic material, but also rites from the Norse, Hellenic, Roman, and Vedic traditions, plus some proto-Indo-European rituals, in an attempt to connect with the most ancient practices. Ellison was initiated into a Celtic Traditional Wiccan coven in 1982. He joined ADF in 1990, serving on the Mother Grove from 1992 until 2010. He was elected to the position of Archdruid in May of 2001, and served until May of 2010, completing his nine years of service in that post. Based in Syracuse, New York, he was the Organizer for Muin Mound Grove, ADF, where ADF maintains a ritual site facility.

Robert Lee "Skip" Ellison

He has been a frequent speaker at Neo-Pagan events, including the Starwood Festival, Sirius Rising, and the Wellspring Gathering. Ellison has been associated with the Grey School of Wizardry (www.greyschool.com) since its inception, and is currently the Provost of Colleges, Bursar, and Dean of Divination, as well as an instructor of Magical Practice, Divination, Performance Magick, Beast Mastery, and Lore. He has written six books, *The Wheel of the Year at Muin Mound Grove, ADF: A Cycle of Druid Rituals, The Solitary Druid, The Divine Liver: The Art and Science of Haruspicy, Ogham: The Secret Language of the Druids, The Fairy Races of the British Isles* and *The Songs of Isaac Bonewits*.

Isaac Bonewits (1949–2010)

Isaac Bonewits was a free-thinking pioneer, articulate, clever, witty, creative, dynamic and assertive, who seemed to attract praise and loathing in about equal measure during his life (not that he cared greatly), but nobody denies the impact his thinking and activism has had on the development of modern Druidism. He was pivotally involved in several early events and developments.

He made enemies among Wiccans very early. He denied that there had ever been an "Old Religion" in the romanticized sense (as he saw it) used by many Wiccans. He accepted that witchcraft had a long tradition, but was adamant that so-called appeals or returns to a European-wide, unified Pagan faith were wrong, both in fact and in principle. He was scathing about what he perceived as either deliberate hypocrisy or at best ignorant self-delusion. In 1971, he wrote:

Isaac Bonewits (Rob Vincent)

> Some of the witch groups claim to be Christian, and except for the fact that they often do their rites in the nude, you could find more Paganism and witchcraft at a Baptist prayer meeting. Other groups claim to be revivals or remnants of the nonexistent "Witch-Cult of Western Europe" (made so popular by author Margaret Murray). They get their "authority" from their Secret Beliefs Handed Down for Generations of Witches in My Family, etc. This sort of witchcraft tends to be a mish-mash of

half-forgotten superstition, Christian concepts, and Hindu beliefs. Thus, their "fertility rites" are done for "spiritual fertility" rather than physical fertility, though they like to hint that their ceremonies are really very exciting (they're not—they are hideously boring to anyone who's been to a good love-in).[9]

But Bonewits was equally scathing about traditional western religion. He considered monotheism, or more precisely the authoritarian monotheism of Christianity, Judaism and Islam, to be an aberration. He wrote that monotheism, "far from being the crown of human thought and religion as its supporters have claimed for several bloody millennia, is in fact a monstrous step backwards—a step that has been responsible for more human misery than any other idea in known history."[10]

Bonewits was born to Roman Catholic parents in Royal Oak, Michigan, in 1949, the fourth of five children. When he was 12, the family moved to San Clemente, California, where he briefly attended a Catholic secondary school before graduating a year early from the local state school. He enrolled in U.C. Berkeley in 1966, graduating in 1970 with a B.A. degree in Magic, the first and perhaps still the only person to graduate from an accredited university with a degree in that subject. While still an undergraduate, he joined the Reformed Druids of North America (see Chapter 7).

In 1966, Bonewits met Robert Larson, an ordained priest of the original Carleton Grove of the Reformed Druids of North America, and together they founded a small Druidic group with connections to various Wiccan covens, and groups which practiced ceremonial magic, which became known as the Berkeley Grove. Bonewits, who had a lively sense of humor but took Drudism very seriously, wanted the RDNA to cast off its student-joke ancestry and become a genuinely Neo-Pagan organization at a much higher level, in terms both of content and organization. The Carleton Grove, which had never truly identified itself as Neo-Pagan (because it wasn't, at least originally) didn't see the point, and friction rapidly escalated into argument and open animosity. Through the 1970s, a flurry of changes occurred, in an attempt to reconcile the arguments, but also—seen in retrospect—because Bonewits had correctly identified that modern Druidism needed to establish more clearly exactly what it was and represented. He welcomed diversity, and freedom of expression, but he was angered by sloppiness, indecision and what he often characterized as hypocrisy, and it was his nature to speak his mind openly and forcefully, which most Druids should approve in principle, even if they don't agree with the message—*y gwir yn erbyn ar byd,* "truth against the world." Several groves broke off from RDNA, calling themselves "Branches," a term which has now become general and no longer controversial. In 1976, a new order was formed, calling itself the New Reformed Druids of North America, or NRDNA, which formed a Council of Archdruids, intended as a forum to settle disputes. A further offshoot of NRDNA wanted to restrict membership to genuine Neo-Pagans and make changes to ritual and organization, and this group became the Schismatic Druids of North America, or SDNA. Subsequently, many members of the SDNA groves left in the 1980s to form Ár nDraíocht Féin (ADF), which I described briefly in the previous chapter.

Throughout all these changes and developments, Bonewits was a loud and vociferous presence. Often it was Neo-Paganism that he attacked—his "own side," so to speak—and he consistently castigated woolly thinking and airy romanticism in simple, blunt, straightforward terms:

> Most Neo-Pagans and Crafters have never done any serious thinking about the implications of their belief system. Most of them—like most Americans—are extremely shallow about religion. Take some of the basic issues that are tearing apart American Christianity—abortion, euthanasia, the morality of war—most Pagans have not thought through on a logical basis what their belief systems really mean in making practical decisions in day-to-day life.[11]

The accusation that most Americans are shallow about religion is a typical Bonewits generalization, and flies in the face of the fact that about 70 percent of Americans still attend church regularly, but flinging insults in all directions was his *modus operandi*. He also insulted Neo-Pagans for being "too loose and liberal." (He called some of them "fat" too, which is childish by anybody's standards.) In conversation with Margot Adler, when she asked Bonewits if there were certain issues on which Neo-Pagans and Crafters would eventually need to reach agreement, he replied, "Yes, I think one would wind up being very concerned about environmental and ecological matters. Most Neo-Pagans are too loose and liberal to be fanatic about *anything*, including their own survival."[12]

He attacked Robert Graves, the idol of many Neo-Pagans (although Graves himself had at best lukewarm feelings about them):

> Graves is a sloppy scholar. *The White Goddess* has caused more bad anthropology to occur among Wiccan groups than almost any other work. It's a lovely metaphor and myth and an inspirational source of religious ideas to people, but he claimed it was a work of scholarship and that people were to take what he said as true.[13]

Bonewits was sometimes a sitting target for attacks from the Establishment. He and several other occultists were filmed in what they thought was a sympathetic documentary. The film, called *The Occult: An Echo from Darkness*, made by Hal Lindsey, soon turned out to be a Christian fundamentalist attack on Paganism and the occult, as Bonewits describes:

> The film is a venomous, vituperative propaganda picture. Its sole purpose is to warp and confuse well-known data of world history and comparative religions, to convince ignorant viewers that all occultism, from newspaper horoscopes and tarot cards to Witch meetings and ritual magic, to ESP laboratories and mind training systems, is a unified Satanic plot to enslave the world and destroy Christianity. Every single person

in the film, except the preachers, is equated with a young girl who "confesses" that she helped burn a baby to death in a Satanic ritual.[14]

At the age of 18, Bonewits had briefly joined the Church of Satan, and allowed himself to be filmed in a 1970 documentary called *Satanis: The Devil's Mass*, so the high horse he rode about false depictions of Satanism was somewhat handicapped by his own activities. Later, in typical joking and cynical style, he explained his brief flirtation with Satanism:

> I had a lot of fun for several months, mostly because we got to dress up in costume and do ritual. I became one of the Satanic altar boys, assisting with the ritual, including occasionally faking some Enochian language to impress the rubes. Eventually I started noticing that everybody else in this organization was extremely right-wing and middle aged and not very well educated and I watched LaVey [Anton LaVey, founder of the Church of Satan] playing his crowd like a musician playing an instrument and I began asking awkward questions there.[15]

However, despite the arguments and controversies, and his readiness to call anyone who disagreed with him a "rube," Bonewits made many positive achievements. He did much to clarify thinking about magic. In his intelligent and highly readable book *Real Magic* (1971), and elsewhere, he comprehensively set out his view that magic does not come from an alien source, but is part of Nature, an art and science that "deals with a body of knowledge that, for one reason or another, has not yet been fully investigated or confirmed by the other arts and sciences." He gives an example:

> The physical Universe (assuming it's there) is a huge *Web* of interlocking energy, in which every atom and every energy wave is connected with every other one. The farthest star in the sky has *some* influence on us, even if only gravitational; the fact that this effect is too small to measure with present equipment is totally irrelevant.[16]

Decades earlier than most others, Bonewits was bold in his exploration of and thinking about magic and the occult in a world increasingly defined by the standards and parameters of modern science. He defended science and technology, but attacked what he called "scientolatry," or "scientism," the paradoxically irrational, closed-mind worship of scientific method:

> I'm a naturalist rather than a supernaturalist. I believe the gods have a mechanistic as well as a spiritual existence, that they follow certain laws and patterns of behavior. But reality is consensual. People define what reality is. In my personal definition of it, I include the fact that you can come up with a moderately logical explanation for everything that happens, provided that you are not hung up on using only Western logic.... Scientism is the worship of nineteenth-century science. It is also the unthinking acceptance of any statement made by any man wearing a white lab coat. That's scientism, and it's a very strong religion in America, mostly among mediocre scientists. You'll find very few topnotch ones who are scientistic in thinking. It's the second-level ones who are terrified of the occult.[17]

Many modern scientists would agree, even if only partially, with Bonewits's view, as stated. Modern science has moved forward. In America, the biggest clash between science and religion is Creationism, which was around in Bonewits's day too, but which has been debated much more vocally and publicly in more recent times. In the face of Christian denials of what to them is plain, hard, undeniable fact about the history and archaeology of the world, scientists have reaffirmed their support for the empirical approach: you observe, you hypothesize, you test, you measure, you describe, but most important of all, you allow and encourage others to re-test your results and review your data. But what might be seen as a strengthening rather than weakening of what Bonewits described as "scientism," modern science (especially, chemistry, physics and cosmology) has in fact opened vast new fields of speculation in which the very nature of matter and existence can no longer be adequately contained within traditional scientific parameters, and a new and far more flexible science has been forced to emerge.

Bonewits was one of the earliest and most outspoken feminists in modern Druidism. He suggested that having more women archaeologists, for example, would address an imbalance caused by androcentric attitudes in how we think about the ancient world, even though such modern "hard" sciences are supposed to be gender neutral. As editor of the magazine *Gnostica*, he adamantly refused any manuscripts that contained or even hinted at sexist or racist attitudes, and stood his ground if challenged. Decades before such gender-equality issues had begun to be accepted (and, of course, they still have a long way to go in terms of being accepted fully), Bonewits wrote powerfully and clearly about gender stereotyping:

> The priestess of Artemis, or Morragu, or Kali is not going to be a simpering idiot or a Kirche-Küche-Kinder sort of woman. She is more likely to be a strong, domineering, combative intellectual. If you find that frightening, go ahead, admit it. But don't accuse her of being "unfeminine" or of trying to castrate every man she meets.... Similarly, a priest of Apollo, or Oberon, or Balder is quite likely to be gentle, intuitive, receptive and very creative. This you may find frightening too. But again, it is more honest to admit your fear than to call him "unnatural," "a queer," "unmasculine," etc.[18]

Bonewits was married five times, the last marriage being a controversial Pagan handfasting to Phedra Heyman while he was still legally married to author Deborah Lipp. He advocated polyamory—relationships with multiple partners with the knowledge and consent of all involved—and attracted some criticism for his views, some of it from the expected conventional sources, but also some from other feminists, who saw polyamory as always favorable to men and potentially harmful to women.

He claimed to be apolitical (although he told Margot Adler that he thought of himself as a "Fabian socialist"), and argued that Druids and other Neo-Pagans should not get involved in politics at all, other than to protect religious tolerance and freedom. In view of the huge amount of effort he put into political work for the Aquarian Anti-Defamation League, that statement seems somewhat ironic, although Bonewits's defense would no doubt be that he was protecting religious freedom, so it didn't really count.

He wrote an organizational description (for the New Reformed Druids of North America) which—perhaps with some changes, depending on the group's particular preferences or priorities—could serve as a model description for any modern Druidic group or organization:

> [Our grove is] … an Eclectic Reconstructionist Neo-Pagan Priestcraft, based primarily upon Gaulish and Celtic sources, but open to ideas, deities and rituals from many other Neo-Pagan belief systems. We worship the Earth-Mother as the feminine personification of Manifestation, Be'al as the masculine personification of Essence, and numerous Gods and Goddesses as personifications of various aspects of our experience. We offer no dogma or final answers but only continual questions. Our goal is increased harmony within ourselves and all of Nature.[19]

He also expressed crystal-clear support for proper scholarship in modern Druidism. While many modern Druids, particularly those who don't know or don't care very much about the Celtic basis of Druidism, value intuition and revelation as highly as, if not more highly than, scholarly study, Bonewits defends scholarship vigorously:

> The emphasis on scholarship was also there because 99.9 per cent of what had been done in the world of Druid revivalism for the last three hundred years had been intensely romantic and fantasy-driven rather than scholarly. While I believe that vision and divine inspiration are absolutely crucial to the creation and perpetuation of modern-day Druidism, I also believe that we don't do the Gods and Goddesses any favors by telling lies about ourselves or about them. That we owe it out of respect, both to the ancient Druids and to the Deities, that we do the hard work to dig out what is actually known about them on the Earth-plane level of scholarship so that we find out what their proper names were, how they were pronounced, the sorts of things that are critical in ritual.[20]

Bonewits died of colon cancer in 2010. Ian Corrigan, a former ADF Archdruid and lifelong friend, praised the man he knew:

> I write today to celebrate the life and mourn the death of Isaac Bonewits, 20th century occultist of note, Pagan and environmental activist, author, bard, humorist and family man. Isaac has gone too young, but will be remembered fondly and with honor by more people than he, himself, could know…. As a chum, Isaac was clever, generous, a fine raconteur, a supporter of home-made music, and an open-hearted guy, interested in new people. He was flexible and adaptive with his ideas, and our many chats and debates about mythography and ritual, magical theory and Pagan culture, changed and shaped both of our ideas…. At heart Isaac was a Pagan—a lover of nature in all its forms, including human nature, he loved the Old Gods and the Old Ways. He was not only a freethinker and an experimental occultist, but was always concerned to bring back the worship of the Gods in modern times…. Isaac valued real scholarship and intellectual honesty. He helped build a Paganism that tries to keep track of what is really known

about the Old Ways, and adapts to new knowledge.... Isaac was always collegial and open-minded, valuing different viewpoints and interested in new inputs. Over the years he worked with many colleagues to refine and rework his outline based on experiment and result. Isaac never resorted to a fixed dogmatism, but remained interested in real effects in the real world.... Isaac's name and ideas will be remembered in ADF. We'll remember with affection his humor and wisdom, his compassion and his effort. We'll remember with honor his work to establish our ways, his strength in the face of criticism and the wisdom of his initial designs.[21]

Philip Carr-Gomm (1952–)

We met Philip Carr-Gomm as the boy pupil of Ross Nichols (above), and saw that he succeeded Nichols as Chief Druid of the Order of Bards, Ovates and Druids (OBOD). Carr-Gomm was born in London and educated at Westminster School. After Nichols died in 1975, Carr-Gomm followed a Bulgarian teacher, Omram Mikhael Aivanhov, for seven years. He travelled to Bulgaria every year for fourteen years, studying the work of Aivanhov's former teacher, Peter Deunov, a teacher and spiritual leader of great status and very wide-reaching training and experience, who is still a greatly revered figure in Bulgarian history. Carr-Gomm absorbed many of these teachings in religion, music, geometry, astrology, philosophy and esoteric science, and in particular Deunov's program of Paneurhythmy, a sequence of physical exercises performed to music, to achieve inner balance and harmonization, first devised in 1932. Carr-Gomm brought this learning back to Britain, teaching Paneurhythmy in England and at the Findhorn settlement in Scotland. In the 1980s, Carr-Gomm became interested in psychology and Jungian analysis, taking a B.Sc. degree at University College, London, with the intention of becoming a psychoanalyst. Instead, he trained subsequently at the Institute of Psychosynthesis and entered private practice.

In 1988, he was elected Chief Bard of OBOD, which position he still holds. His major initial achievement was to transform the Order's considerable academic library and resources into a major teaching program, which is now the largest in the world. In addition, along with his partner Stephanie, he has described the animal and plant lore of Druidry

Philip Carr-Gomm
(Vanessa Haines)

in the form of two books and oracles, *The Druid Animal Oracle* (1994) and the *Druid Plant Oracle* (2008), and a further six books on Druidism, including a biography of his predecessor Ross Nichols.

He has also used the term *Druidcraft* to celebrate what he sees as the mutually compatible elements of Druidism and Wicca, claiming that the differences between them didn't originate in some ancient Pagan past, but merely as a result of (historically) recent amicable, minor disagreements between Gerald Gardner and Ross Nichols (see above). Many modern Druids have a friendly respect for Wicca, but no more than that. Even if they accept the Wiccan emphasis on sexuality as valid, they do not necessarily give it the same value or importance. Carr-Gomm, however, sees the Druidcraft combination as a genuinely enriching synthesis, and has explored this synthesis in his books *The DruidCraft Tarot* (2004), and *DruidCraft: The Magic of Wicca & Druidry* (2002), in which he writes:

> At the heart of Wicca lies the theme of God and Goddess united as one. The introduction of this theme in modern times was inspired. It restored to indigenous, Pagan spirituality the fundamental understanding of the importance of the relationship between the two great manifestations of divinity, which we call Masculine and Feminine. This understanding has a noble lineage, reaching its greatest sophistication in the Taoist and Tantric philosophies of the East, and the Alchemical wisdom of the West. And this is where the two circles of Druidry and Wicca meet and merge—in the alchemical wedding of God and Goddess.... It is as if the two founding fathers of modern Wicca and Druidry, Gerald Gardner and Ross Nichols, caught different parts of the mystery as they dipped their hands into the well. Nichols caught the magic of the Bard, the magic of history and the written and spoken word, Gardner caught the magic of God and Goddess, the thrill of the spiral dance and the union of cup and wand.... Combined, their contributions to modern Paganism blossom, gaining authenticity and breadth, vitality and depth. Enriched with that sense of continuity and tradition that comes from the Bardic stories, Gardner's Wicca can draw upon myths and images from the land and culture in which it was born. Enriched with an awareness of the inherent sexuality of life within spirituality, Nichols' Druidry is refreshed at its roots.[22]

Ellen Evert Hopman (1952–)

Ellen Evert Hopman is a woman of many parts and talents, a writer, teacher and religious leader. In over thirty years of research, writing, teaching and organizational leadership in modern American Druidism, Hopman has developed a thoroughly researched, reconstructivist approach to the organization and development of modern Druidism. In the course of that work, she has also acquired a deep and extensive knowledge of Druidic history and lore, particularly in early Irish mythology and vernacular literature, and in traditional and modern herbalism.

She was born in Salzburg, Austria, and has traveled very widely, but now lives in Massachusetts. She graduated *Summa Cum Laude* with a B.Sc. in Art Education from Temple University in Philadelphia, followed by a Master's degree in Mental Health Counseling from The University of Massachusetts, Amherst, in 1990. She was trained in Herbalism by William LeSassier in New York and at the Findhorn settlement in Scotland, under the tutelage of Barbara D'Arcy Thompson. She also received professional training at the National Center for Homeopathy, and is a professional member of the American Herbalists Guild. She is a founding member and was for five years Co-Chief of the Order of the WhiteOak (*Ord na Darach Gile*), serves on the Grey Council of Mages and Sages, and was a professor of Wortcunning at the Grey School of Wizardry. She is a published novelist, herbalist, and certified teacher of writing with Amherst Writers and Artists.

Ellen Evert Hopman

Her book *A Legacy of Druids: Conversations with Druid Leaders of Britain, the USA and Canada, Past and Present* (2016) is a fascinating collection of interviews with Druids and other Pagans from a very wide variety of backgrounds and interests, which illustrates in a very personal and readable way just how diverse and eclectic modern Druidism is. Mael Brigde of Daughters of the Flame summarizes it as:

> A thoughtful, chatty book—reading it is like visiting, mead in hand and cross-legged on the forest floor, or sipping tea and nibbling dainties in an overstuffed chair, one fascinating person after another as they reflect, through their spiritual history, opinion and advice, an exciting time in the evolution of modern Druidry and Celtic Neo-Paganism. Far from giving a single self-praising paean, the subject is pondered with care, scepticism, and occasional grumpiness from a multitude of viewpoints.[23]

To give a flavor of this delightful and interesting book, here is a brief extract from the 1996 interview with Susan Henssler, the coordinator of the Bardic tutoring program for the Order of Bards, Ovates and Druids, which offers the added bonus of further insight into some of the differences between American Druidism and British Druidry. (I have added the names of the interlocutors for clarity.)

HOPMAN: One of the things that American Druids sometimes find hard to understand about OBOD is the way that one can be a Christian and be a Druid at the same time. Can you talk about that?

HENSSLER: Well, one of the things that some of us in OBOD have said is that OBOD Druidry is not so much a religion as a way of life. It is a spiritual path and a way of working with the world, its metaphysics and also a guide to action and right action and conduct in the world ...

...HOPMAN: There are some American Druid groups that put a great emphasis on scholarship. It seems that the OBOD course puts more emphasis on the inner life and on the intuition. Can you address that a little bit?

HENSSLER: That has to do with what one considers Druidry to be. If you look at it as a historical entity, as the scholars do, then you have to go on the documentation and you concern yourself with what people in the past believed.... For me and for us in OBOD, Druidry is a living thing. It is an essential part of the human spirit by whatever name. So what the ancient Celts happened to think or do is certainly of interest and is very valuable to uncover, but that's not what Druidry is now.... The connection with the earth that I've had through places like Iona where I go every year on retreat with the Order, Stonehenge, Glastonbury, and Avebury where I go half a dozen times a year, has become very significant for me. It's the first time that I have really felt the living energy of the planet ...

...HOPMAN: In the States I have been finding that by working with the Native Americans. They have been there for at least 40,000 years and they definitely have a sense of place. A lot of Druids in America find that extremely controversial for some reason. They have a very hard time with that.

HENSSLER: Here in England we look at the association of Druidry and the Native American tradition as a very natural and positive thing. We certainly applaud whatever route people take to find something that works for them, that is meaningful.[24]

Per Vari Kerloc'h (1952–)

Per Vari Kerloc'h is the current Grand Druid of *Gorsez Breizh*, the successor to Gwenc'hlan le Scouëzec (see above). (While Grand Bards serve a term of three years in the Cornish *Gorsedh*, Grand Druids of the Breton *Gorsez* are elected for life.) He was born in the fishing town of Douarnenez. Not only is he a native Breton speaker, he has also taken the trouble to learn Cornish, the first Breton Grand Druid to do so. He was a trade union representative with *La Poste*, the French postal service, and has experience in political negotiation as well as religious leadership. He has visited Wales and Cornwall frequently. While maintaining the balanced and even-handed leadership established so well by Le Scouëzec, Kerloc'h has also brought back to the *Gorsez* some of the fire in the belly which has always been a characteristic of Breton nationalism.

Arthur Uther Pendragon (1954–)

Another character of determination and self-actualization is Arthur Uther Pendragon. Born John Timothy Rothwell to a working-class family in Yorkshire, England, his origins suggest little or no connection with either Celticism or Druidism. However, after a spell in the British army, followed by a time as leader of a biker gang called the Gravediggers (subsequently the Saddletramps), this energetic and colorful character (nicknamed King John by his fellow bikers) discovered within himself a passion for Arthurian legend. He eventually came to believe that he is a reincarnation of King Arthur, and in 1986 he changed his name by deed poll to Arthur Uther Pendragon. In 1991, he was elected Pendragon and Swordbearer to the Glastonbury Order of Druids. At all Druidic events, he dresses in Druidic robes and carries a ceremonial sword representing Excalibur.

As Chosen Chief of the Loyal Arthurian Warband (LAW), he has subsequently been a main player in the never-ending conflict surrounding access to Stonehenge. He was one of the leaders of the campaigns throughout the 1990s to remove English Heritage's original four-mile ban on Druid access to the Stonehenge site. With help from Liberty and other supporters, Pendragon took the case all the way to the European Court of Human Rights in Strasbourg, which ruled in favor of the UK government. However, the British House of Lords later ruled that there is a right of way to the monument, which Druids may use, and an uneasy arrangement continues between

Arthur Uther Pendragon

English Heritage, as managers of the site, and the many Druids, other Pagans and individual worshippers who now insist on their right to worship before the stones, particularly for the sunrise ceremony on Midsummer Day. Pendragon established a protest camp at the site in June of 2008. In April 2009, he was ordered to leave by Salisbury County Court, who claimed he was endangering the free movement of traffic. He refused initially, but finally ended his protest in May 2009, after English Heritage announced plans to divert the main road, the A303, through a tunnel beneath the monument.

In 2011, Pendragon brought an appeal to the High Court on a different but related topic. He argued that the remains of more than 40 bodies, which had been excavated by archaeologists from Sheffield University in 2008, should be returned to Stonehenge for reburial. The High Court rejected his appeal. He further argued that, out of respect for the ancestors, skeletal remains in the English Heritage visitor center should be replaced by replicas, so that the original bones could be re-interred.

Pendragon has been arrested over 30 times for his protest activities, mostly for trespass. In prison, he has refused to wear prison dress, insisting on the right to wear his Druidic robes, and as a consequence has been put naked into solitary confinement, although there have been occasions when the administrators of Her Majesty's Prisons have subsequently allowed Druids to keep their robes in prison, following Pendragon's persistent challenges.

He describes his activism defiantly, challenging what he perceives as the ineffectual weakness of Druids who, to use the American expression, "talk the talk" but don't "walk the walk":

> Basically what I have done is I have gone out there and invented perhaps the first Druid conundrum for two thousand years. When I went to Newbury I was faced with a problem. Who was the real Druid? The protester in the tree risking his life or the guy on the ground in the white frock from another Druid Order? Well, the answer I came up with was the guy in the tree, in the white frock, wearing it, and that was me. And that's what I've done.[25]

The allusion to living in a tree is real, not metaphorical. Pendragon not only lived in a tree to protest a proposed new road, he fixed his personal mail box to the tree and received mail:

> In the case of the proposed Newbury bypass I spent a month living up a tree, basically saying you will not chop this tree down while I am in it. And subsequently I have done five court appearances because of it.[26]

John Michael Greer (1962–)

John Michael Greer is an American author and religious leader who has established a reputation among academics, scholars and politicians, as well as among Druids and other Pagans, for his authoritative knowledge of and opinions about the environment. He was Grand Archdruid of the Ancient Order of Druids in America from 2003 to 2015. He has subsequently devoted himself to the Druidic Order of the Golden Dawn, which he founded in 2013. His book *The New Encyclopedia of the Occult* (Llewellyn, 2003) has been widely accepted as a standard reference book. His clear warnings about the potentially disastrous effects of ignoring continual damage to the environment have been widely acknowledged and praised. Just the titles of his most influential publications give an indication of some of his concerns: *The Long Descent: A User's Guide to the End of the Industrial Age* (New Society Publishers, 2008); *The Ecotechnic Future: Envisioning a Post-Peak World* (New Society Publishers, 2009); *The Wealth of Nature: Economics as if Survival Mattered* (New Society Publishers, 2011); *Star's Reach: A Novel of the Deindustrial Future* (Founders House, 2014); *After Progress: Reason and Religion at the End of the Industrial Age* (New Society Publishers, 2015); *Dark Age America: Climate Change, Cultural Collapse, and the Hard Future Ahead* (New Society Publishers, 2016).

Emma Restall Orr (1965–)

Despite many decades of feminism within the modern Pagan and Druidic traditions, it is still rare for women to be elected to senior leadership roles in organizations. We noted earlier that Ann Trevenen Jenkin was the first female Grand Bard of the Cornish Gorsedh. Emma Restall Orr, who is both female and comparatively young, has bucked the unfortunate trend of male chauvinism. She studied Druidry from the mid 1980s, working for The Order of Bards Ovates and Druids, then The British Druid Order, where she was joint chief for some nine years alongside Philip Shallcrass. In 2002 she left to found The Druid Network, which now runs without her. She says that while her time within Druidry was enormously valuable, she would no longer term herself a Druid.

In 2004 she founded Honouring the Ancient Dead, an advocacy group working for the respectful treatment of ancestral material, "human remains," particularly those of our pre–Christian past. With very little involvement in any organization now, beyond personal study and writing, her focus is wholly upon Sun Rising Natural Burial Ground, a natural burial ground and nature reserve in South Warwickshire, England.

In her book *Thorson's First Directions—Druidry* (2000), she gives detailed but very friendly and accessible information about ceremonial, ritual and prayer, to which we shall return in Chapter 11. She gives simple but memorable advice to neophytes on how to get started: stop reading, and start living, by going out into Nature with "good boots and a compass" and "walking, watching, feeling, sitting, listening":

When you feel that your presence has begun gently to merge with the environment through which you wander, allow your mind to ponder upon your quest, your desire to know more about the old tradition of Druidry. What is your motivation? What do you hope to gain? What are you expecting? If you are listening with an open mind, quiet from blending your sense of self with the natural world, the answers that emerge will be your first taste of Druidry. Woven through them will be a clarity that will teach more than any written words. Through them will emerge, too, an understanding of the first step you must take on your journey into the tradition.[27]

Brendan Cathbad Myers (1974–)

Brendan Cathbad Myers is a Canadian Druid and professional philosopher. He has a reputation for extensive knowledge as well as wisdom. Isaac Bonewits (see above), a clever man who took no prisoners and certainly did not lack self-confidence, said of him, "Brendan Myers is smarter than me."[28]

Myers was born and raised in Wellington County, Ontario, the eldest son of an Irish-Canadian family. He gained a Bachelor's degree in drama and philosophy and subsequently a Master's in philosophy, both from the University of Guelph. From 2001 to 2005, he completed his Doctoral studies in Galway at the National University of Ireland, traveling extensively in Europe, particularly in England and Germany.

Myers began his involvement in Pagan activism while still an undergraduate, converting from Catholicism. He became a convinced and active environmentalist. His Master's degree dissertation, which was published in 2000, was entitled *Animism, Spirit, and Environmental Activism*. His Doctoral thesis was *Time and the Land: Four Approaches to Environmental Ethics, Climate Change, and Future Generations*. He returned to Canada towards the end of 2005, and taught philosophy at different colleges and universities in Ontario and Quebec for two years. In 2007 he completed a report for the Canadian Government on the relationship between aboriginal values and ethics in relation to policing, peacekeeping and consensus government. Recognized as an academic of the highest order (and the subject of philosophy tends generally to attract a kind of intellectual conservatism and rigor rarely, if ever, found in Druidism), Myers was awarded the Mount Haemus Award for research in Druidry by OBOD in 2008. He now lives in Gatineau in Quebec, working as professor of philosophy and humanities at Heritage College, the only English-speaking college in western Quebec, and asserting his right to be known as the only openly Pagan professor of philosophy in the world.

9. Sacred Sites

The Nemeton

We know that ancient Druids conducted ceremonies in the open air, probably in daylight, and that a general name for the sacred places was *nemeton*, usually translated as "grove," although modern Druids now use the word to refer to any sacred space or site used for ceremonial. The word *nemeton* (sometimes in slightly modified form) reappears in place-names as far apart as Scotland and Spain north to south, and Ireland and Anatolia (modern-day Turkey) west to east, indicating not only that it was common in every Celtic region, but that it must also have held great significance within Celtic communities, corroborating Caesar's description of religion being deeply embedded and highly important in Celtic culture. Moving west to east, we have Nemed in Armagh and at Sliabh Fhuait in Ireland; the Névet Forest in Brittany; Nonant, Nonant-le-Pin, Nampon and Nanterre in France; and Strabo's recording of the great Galatian Druid assembly in Anatolia (modern Turkey) at Drunemeton. Moving south to north, we find an identified *nemeton* site at Matabodes near Beja in southern Portugal; Nymet and Nympton in Devon, England; an inscribed dedication to the Goddess Nemetona at the Romano-British temple in Bath, made by a visitor from the Belgic Treveri tribe who had traveled all the way from Gaul; the Roman place-names *Vernemeton* at what is now called Willoughby-on-the-Wolds in Nottinghamshire, and *Aquae Arnemetiae* ("waters of the *nemeton*," now Buxton), England; and the Roman name *Medionemeton* ("the central *nemeton*") near the Antonine Wall between what are now Glasgow and Edinburgh in Scotland.

Craig Weatherhill has identified four *nemeton* sites in Cornwall, where the word appears as *neves*, through mutation. They are Lanivet (*lann* + *neves*); Carnevas, St. Merryn (*krug* + *neves*); Trenovissick, St. Blazey (*tre* + the adjective *nevesek*); Trewarnevas, St. Anthony in Meneage (*tre* + *gor* + *neves*, the *gor*- element meaning "great" or "major"). The last of these, he says, "is really interesting." He asks, "Why "*gorneves*" (*uor-nemeton*), unless it was a major Druidic center, located in forested land on the south side of the Helford River? Was it Cornwall's primary Druidic site?"[1] If it was—and that seems reasonable, on the clear evidence of the place-name alone, another speculation is that it might have become such after the Roman destruction of the Druidic center on Ynys Mon or Anglesey in 60 CE and that the surviving Druids from that catastrophe may have hurried south to take refuge in the distant and secret forests of Cornwall.

The question of the extent to which the Druids also used the ancient stone circles, monuments and alignments remains moot. Pliny and other classical writers assert that they did not. But we have to remember that these Roman historians were going out of their way to portray the Celts in general and the Druids in particular as utter savages, so they wanted to make everything about them sound as wild and barbaric as possible. Even stone circles would have been too civilized for them. Or, if they did use them, it was in the most bloody and barbarous way possible. Here, for example, is how Lucan describes the *nemeton* at Massilia or Massalia (now Marseilles) in France:

> No bird nested in the *nemeton*, nor did any animal lurk nearby; the leaves constantly shivered though no breeze stirred. Altars stood in its midst, and the images of the Gods. Every tree was stained with sacrificial blood. The very earth groaned, dead yews revived; unconsumed trees were surrounded with flame, and huge serpents twined round the oaks. The people feared to approach the grove, and even the priest would not walk there at midday or midnight lest he should then meet its divine guardian.[2]

My personal belief is that the ancient Druids would not have ignored these incredibly powerful places, for the simple reason that Druidism ancient and modern is so closely bound to the Earth and to nature, and these places shout out their power as plainly as hitting your thumb with a hammer. The Druids may have deliberately avoided them for reasons unknown, or they may have used them for ritual and ceremonial purposes while knowing that others had created them, or, if the continuity theory of Cunliffe and others is correct (see below), they may have simply continued using these holy places in the same way that their ancestors did. We have no way of telling, although archaeology generally finds detritus from prehistory all the way through to the Middle Ages either at or close to these famous prehistoric sites, and common sense tells us that the ancient Druids would certainly have known that the monuments were there, almost equally certainly would have understood their solar, lunar and astronomical alignments, and almost equally certainly would have treated them with enormous reverence and respect, regardless of whether they also actually used them for gatherings or ceremonies.

Sacred Sites in Europe

The stone circles and megalith alignments in Britain (of which there are many hundreds, some of them quite small and almost forgotten now, and sadly neglected) were built at different times, mostly between approximately 3300 BCE and 1500 BCE. According to standard historical (or pre-historical) scholars, the people who built them are unknown, but they were succeeded and ousted from about 1800 BCE onwards by an invading people now called the Beaker People, because they made and used clay beakers, fragments of which they left behind them for archaeologists to find much later. According to the same historical tradition, the Celts arrived from mainland Europe, initially from the Belgic tribes of Gaul, at an unspecified date but certainly no earlier than 900 BCE at the very earliest, and more likely closer to 600 or possibly even as late as 450 BCE. This suggested sequence coincides well with the traditional Irish vernacular mythology of a series of invasions, with the various Gods and supernatural beings of the myths representing a series of historical invasions by actual historical tribes or ethnic groups.

However, recent work by Barry Cunliffe, John T. Koch and others has radically suggested that, while the expansions northward into Britain from 450 BCE onwards may indeed have taken place, the Celts originated much earlier in western Europe and the Iberian peninsula, perhaps as early as the late Bronze Age, descendants of a population which had occupied western Europe ever since the retreat of the last Ice Age about 10,000 years ago, with Celtic developing as the *lingua franca* of the Atlantic seaboard from *circa* 5000 to 2700 BCE, expanding thenceforward from west to east, rather than east to west. If this theory is true (and I think its status is still probably "startling" within the traditional academic community), it would mean a continuous linguistic and cultural connection through Celtic areas dating back almost ten thousand years, and could bring the standing stones and monuments back into the Celtic and Druidic fold.

Leaving aside the question of whether ancient Druids used them or not, these are still sites of great importance to modern Druids, who should try to visit them if they can. There are literally thousands of prehistoric sacred sites in Britain, Ireland and Brittany, but space limitations require me to make a very brief and subjective list of only a few of the most important ones. To begin, I list below what I consider to be the nine best stone circles (i.e., most sacred and most powerful, from a Druid's point of view) in Britain and Ireland. The comments reflect my own experiences, and others may feel differently about them:

Stonehenge in Wiltshire: This very famous monument was built between 3000 and 2000 BCE, and was then apparently abandoned about 1800 BCE, but nobody knows why. Extensively researched and investigated, it is probably the most famous Neolithic monument in the world. It is horribly commercial, overcrowded and unbearably busy and noisy in the summer, there is a hefty entrance charge, and the site is frustratingly regimented—you are kept well away from the stones by ropes, and a requirement to stay on the designated concrete path—but it is still worth a visit. It's best to come very early, on a cold day out of season, or go the whole hog and try to join in the dawn celebrations actually inside the circle on Midsummer's Day—that's the only way you will ever be able to approach or see the stones uninterrupted and use Stonehenge as a temple or as a site for deepest prayer and sacred contemplation. I can remember as a young man being able to walk right up to the stones and touch them, and talk directly with them. I was always surprised at the tremendous heat they gave out at night, and the enormous, silent strength they possessed. Now, unfortunately, in almost every aspect, Stonehenge is no longer perceived as a sacred site, but rather as a cash-cow, a huge, commercial enterprise: it attracts about a million visitors per year, earns about $12 million directly and another $40 million indirectly to the British economy. The shop is overpriced throughout, but there are some good books available.

Stonehenge, Wiltshire, England (Mavratti)

Avebury in Wiltshire: Called Caer Abiri by the British Druid Order, Avebury is actually a group of three circles, much larger than Stonehenge in terms of area covered, and was built about 2600 BCE. Part of the village is actually inside the largest circle. It is nowhere near as commercialized as Stonehenge: there is no entrance fee. The site has two ceremonial avenues and several barrows and tumuli, and attracts a great deal of interest and attention from Pagans of every kind. The BDO founded the Gorsedd of the Bards of Caer Abiri here in 1993, with ritual written by Philip Shallcrass. The circle complex is large enough to accommodate many visitors and still leave space for prayer and quiet contemplation. The stones are beautiful in winter, especially if there is snow on the ground. The locals are patient with visitors and sympathetic to Pagans. This is the *nemeton* of the first cycle of my triple handfasting with my wife (see Chapter 11).

Ring of Brodgar, Isles of Orkney, Scotland: The circle is remotely located, and requires a two-hour ferry journey from the Scottish mainland, but it is sited in a spectacularly beautiful location, typically Orcadian, with low hills and the sea always crowding close by. Built around 3300 BCE between two lochs, the circle is close to many other interesting sites and features on the nearby Ness of Brodgar. There is always a lot of

Avebury, Wiltshire, England (Wikimedia, photograph by Diliff)

The Ring of Brodgar, Orkney, Scotland (Wikimedia, photograph by Shadowgate)

active archaeology going on here. The whole area is packed densely with ancestral spirit. Five thousand years ago, this place was probably even more important than Stonehenge became later. This is the *nemeton* of the third cycle of my triple hand-fasting with my wife.

Callanish (Tursachan Chalanais) on the Isle of Lewis in the Outer Hebrides, Scotland: This monument was built probably about 2900 BCE, possibly earlier, and is set in a spectacular coastal location in the remote Hebrides. (Visiting Lewis requires either a fairly long ferry journey or air flight from the Scottish mainland.) Callanish (or Calanais in the Gàidhlig spelling) is associated with Midsummer celebrations, and is popular with Pagans as well as with regular tourists. In fact, it becomes very busy with busloads of tourists in high season, and can sometimes be crowded and noisy. It's a small site, with a café and little gift shop, which can easily become swamped if too many tour buses arrive all at the same time. For me, the whole site is dominated by the sea and the immanent presence of Manannán mac Lir, but it is best to be there either early or late, when the site is quieter—otherwise it is dominated by squawking tourists and endless snaps and selfies on smart phones. In

Calanais Stone Circle, Isle of Lewis, Scotland (Wikimedia, photograph by Chmee2)

high summer, the midges eat about a pound of human flesh per hour, especially in the evening after rain showers, so smother yourself with repellant. (The Hebrides are so far north that in June the sun barely sets at all, making 11 o'clock at night or 3 o'clock in the morning, when the shop and café are closed and no buses are around, ideal times for using the stones as they were meant to be used, i.e., as a sacred site.)

Castlerigg in Cumbria, England: This is quite a compact circle, with some interesting features, set on a hill summit and surrounded by a circle of mountain peaks, including Skiddaw and Lonscale Fell, so it is visually stunning, almost Alpine in feel. Its panorama literally took my breath away the first time I made the short climb up to the circle, which appears suddenly as you crest the gentle upslope. Castlerigg gets a steady stream of visitors, but there is nothing crowded or commercial about the site, even in high summer. It is dominated by the big, open sky and the quietly massive mountain peaks. The first time Odin spoke to me, many years ago now, was at Castlerigg, so for me it has a powerful northern feel and association.

Long Meg & Her Daughters, Cumbria, England: Properly called Maughanby Stone Circle, this site is large (51 stones still standing of an estimated original 70) and very open, probably completed about 1500 BCE, so quite young by comparison with other sites. Long Meg is a single stone set outside the circle, reputedly a witch turned to stone—it has a cup and ring marking, plus spirals and concentric circles. This is a powerful circle, charged with a great deal of spiritual static—it changes appearance and mood very quickly according to the prevailing weather.

Stanton Drew, Somerset, England: These are three interconnected circles in the Chew Valley in Somerset, making a very large complex overall. Many of the stones are deeply weathered, and have large holes or fissures in them. The site is much used by Pagans, quite a few of whom leave offerings in the holes in the stones—do not, under any circumstances, remove or interfere with them. Several hand-fastings have taken place in the Great Circle, which is the second largest in area in Britain (Avebury is the largest). The nearby village of Stanton Drew is charming and friendly.

Rollright Stones, Oxfordshire, England: The main stone circle has 77 megaliths, all shapes and sizes, nicknamed The King's Men. Other stones outside the circle are called The King and The Whispering Knights. The limestone megaliths are heavily weathered, and invite close observation, because so many different faces, objects and other apparitions can suddenly hit your eye if you just stare long enough at them. Strange lights have been reported quite frequently at the site, and the pocked, oddly-shaped stones are very lively and talkative in misty weather or in the dawn or dusk gloaming.

Arbor Low, Derbyshire, England: This is a most unusual stone circle, in that the stones are laid horizontally rather than upright. It was built about 2500 BCE. It consists of about 50 well-preserved limestone megaliths on a low hill in an open-sky part of the Peak District. The site was used well into the Bronze Age, and still feels very active. It is said to be the focus of several strong ley-lines. Local Pagans have used the site regularly, and it feels alive, healthy and well cared-for.

Apart from the many stone circles, there are many other ancient sites in Britain, Ireland and Brittany which are of special interest to Druids, and which are definitely worth visiting, a few of which I describe below. Again, the selection is limited to places I know, and the brief comments reflect my own experiences, which may differ from those of others.

England

West Kennet Long Barrow and Silbury Hill, Wiltshire, England: These two monuments are either side of the main A4 road between Marlborough and Caine, not far from Avebury and Stonehenge. Silbury Hill is a manmade chalk mound, built about 2400 BCE. It has been excavated several times since the 18th century, but no major artifacts have been found. Nobody knows what its original purpose was, although there has been a great deal of speculation, but its size and the incredible amount of labor required for its construction clearly indicate that it was a site of great importance to the people who built it. There is no longer any direct access to the hill itself. The West Kennet Long Barrow is a sizeable Neolithic burial chamber, a short walk away to the south from the main road opposite Silbury Hill. Its construction was begun about 3600 BCE, i.e., earlier than Stonehenge. The chamber is open and accessible, and there is no entrance fee. Inside are small stone burial chambers either side of a narrow entrance passage. Excavations found evidence of at least 46 human burials in the barrow, dated between 3600 and 2500 BCE, so the site was in continuous use for about 1,100 years, which is a remarkable fact in itself. The discovered bones were disarticulated, and some skulls were missing. The first time I showed my wife the interior of the barrow, she immediately burst into tears, and had to go outside again. The continuing presence of the ancient ancestors there is incredibly strong. Archaeologists have speculated that selected bones, and possibly other relics, were regularly removed from the barrow, perhaps for ceremonial or ritual purposes, and then returned. The Long Barrow and Silbury Hill were both visited by early Druids John Aubrey and William

West Kennet Long Barrow, Wiltshire, England

Stukeley, and by countless thousands of visitors since. The sense of connection to the ancient land and people here is so powerful it is almost palpable, as my wife's tears attest.

Glastonbury, Somerset, England: The town of Glastonbury and its famous Abbey (where King Arthur and Queen Guinevere were reputedly buried) have a huge amount of interest to offer all by themselves, and the town has been visited over the years by so many hippies and Pagans of all kinds that it has a unique atmosphere. It holds a summer festival every year that attracts thousands of additional visitors. The town area has been continuously occupied since Neolithic times, so it is jam-packed with history and sites of interest. This is where Joseph of Arimathea (Jesus Christ's uncle) is said to have struck his wand or staff into the ground, where it grew into the Glastonbury Thorn tree. In addition to the town and the Abbey, there are two sites of great spiritual power within or close by the town. The first is Glastonbury Tor, a steep hill that rises up close to the town, which shows traces of a spiral pathway added during Neolithic times, and which has the ruin of a tower, dedicated to St. Michael, at its summit. The Tor, which is free of access, is very popular with visitors, but is big enough not to feel too crowded, even in high summer, when hundreds of people come to picnic, play, and generally skylark. The whole place crackles with energy. I saw my first Unidentified Flying Object (UFO) from the summit of Glastonbury Tor one frosty February night about fifty years ago, and have never forgotten it. If you go to the Tor, expect anything, and be prepared to be

Glastonbury Tor, Somerset, England (Flikr by Laika ac)

involved in anything, from prayers to picnics, and for strangers to strike up conversations with you about every topic under the Sun. At the foot of the Tor is the second site of great power, the Chalice Well, a natural healing spring which has never failed, even in the most severe drought. There is now an entrance fee to this site. The reddish, iron-oxide rich waters (the taste is very metallic and bitter) have been reputed to have healing powers for countless thousands of years. The site is popular with Pagans of all kinds, and was dedicated as a World Peace Garden in 2001. Across the road, a Victorian well house has been recently converted into the White Spring Temple, whose calcite-whitened waters are also reputed to have healing powers. Both springs flow from the Tor.

South Cadbury: South Cadbury (or, more properly, Cadbury Castle) is a natural hill with added man-made earthen ramparts, just south of the main A303 road about eight miles north-east of the town of Yeovil, which was used as a hill fort from Neolithic times. The hill fort is large—about 20 acres (8 hectares)—and from its summit you can see right across the flat flood-plains to Glastonbury Tor about 13 miles away. The hilltop was partially excavated by Leslie Alcock in the 1960s, when the remains of a large assembly hall were discovered, adding signifi-cantly to the long-held belief that this was the site of King Arthur's palace of Camelot. The walk up to the summit is short and very steep, but the view, the big and open sky, and the powerful sense of ancestor connection once you reach the level plain and the still clearly visible earth ramparts make the climb well worth the effort.

Cerne Abbas Giant: The Cerne Abbas Giant is a hill figure made by cutting turf and filling the spaces with chalk, of unknown date, near the small village of Cerne Abbas in Dorset. The figure represents a naked male with a huge, erect penis, carrying a huge club in his hand. There is evidence that there was once also a cloak or animal skin below his left hand. Although the earliest reference to the figure is dated 1694, the style and content of the figure suggest that it was made well before the 17th century. It is assumed to represent a hunter or warrior God of the Hercules type, created as a religious image by the extensive labor of per-sons unknown, but who were clearly either non–Christian or pre–Christian. It is not possible to walk on the figure itself—you simply park on the very small and quiet country lane next to it.

Uffington White Horse: At Uffington in Oxfordshire, there is another very well-known carved chalk figure, this one being a highly stylized horse. The figure is 360 feet (110 meters) long, and you can walk across it (there is no entrance charge), although visitors are obviously requested not to walk on or damage the chalk inlays themselves. There are several other carved white horse figures in Britain, but the Uffington is the oldest and most distinctive. The precise date of construction is not known—it varies all the way from late Bronze Age (1000 to 700 BCE) to the Anglo-Saxon period, with late Bronze Age or early Iron Age being the most likely. My wife and I have spent some time walking over the figure, finding the eye in particular a strong center of energy. This place belongs to the Goddess Epona. The figure has been vandalized many times, and requires regular maintenance to remain visible. The site is currently owned and maintained by the National Trust and is a Scheduled Ancient Monument.

Wayland's Smithy: About a mile to the west of the Uffington White Horse is Wayland's Smithy, which is a Neolithic long barrow and chamber tomb built in two phases, from 3590 to 3550 BCE and from 3460 to 3400 BCE. The site was extensively excavated by Stuart Piggott and Richard Atkinson in the early 1960s, which was also about the time I first visited it. The unusual name was given to the site by the Saxons, thousands of years after it was built (the name is first recorded in a charter of 955 CE). It refers to the legend of a Germanic deity, Weyland or Woland, who was a divine blacksmith. According to the legend, if your horse lost or damaged a shoe, you could bring it to the barrow, leave it and a bag of coins overnight, and in the morning the coins would have gone and the horse would be re-shod. Just like West Kennet Long Barrow, this is a simple, quiet, very sacred place where the presence of the ancestors is almost palpable.

CORNWALL

St. Nectan's Glen: St. Nectan's Glen is a pretty, wooded valley near Tintagel in North Cornwall. At the end of a pleasant walk of about a mile through the woods next to the River Trevillet (there is no road access), you come to Nectan's Kieve (from Cornish *Kuva Nathan*, "Nectan's or Nathan's Sawn-Down Barrel or Tub"), a spectacular 60-foot (20-meter) waterfall that shoots out from a hole in the rock into a deep pool that it has carved out below. The rock above the pool is dedicated to the 6th-century Christian saint who had a hermitage there, but this was clearly a Druidic site of worship long before him. The trees by the pool are now covered with clooties (Scots for "cloths") or tree-ties, put there by current Pagans and others to bind their prayers to the site.

Madron Well: The little village of Madron has a church, in which St. Madron (or Maddern as locals pronounce it) is depicted with a white beard and carrying a great staff or wand, rather Druidic in appearance. However, we know by the name alone that the Christians converted a

St. Nectan's Glen, Cornwall (photograph by Nilfanion)

female Goddess into a male saint, because Madron means simply "Mother," and clearly refers to the Goddess. Madron Well Chapel, more often called The Baptistery by locals, is a tiny chapel, now in ruins, outside the village, within which a small baptismal pool is formed by the adjacent stream. This building is clearly Christian in origin, although the baptismal pool was almost certainly Druidic before the Chapel was built. My wife and I once spent a whole night sleeping in the Chapel as part of a dream-recording project run by Paul Devereux. To the left of the pathway that leads to the Baptistery, there are woods. Deep among these is the ancient Madron Well, the original sacred, Pagan well. It was here that the Goddess gifted to me my rowan wand or staff, *Sarf Nija*. The water table is very close to the surface in these woods, and the many floods there have led some visitors to tie their prayer clooties to trees next to the path, thinking they were at the well when, in fact, they were only close to temporary flood water, so don't be misled by the many clooties tied close to the path. The real well is hidden deep within the woods, a good distance away from the path, and you may have to take off your socks, shoes and pants to wade through the floods to find it, as I have done on a few occasions—and you will need to ask the Goddess Madron, by name, to help you, because the well is difficult to find. (A clue: it is set down into the ground, with no wall or other structure above ground, making it difficult to see from any distance, but it is lined with bricks and large stones and is quite unmistakable once you have come close enough to see it.)

WALES

Cadair Idris: Cadair or Cader Idris (Welsh for "Idris's Chair") is a mountain in Gwynedd, near the interesting little town of Dolgellau. Idris was either an ancient mythological giant, or the 7th-century Prince Idris ap Gwyddno, or even, as some have suggested, Prince Idris who also happened to be a giant. Just below the mountain's summit is Llyn Cau, a stunningly beautiful *tarn* or glacial mountain lake. There are three trails to the top of the mountain: *Llwybr Pilin Pwn* ("The Pony Path"), from Dolgellau in the north, is the easiest, but also the longest at just over three miles; *Llwybr Madin* ("The Fox Path") is less than two-and-a-half miles, but involves a climb and subsequent descent through loose scree, and is dangerous unless you are a very experienced climber or hill-walker; *Llwybr Minffordd* ("The Minffordd Path"), from the south, is 2.7 miles long and includes a couple of steep climbs, but begins by the glacial Tal-y-Llyn lake and passes close by the lovely Llyn Cau. Cadair Idris is impressive in all weathers, but you certainly wouldn't

Cadair Idris, Wales (photograph by Matěj "Dědek" Bat'ha)

want to be caught out on the mountain in a bad winter storm. Its slopes are said to be the hunting grounds of Gwynn ap Nudd and his *Cwn Annwn*, or Hounds of the Underworld. Traditionally, Bards would sleep on the sides of the mountain seeking *awen* or divine inspiration. There is still a strong local belief that if you find yourself trapped by bad weather and forced to sleep on the mountain against your wishes, you will wake up insane (or dead).

Bardsey Island: Bardsey Island (*Ynys Enlli* in Welsh) is not a place to visit without forethought and planning. It is a sea journey of only two miles from the tip of the Lleyn Peninsula on the Welsh mainland, but the island is tiny, has no electricity, water supply or sewage, and can be reached only by prior arrangement with the owners of the few properties on the island. You have to carry in your own water and food and all other supplies, and carry all your own belongings and trash out with you after your visit is over—the owners use a tractor and trailer to help you transfer everything to the boat. You have to use self-composting outside toilets, bringing your own candle and hoping the wind doesn't blow it out. Bardsey has been called "the island of 20,000 saints," because it has been a sacred burial ground since time immemorial. The island has been inhabited since Neolithic times. It was a place of refuge for Christians in the 6th century. *Afal Enlli*, the Bardsey Apple, an extremely rare variety originally grown by monks on the island, survived on Bardsey for over a thousand years until it was brought back into general cultivation on the mainland in the 1990s. The island, remote and rugged, teems with wildlife and has inspired many bards, authors, artists and musicians. My wife and two members of our American "prayer family" spent a week praying and meditating on Bardsey in 2007, and came back with many tales of vision and inspiration.

Dinas Emrys: Dinas Emrys is a rocky, wooded, little hill near Beddgelert in Gwynedd. The site itself, although pleasant, offers little to see these days, but this is where Merlin is supposed to have revealed the white and red dragons (Saxons and Britons) hidden in the pool beneath the castle that the tyrant King Vortigern was trying to build. This is the Dinas, or fortress, of Emrys, or Ambrosius, which as we saw in Chapter 5, means "the immortal one," and may refer to Merlin. The site of the revealed pool can still be seen.

SCOTLAND

Dunadd: Dunadd is in Kilmartin Glen, between Inverary and Oban in Argyll. It is a large rocky outcrop, on the top of which a footprint and a small basin-shaped depression were anciently carved into the rock, which are still clearly visible. During the early Middle Ages, the fortress of Dunadd was the center of the kingdom of Dál Riada. Kings were crowned there, with part of the ritual being the placing of the King's naked foot into the carved footprint space (nobody is quite certain what the basin was used for, but ritual washing is probable). My right foot (size 10 British, 11 American) is fractionally larger than the carving, but placing your naked foot in exactly the same spot where many kings anciently placed their naked feet to celebrate their sacred connection to the Earth is a strangely satisfying and uplifting experience, and definitely a very practical way to connect with the past. Kilmartin Glen has 350 ancient monuments within six miles of the village, 150 of them being prehistoric.

The Clootie Well, the Black Isle: As noted above, clooties (also spelled cloutie or cloughtie) is the Scots word for "cloths," and is used, as we saw in relation to St. Nectan's Glen and Madron Well, to describe the very common Pagan practice of tying strips of cloth or rag to the branches of a tree close to a holy well, the idea being that the prayer made at the well will continue to be effective for as long as the cloth remains hanging in the tree. For prayers of healing, the cloth is dipped in the well, perhaps placed against the affected body part, then as the cloth dries and fades in the tree, so the sickness abates and disappears. The strips can come from anywhere, from the pieces torn off a handkerchief which I usually tie, to the complete pair of child's jeans that I once saw hanging from a tree limb by the Sancreed Holy Well in Cornwall. The Clootie Well on the Black Isle in Scotland is near the village of Munlochie on the A832. I include it as just one example (although a particularly impressive one) of the many clootie wells found in Britain. The Munlochie well always has literally hundreds of clooties on the surrounding trees, and it is obvious that Pagans come from far and near to visit it.

St. Ninian's Cave: St. Ninian's Cave, near Glassertown in Wigtownshire in southern Scotland, is associated, as the name obviously tells us, with the 8th-century Christian saint Ninian (also called Ringan or Trynnian) who built the first Christian church in Scotland, the *Candida Casa* at Whithorn in Galloway. The cave is on the seashore, found after a short walk through woods and across a very pebbly beach (there is no vehicular access). The minute you see it and stand in it, it is obvious that this cave has been a sacred site for millennia. St. Ninian may well have used it—good luck to him—but he wasn't the first, by any means. The cave is tall, dark, beautiful, wet, shining, and—as my wife unforgettably described it to me the first time we visited—it is Mother Earth's vagina, as clear as daylight (except that she didn't use the word "vagina"). The waves pound rhythmically on the pebbled shore outside, while the cave is cool and silent inside, but from within its silence you can still see the beach and the surf and the sky, living and moving and breathing. Being inside the cave and looking out is like watching the world while you're waiting to be born. You understand immediately how and why it might be a place for someone, Christian saint or ancient Druid, to leave the world behind and enjoy the peace and security of absolute solitude and calm.

Drumelzier: Drumelzier (pronounced *drum-el-yuh*, with the accent on the second syllable) is a sleepy little village on the B712 in the Tweed Valley in the Scottish Borders. It has a castle, and other village amenities, but it is famous among Pagans as the place where Morgan le Fay imprisoned Myrddin or Merlin in a tree, which grows to this day on a river bank below the village and can be found if you know where to look for it. (I did look, and I did find, but this is a quest you must make alone, if you choose to make it yourself.) He is buried beside the Powsail Burn ("burn" means "stream" in Scotland), the burial place marked by a

thorn tree, which it is obvious many others beside myself have found
and recognized. A prophecy was made:

> When Tweed and Powsail meet at Merlin's grave,
> Scotland and England shall one monarch have.[3]

On the very day that James VI of Scotland was also crowned James I
of England (the 24th of July, 1567), the shallow, slow-moving Tweed
flooded its banks and overflowed into the Powsail Burn, something it
had never done before and has never done since, and thus the prophecy
was fulfilled.

IRELAND

Newgrange, Boyne Valley, County Meath: Newgrange, called *Sí an Brú*
(*shee-an-broo*, "Fairy Mound of the Hostel") or *Brú na Boinne* (*broo-na-
boyn-yuh*, "Hostel of the People of Boann") in Irish, is one of the most
beautiful and astonishing Neolithic monument complexes anywhere in
the world. Built around 3200 BCE, it is older than both Stonehenge and
the Pyramids of Egypt. It stands about five miles west of Drogheda,
about thirty miles north of Dublin, on the north bank of the River
Boyne, whose tutelary Goddess is Boann. In the Irish legends the *Brú*
were the senior clan of the *Tuatha Dé Danann*, their leaders being the
father-god the Dagda, his wife Boann and his son Oengus. (The word
brú, as well as being a name, has three literal meanings: a hostel or guest
house; a brink or edge, as in *ar bhrú*, "on the brink"; and a crush or
pressure, as in *brú fola*, "blood pressure," or *brú croi*, "oppression or
crushing of the heart.")[4] The main feature of the site is a large, circular
mound with internal passageways and burial chambers. The entrance
aligns with the midwinter sunrise, so that once and once only every year
shafts of light from the rising sun penetrate all the way to the center of
the mound, similar to Maes Howe in Orkney, and Bryn Celli Ddu in
Wales. The stones around the mound's entrance are carved in an astonishing variety of patterns, which may be purely abstract, but almost certainly originally had religious significance—they are mesmerizing.

Tara, County Meath: Tara, or more properly The Hill of Tara, is
between Navan and Dunshaughlin in County Meath. The site is called
Cnoc na Teamhrach (literally "Hill of the Hills") or *Teamhair na Rígh*
("Hill of the King") in Irish. Although the site is not especially pictur-
esque, it is where the *Lia Fáil* or Stone of Destiny still stands. According
to ancient legend, this sacred stone would scream out its affirmation
when approached by a would-be High King of Ireland (the screech was
said to be loud enough to be heard across the whole land), so the *Lia*

Fáil represents the Goddess herself accepting the High King in the sacred marriage that brings fertility and prosperity to the nation. Close by is a hill-fort called *Ráith na Ríogh* ("the Rath or Fort of the Kings"). Below its summit is *Teach Chormaic* ("House of Cormac"), the burial chamber of Cormac mac Airt, the High King of Ireland from 227 to 266 CE, who appears in many of the early Irish tales.

BRITTANY

Carnac, Morbihan: Carnac (*Karnag* is the Breton spelling) is a small community beside the Gulf of Morbihan on Brittany's south coast. The Carnac Stones (*Steudadoù Karnag*) consists of more than 3,000 shaped and carved stones, many of them weighing several tons, set out in a complex pattern of avenues, alignments and single menhirs, with tumuli and dolmens also in the complex. It was built no later than 3300 BCE, but archaeologists believe that many of the stones date from as early as 4500 BCE. The site has not been well managed—local farmers have even stolen stones to build huts for livestock or chickens—but it is still massively impressive. As with the largest stones at Avebury, you try to imagine how anybody could possibly move such massive objects into such precise alignments, and you also find yourself drawn towards individual stones which exert a special magnetic pull.

Baie de Douarnenez: This huge bay (it's about 10 miles wide and 13 miles deep) is in the far west of Brittany. The fishing town of Douarnenez is the only settlement of any size in the entire bay. This is wild country. This is the site of the legendary city of Ys, built by Gradion or Gralon the King of Cornuaille (*Kerne* in Breton, the same name as Kernow or Cornwall) at the request of his daughter Dahut. The disreputable, selfish princess (a Pagan or Druid, according to Christian versions of the legend) stole from her father the key to the gates which kept the ocean from entering the city, but left the gates unlocked and the city and all its inhabitants were drowned. The Breton musician Alan Stivell wrote a magnificent piece of music for harp and orchestra to celebrate the legend, called simply *Ys*. There is a saying which involves a pun in Breton: *Pa vo beuzet Par-Is, Ec'h adsavo Ker Is*—"When Paris (Par Is, "like Ys" in Breton) drowns, the Fortress of Ys ("*Ker Is*") will arise." If you are in Douarnenez (or quite a few other of the Breton fishing towns or villages) look out for a local *Degoûtation de Fruits de Mer* ("Tasting of the Fruits of the Sea"), at which fresh fish, mostly sardines and tuna steaks, will be served straight from the boats to grills on the pier and served very simply (and cheaply) with wine and bread in vast quantities. *Crêpes*, thin pancakes which may be sweet or savory, are good anywhere in

France, but are outstandingly good in Brittany. (This gratuitous advice is offered to encourage your Druidic sense of adventure and exploration.)

Sacred Sites in Canada and the USA

Back in Chapter 1, I noted that almost all of the well-known sacred sites in the USA are Native American. This raises a question which has been present in modern Druidism in Canada and America for a considerable time, but which remains unresolved. What is the appropriate relationship between Druids and the indigenous peoples of the Americas? Druidic culture is founded on the traditional Celtic territories in Europe, now almost entirely represented by the Celtic nations of the Atlantic seaboard, Scotland, Ireland, the Isle of Man, Wales, Cornwall, Brittany, Galicia and Asturias. The indigenous cultures of the Americas are based on the territories of several different groups: the Inuit (the indigenous people of the Arctic); the First Nations (the 634 recognized indigenous nations in Canada south of the Arctic), a title also used by some tribes of the Pacific Northwest in the United States; the Métis (descendants of marriages between European settlers and members of several northern tribal nations, including the Mi'qmak, Algonquin, Saulteaux, Cree, Ojibwe and Menominee); the more than 500 North American indigenous nations of pre–Columbian origin, variously referred to as nations, tribes, Native Americans, American Indians and simply Indians (although "Indians" is both geographically incorrect and considered insulting and demeaning by some); the many different peoples of central American countries, including Mexico; and the many different indigenous peoples of South America. For Druids in America (which generally means in the United States or Canada), the problem can be simply summarized: they want to continue a Celtic religious tradition which is Earth-based, territorial, and intimately intertwined with the Gods and spirits of particular places. From the Native American point of view, the same problem can be equally simply summarized: every square inch of those places belongs to our nations, but our territories were stolen from us, and we resent you trying to impose your European culture and Gods on our native lands. The Rev. John R. Adelmann, also known simply as Fox, founder and Senior Druid of the Shining Lakes Grove of ADF, describes his personal experience of the problem:

> Over the next few years I became very involved in Deep Ecology, the environmental movement and Native American spirituality. I taught myself to live off of the land, became an environmental activist, made my own clothes and shoes, and generally tried to lead a life in balance with the natural world. Ultimately, this interest led me to spend a year with the Shawnee Indians. Life with the Shawnee was a dream come true. For the first time I knew what it meant to have an all-encompassing faith, where every

action and thought had relevance to the spirit. I developed a great fondness for the feeling of belonging, for tribal life among a supportive community and knew a profound kinship with all beings of the world. During this time, as the result of a vision, the Natives dubbed me "Chakwiweshe," or "Fox." But, alas, the idyllic life didn't last.... Little by little it became apparent that I, a man of purely European descent, had intruded where I was not completely welcome. The native people have suffered so much at the hands of my culture and still bear the scars. Although they made every attempt to welcome me among them I began to feel like a guest whose visit had gone on for a bit too long. It all finally precipitated into a confrontation with a man that I had taken as my adopted brother. He told me that I should leave Native American culture to his people and to seek my own native heritage. I protested that my people had not lived in harmony with nature or in tribal communities for so long that surely there was no trace to be recovered![5]

Michel-Gerald Boutet describes a different kind of problem emerging after Canadian Druids made contact with Indians:

The elders had lots of conversations with the Indians. If they [the Druid elders] didn't go to Mass for seven years they were cursed by the parish priest as being "Warlocks" or "Werewolves." There was a Werewolf society in Quebec called *Loup-garous* in French. What they were doing was they had contact with the Scottish Masonic lodges and the Algonquin *Midewiwin* (Medicine Societies). The *Midewiwin* were what I would call a Masonic lodge within Indian society. They were like the Druids, they were the gurus, the ones who had the responsibility of transmitting information or initiation or science or herbology, astrology, all these things, to the next generations. In the French-Canadian society, because of the parish priest and the strong Catholic influence, this was seen through very bad eyes.[6]

I offer no simple solution to the problem of potential conflict and misunderstanding between modern Druids and native Canadian and American peoples (I don't think there is one), but I can offer a few thoughts from my personal experience. I lived in the United States for fifteen years. Our "prayer family," which I have mentioned a few times already, is not a grove or henge, or even Druidic: it is quite a large group of close friends and families in Oregon, who all share a Pagan outlook. This group was founded by "the Old Man," an individual who had himself learned a great deal directly from indigenous people about Native American traditions but who was also a solitary Druid. He passed on his skills and knowledge to many, including a young woman who subsequently has become the leader of our group (we have no formal roles or titles) because she has what Native Americans call "the medicine," the gift of healing and vision (the closest Celtic term is perhaps *imbas forasnai*) and a natural connection with the world of spirit. On a spontaneous and informal basis, this group or family has created a long-lasting and (from my point of view) very powerful and effective synthesis of Celtic and Native American traditions, with a touch of house-witch thrown in for good measure, which has lasted for many years now. We have a sweat lodge, built with help and advice from Native Americans; we organize an annual vision quest (a period spent alone in a wild place, fasting and without water, to pray and invite sacred visions, common among many tribal nations), which is undertaken by volunteers, supported by the rest of the group in preparation, training, auxiliary prayer and safekeeping; we meet regularly for prayer, usually in the sweat-lodge, with individuals permanently assigned to regular responsibilities, like fire building and tending; we conduct ritual and ceremony, which is mostly improvised from a mixture of Celtic and Native American sources and traditions. For some years now, my wife and I have lived in Scotland, 8,000 miles away from our "family," but we are still part of that family and still very much involved in what goes on, on a daily or weekly basis. I think if we fall back on the Druidic basics of respect, responsibility, *fír fer*, fitness of things, and truth against the world, there is hope for us. I would like to see a great deal more co-operation between modern American Druids and Native Americans; we have a lot to learn from each other.

In that spirit of co-operation and respect for indigenous traditions, therefore, I give below some very brief observations on a few of the very many sacred sites in Canada and the USA, most of them being sites which I have visited myself, and the other three being sites I have learned about personally from others:

CANADA

The Sacred Headwaters, British Columbia: Klabona or Klappan Valley is the name given by the indigenous Tahltan people to this subalpine rock basin in British Columbia where three wild-salmon rivers have their source: the Skeena, the Nass and the Stikine. The area also has grizzly bears, caribou and wolves. I'm not a hunter, but I have been told that this is the most magical place to hunt and fish in the entire world.

Klix-in, British Columbia: Klix-in, previously known as Keeshan (to represent the sound of waves crashing against rocks) is the original home of the Huu-ay-aht group of the Nuu-chah-nulth people. It was made a National Historical Site of Canada in 1999. It preserves buildings from a village occupied by the Nuu-chah-nulth "since time began," and gives the modern visitor a good idea of what it might have felt like to live in a tiny, indigenous, native community decades or centuries ago.

Saoyú-ʔehdach, Northwest Territories: Saoyú-ʔehdach (pronounced very approximately *sa-oh-yu-ed-ak*), known in English as Grizzly Bear Mountain and Scented Grass Hills, is an area of cultural and spiritual significance to the Sahtú people. The sacred land consists of two connected peninsulas in Great Bear Lake, the largest lake entirely within the land mass of Canada itself. In modern times, local natives were employed to gather and transport radioactive materials found near the lake to be used in the Manhattan Project, and it is still not clear how many died as a result, or how many are still suffering. A similar issue arose with uranium mining in Monument Valley (see below)—some people believe that John Wayne developed cancer from spending so much time filming there. (Paul Devereux has a theory that human beings are instinctively drawn towards places with naturally high levels of background radiation, and has tested it by measuring natural radiation at many different sacred sites, but I don't know whether he ever made any conclusive discoveries.)

CANADA/USA

Niagara Falls, Ontario: A world-famous, heavily commercialized tourist trap, Niagara Falls is nevertheless still a sacred site of great significance, and well worth visiting. Actually three falls (Horseshoe Falls, American Falls and Bridal Veil Falls), the site was first recorded by the French explorer Samuel de Champlain in 1604. Maps of the 17th century record the inhabitants as the Niagagarega people, a group of the Iroquois, although the 19th-century American geographer Henry Schoolcraft claimed that the name was from the Mohawk language, originally pronounced *oh-ne-aw-ga-ra*. If you can ignore the other tourists, the massive flow of water (more than six million cubic feet or 168,000 cubic meters every minute at its peak) releases huge psychic and spiritual as well as physical energy. I have visited three times, and always enjoyed myself. The optional boat trip around the bottom of the falls is expensive but worth doing at least once, just for the experience—rain ponchos (waterfall ponchos, strictly speaking) are provided, and you need them, because it gets really wet down there.

THE USA

Denali, Alaska: Denali, the original Koyukon-Athabaskan tribal name of the tallest mountain in North America (20,310 feet or 6,190 meters), was renamed Mount McKinley in 1896, but the indigenous name was used again by the Alaska Geography Board since 1975, and officially restored nationally by Barack Obama in 2015, despite some opposition in Congress. The mountain now also has a national park all to itself. Over 100 mountaineers have died trying to reach Denali's summit, which was first reached in 1913, after many previous failed attempts. Athabaskan is the official, academic name of a very large language group, spoken all the way from Alaska down to Mexico, but its various native speakers prefer their own name, Dené. Denali (which also has

Niagara Falls, Ontario, Canada (Wikimedia Commons)

minor variants in the 32 languages of the North Athabaskan group) is considered a sacred site of great power by many tribes of Alaska and the Pacific Northwest.

Olympic Peninsula, Washington: The Olympic Peninsula in Washington State contains the Olympic National Forest, within which there are five designated wilderness areas. The temperate rain forest of the area is especially dense and ancient. The large trees, thick mosses and ferny undergrowth create a very wild and rugged place. Once you leave the main coastal road, you are in forest which has scarcely seen a single human footprint, if ever, even from the natives of the reservation lands close to the coast. It's as difficult to penetrate (on foot—there's no other way) as if it were tropical jungle, and I have felt both quickly tired and claustrophobic on my small number of expeditions. If you want to escape modern civilization for a while, this is the place to go, but be prepared for constant damp and mildewed tents—the rainfall, particularly on the western Pacific coast side, is spectacularly high.

Mount St. Helen's, Washington: Mount St. Helen's, about 50 miles to the northeast of Portland, is most famous today on account of its spectacular eruption in 1980, the deadliest and costliest volcanic eruption in American history (so far)—57 people were killed, and 250 homes and miles of roads and railway were destroyed. I have visited the volcano several times, and the vista from the side where the eruption burst forth is still awe-inspiring: the mountain exploded out from one side, rather than from the peak, and the millions of tons of ejected rock have created a vast, sterile scar of a slope. Close by the mountain there is a lava tunnel, created by retreating lava when the volcano was first formed. Fighting off my severe claustrophobia (I struggle even with ordinary elevators), I have managed to walk through the entire tunnel, and found it an inspiring and moving experience—the polished, glass-like rock is very beautiful.

Mount Hood, Oregon: The slopes of Mount Hood are where members of our "prayer family" go on solo vision quests. My wife had an interesting encounter with a lynx on one of her quests, and still talks about the experience to this day, feeling the animal's protective spirit to be always with her. Mount Hood is also where we have gathered large stones for our sweat-lodge fire. The still potentially active volcano is called Wy'east by the local Multnomah tribe. It stands about 50 miles to the southeast of Portland, and is prominently visible, even from that distance, often remarkably beautiful at either sunrise or sunset, when the snow-covered slopes (even in high summer) turn radiant pink. According to Multnomah legend, Sahale or the Great Spirit had two sons, Wy'east and Pahto, who both fell in love with the same young woman, called Loowit by the Klickitats and Lawetlat'la by the Cowlitz people, who could not choose between her two suitors. In their jealous arguments, the three destroyed much land and many villages. In fury, Sahale turned them all into volcanoes: Loowit or Lawetlat'la became Mount St. Helen's, Pahto became Mount Adams, and Wy'east became Mount Hood.

Mount Hood, Oregon (U.S. Department of Transportation/Federal Highway Administration)

Yellowstone National Park, Wyoming/Montana/Idaho: Yellowstone was the first national park in America, and probably in the world. Its existence was signed into law by President Ulysses S Grant in 1872. It covers just under 3,500 square miles (9,000 square kilometers) and has a huge range of habitats, plants and wildlife, including free-ranging bison, wolves, elk and grizzly bears. Native American tribes have lived in the region for over 11,000 years. Obsidian weapon points, either arrowheads, knife blades or spear points, have been found dating from that antiquity, and there is evidence that the Clovis people traded such artifacts to very distant locations. The Shoshone, Nez Perce and Crow tribes have also been settlers in Yellowstone. The park's most famous attraction is Old Faithful, a geothermal geyser, but Old Faithful and the park's many hot springs are a reminder of the underlying volcanic activity, and several authorities have expressed concern that a major eruption or other volcanic event is long overdue at Yellowstone. Huge as the park is, it is so popular that certain areas become quite crowded in high summer, but it is always worth a visit, and the huge variety of living plants and animals, as well as wild terrains, is guaranteed to please any aspiring or practicing Druid.

El Capitan, Yosemite National Park, Mariposa County, Northern California: *El Capitan* is a 3,000-foot (900-meter) natural rock formation in Yosemite National Park, a favorite place for rock climbers and base jumpers (now banned, after a death and several serious injuries), as well as a few devout Druids. It is massively inspiring. The name Yosemite comes from the Miwok people and means "killer," referring to the driving out and perhaps slaughter of a renegade tribe from the area, but with a new relevance following the base-jumping deaths. The Yosemite National Park is a great representation of the Druidic commitment to nature and the protection of our planet. President Abraham Lincoln and the pioneer Scottish-American environmentalist John Muir were instrumental in its creation, and it led to the development of the entire national park movement. About half of California's 7,000+ plant species are found in Yosemite, which has five different vegetation zones: alpine, subalpine, higher montane forest, lower montane forest and chaparral.

Cahokia Mounds, Missouri: Cahokia Mounds is a National Historic Landmark and one of only 23 UNESCO World Heritage sites in the

El Capitan, Yosemite National Park, Northern California (Mike Murphy)

United States. First settled in about 400 CE, from about 600 CE to about
900 CE it was the site of a pre–Columbian city, which, in the nature of
Native American settlements, is something of a rarity. It is the largest
and most complex pre–Columbian archaeological site north of Mexico.
Several different tribes are believed to have co-existed in the same area,
including the Omaha, Osage, Kaw and Ponca. A suggestion is that the
three-crop rotation of maize, beans and squash, which later became
standard agricultural practice in many tribal nations, was first introduced and developed at Cahokia. As mentioned in Chapter 1, a wooden
circle called Woodhenge has been built at the site which imitates the
Woodhenge near Stonehenge in England.

Crater Lake, Oregon: Quite apart from its sanctity, Crater Lake, which
is sacred to the Klamath nation, is simply one of the most beautiful
places I have ever seen in my life. The drive up to the caldera rim takes
you to an elevation between 7,000 and 8,000 feet, so I suppose I should
not have been surprised to see patches of snow on the ground even in
high summer, the first time I drove it. But it is the depth and color and
clarity of the water inside the caldera that takes your breath away. No
stream or river feeds the lake, or flows out of it: its water evaporates and
is replaced by snow and rain. It has been estimated that it takes about
250 years for all the water in the lake to be replaced. It is the deepest
lake in the United States, and its blue is of an intensity and clarity which
is impossible to describe—you have to see it. There are two little islands
in the lake, one appropriately called Wizard Island. There are pleasure
boats on the lake itself, but I have never been on one. The caldera is
about five or six miles across its diameter, and driving around the whole
of it takes a surprising couple of hours or more on the slow, narrow
road.

Mount Shasta, California: Like Mount Hood, Mount Shasta is a still
potentially active volcano. It is sacred to several tribal nations, including
the Okwanuchu and the Siskiyou. Unlike Mount Hood (and most other
volcanoes, for that matter) it has a city of about 3,400 people close to its
summit (less than 9 miles), also called Mount Shasta although it was
once called Sisson. Fishing, hiking, climbing and skiing are all popular
activities for locals and tourists alike. Even more than with Mount
Hood, if the volcano ever does erupt, the damage and loss of life would
be considerable.

The California Redwoods: Druids love trees, none more so than me, so
the California Redwoods are very special to me. The size of the trees is
legendary, but it is not until you are in amongst them that you realize
quite how huge they are. I have a photo of me and my son driving in our

little red Toyota truck through the trunk of a California Redwood: the tree was so big that they cut a road-wide tunnel right through its base, but I understand that particular tree has since died and fallen. Cumulatively, a forest of these giant trees is almost overwhelmingly beautiful and inspirational. A good starting place is Big Basin Redwoods State Park, about 22 miles northwest of Santa Cruz.

The Devil's Tower, Wyoming: You have already seen this very famous landmark if you watched the film *Close Encounters of the Third Kind*. Also called Bear Lodge Butte, it stands a dramatic 1,267 feet (386 meters) high near Sundance in northeastern Wyoming. President Teddy Roosevelt declared it the first United States National Monument in 1906. It now attracts about 400,000 visitors a year, of whom about 4,000 are climbers. William Rogers and Willard Ripley did actually fix a wooden ladder to it in 1893, which was used by some 215 people, the last of them in 1927, the bottom 100 feet later being removed for safety reasons in the early 1930s.

The Medicine Wheel, Bighorn National Forest, Wyoming: The Medicine Wheel is a stone circle, about 80 feet (24 meters) in diameter,

The Devil's Tower, Wyoming (photograph by Doug Olson)

which functions as an astronomical alignment in the same way as many of Britain's ancient stone circles, although the largest of its stones is only about the size of a home-made bread loaf. It lies close to the summit of Medicine Mountain in the Bighorn National Forest, in the territory of the Crow nation, although the Crow deny having built it, saying that it was put there by ancient ancestors. For the Crow and others, the circle and the mountain in general are used for fasting and vision quests. Although the Medicine Wheel is in Crow territory, it is also used by the Arapaho and other tribes. The sacred stones are close to the summit of the mountain (9,462 feet or 2,939 meters), which makes reaching the monument a long and steep climb. The trail shows many ancient signs of grooving and cutting away of the rock by travois, the traditional native two-pole sled, supporting the Crow claim that the site was created and first used thousands of years ago.

Monument Valley, Arizona/Utah: The massive buttes of Monument Valley first became widely known through the films of John Ford, but they have since been used so often by other film makers that one look at them is enough to signal, "This is the Wild West," even though the valley itself is only about five square miles in area, while the rest of the West is thousands upon thousands of times bigger. The valley is located

Monument Valley, Arizona/Utah (photograph by Massimo)

in Navaho County on the Arizona/Utah border, not far from the Four Corners. It lies within the tribal area of the Navaho National Reservation, and its Navaho name is *Tsé Bii' Ndzisgaii* ("Valley of the Rocks"). There are guided tours (for a fee), or you can pay an access fee to drive your own car on a 17-mile long dirt road, which may take two to three hours, weaving around and between the desert rocks and stopping to take lots of pictures.

Sedona, Arizona: Sedona is a modern city of about 10,000 people in the northern Verde Valley region of Arizona. It has sandstone rocks as red and almost as distinctive as those in Monument Valley, but it is of interest to our current purpose because it was the site of one of the earliest Native American settlements, dating back to about 9000 BCE and possibly even as far back as 11500 BCE. These unnamed early hunter-gatherers had left by about 300 CE. About 650 CE, the Sinagua people came to settle in the valley. They in turn left in about 1400, but left rock art and other artifacts behind them. The Yavapai arrived about 1300, living separately from the Sinagua. The Apache nation arrived about 1450. Both the Yavapai and Apache were nomadic or semi-nomadic, often following the buffalo herds. In 1876, in a forced march which has since become infamous, the Yavapai and Apache tribes of Verde Valley, about 1,500 people in all, were rounded up and made to walk, in mid-winter, the 180 miles to the San Carlos Indian Reservation. Several hundred of them died. In 1900, about 200 survivors or descendants of survivors of the march abandoned the San Carlos Reservation and returned to the Verde Valley, where they lived as a combined Yavapai-Apache nation. Sedona and the Verde Valley are therefore sacred sites of great significance to today's Native Americans, both those of the Yavapai-Apache nation and those of other nations, who still think of the forced march to San Carlos as a callous and calculated act of genocide, never to be forgotten.

10. The Tree Alphabet
and Calendar

You could spend a whole lifetime studying Celtic and Druidic lore and tradition (many people already have) and still find yourself with countless further undiscovered areas to explore. In this brief introduction, I shall restrict myself to a single topic, the Celtic Druidic tree alphabet and associated calendar.

The Ancient Celtic Agricultural Cycle

Bede, writing in the 8th century CE, began his ecclesiastical history of Britain with an impressive, almost lyrical, description of its natural resources:

> Britain excels for grain and trees, and is well adapted for feeding cattle and beasts of burden. It also provides vines in some places, and has plenty of land and water-fowls of several sorts; it is remarkable also for rivers abounding in fish, and plentiful springs. It has the greatest plenty of salmon and eels; seals are also frequently taken, and dolphins, as also whales; besides many sorts of shell-fish, such as mussels, in which are often found excellent pearls of all colours.... There is also a great abundance of cockles, of which the scarlet dye is made.... It has both salt and hot springs, and from them flow rivers which furnish hot baths.... Britain also has many veins of metals, as copper, iron, lead and silver; it has much and excellent jet, which is black and sparkling, glittering at the fire, and when heated, drives away serpents.[1]

Agriculture and husbandry have changed enormously since the time of the ancient Celts, of course, but the main crops and livestock are still familiar to us today: oats, barley and wheat, cattle, horses, pigs, goats and chickens. The main differences between then and now would be the size of the overall population (probably less than two million then as opposed to today's approximately 65 million) and the area of land under cultivation (less than 1 percent as opposed to today's approximately 25 percent). The so-called Roman roads (because the Roman military paved them, although there is increasing evidence that it was the Celts themselves who created them in the first place) would have traversed country thick with seemingly endless native forest, crossed many a moor and marsh, and great tracts of land would still have been wild.

Pliny tells us that the Celtic year began in July, like the Athenian year. Although Robert Graves and others have reconstructed a Celtic calendar which begins and ends around Midwinter, early Celts may well have reckoned the years from Midsummer to Midsummer. The famous Coligny Calendar, from first-century Gaul, is definitely Celtic, but it is too heavily influenced by Roman traits to be relied on for absolute evidence of early practice. Presumably the general administrative calendar would have been Romanized entirely, although the extent to which rural tribes would have paid any attention to it remains moot. While there may well have been Roman feasts and holidays (including Christian ones after the Empire converted in the 4th century), the Druidic lunar calendar survived well into the 18th century in rural areas of England and Scotland and was probably all that was needed by early Celtic farmers. There are still remote areas in the Highlands and Islands to this day where local people use the phases of the Moon to describe short stretches of time and hardly refer to the regular solar calendar at all. Even the names of the solar months came into Gàidhlig comparatively recently.

Hunting continued as a main source of food provision, but the territorial nature of Celtic tribal society early established pasture land, grasslands, meadows and crop fields as essential, and it seems likely that the ancient slash-and-burn system was also replaced very early by some form of crop rotation or laying fields fallow in grass, rye or clover to recover their fertility. Fuel would have been abundantly available from the forest, and there is evidence that gorse would have been used for hedging and a variety of other timbers for buildings, tools and weapons. Charcoal burning would have been an important local industry to provide fuel for the blacksmith. The Cornish place-name Kenidjack is derived from *keunys*, meaning a place abundant in kindling or fuel; the Welsh and Breton cognates are *cynnud* and *keuneud* respectively.

A reliable water supply from streams, rivers or wells would also have been of paramount importance, and there is considerable evidence of sources of water, including springs, lakes and natural holy wells, being venerated since earliest times in Druidism. Fishing would have added freshwater fish and seafood, like crabs, clams and mussels, to the tribe's diet, as well as dabs, codling, sea bass and other fish caught easily close to shore. Salmon were netted during the annual spawning, and were specially venerated in Druidic lore, as they still are.

Aristocrats and Druids may well have avoided manual agricultural labor, but the vast majority of the population would have contributed at some point to the highly labor-intensive work of food production. Pliny says there were two hay harvests, one early and one late in the year, which accords with his suggestion of a calendar which began at Midsummer. The amount of fodder would determine how many animals could be kept alive over winter. The rest would be slaughtered in autumn and the meat salted. Early Celts used both wooden and metal agricultural tools, including iron-soled ploughs. As soon as the first winter frosts had broken up the ground, the fields were double-ploughed, first north to south, then east to west, so that the fields were generally square in shape. (The English later ploughed their land in narrower strips, a "furrow long"—the origin of the word furlong.) The draught animals were mostly oxen—Celtic horses were generally too small and light for such work. Crop fields were not hedged generally; it is possible that they were protected from predatory animals by child lookouts. However, livestock could be contained by light wickets or fences of ash stakes with hazel twigs woven between them, or by improvised fences of gorse and bramble.

Winter was a lean time. The select livestock, from which next year's herds would grow, were fed on hay and restricted to enclosures; the rest were slaughtered. Pigs, horses and sometimes cattle would share living space with humans, all helping each other to keep safe and warm. The seeds of the fat hen plant, dried mushrooms, dried fruit and berries, and nuts—especially the highly-prized hazelnut—would supplement the basic winter diet of oat porridge, barley meal and very occasional salted meat or fish. Leaves of brooklime, bittercress and other watercresses were gathered and chewed for their "magical" healing properties, which actually consisted in their high vitamin C content.

The Romans brought new foodstuffs with them to Britain, including cherries, rabbits and peas, and developed oats (which were known and eaten in Scotland, but considered a wild weed in the south) as a cereal crop. Of these, peas were by far the most important. The Roman army diet was, in fact, essentially vegetarian, consisting almost entirely of bread and pease-porridge or pease-pudding made from dried peas, which were easy to grow, easy to dry and store, easy to carry in bulk, easy to cook, high in protein, filling and sustaining, and reasonably tasty, especially with a little salt and some local wild onion or wild garlic or other vegetables and hedge fruit. There is, however, some evidence from bones and other archaeological remains in British and German forts that the army also occasionally ate ox, sheep, pork and goats, as well as poultry, fish and shellfish where available.[2] The Celts probably added peas to their diet as a winter staple very soon after the Roman occupation (unless, like beans, they may have been considered taboo, as they were to Pythagoras and his followers, because breaking wind was thought to be the sound of another soul leaving the body).

Cattle raids, which are frequently mentioned in the vernacular tales, would in reality most frequently have been undertaken by desperate and hungry tribes or clan septs against richer and more powerful neighbors. Winter was not a good time for warfare, and cattle raids were merely a special kind of warfare, conducted mostly as autumn turned into winter. The Táin Bó Cúailnge or Cattle Raid of Cooley, the central text of the Ulster Cycle in early Irish Celtic mythology, tells the story of the Connacht queen Medb and her husband Ailill raiding Ulster to steal the magical stud bull Donn.

The Festivals

There were great mythological and calendrical cycles embedded in the agricultural cycle, and they survive to this day in the themes of the annual festivals. Although the actual dates would almost certainly have been set by a lunar calendar, they are celebrated nowadays on or near solar dates of the modern calendar, as follows: Imbolc or Oimelg, the festival of milk, of lambs, of birth, of the new spring, on or about February 1st; Beltan or Beltaine, the *tan* or "fire" of the God Belinus or Beli Mawr, the celebration of the Son or young male God, when livestock and humans passed between two fires for purification and fertility, on or about May 1st; Lughnasadh or Lughnasa, the *nasadh* or "commemoration" instituted by Lugh or Hugh, the great Father-God, the festival of the great harvest, on or about August 1st; and Samhain, the closing down of the year, the beginning of winter, on or about November 1st. These four festivals marked the original great stations of the ancient Celtic year, and, along with the spring and autumn equinoxes and Midsummer and Midwinter, the eight annual festivals are now widely acknowledged and celebrated by most Pagans in many countries.

Professor Alexander Thom suggested that prehistoric peoples divided the year into sixteen equal periods, rather than eight.[3] Aubrey Burl, who wrote extensively about Stonehenge and later collaborated with Thom, produced a table correlating an eight-station Celtic cycle of festivals with the later Christian festivals which came to overlay them:

Solar Alignments Related to Celtic and Christian Festival Dates

		AZIMUTHS AT 55°N		FESTIVALS	
DATE	DECLINATION	SUNRISE	SUNSET	CELTIC	CHRISTIAN
8 May	+ 16.6°	60°	300°	Beltane	Whitsun
21 June	+ 23.9°	45°	315°	Midsummer	St. John's Feast
9 August	+ 16.7°	60°	300°	Lughnasadh	Lammas
23 September	+ 0.4°	90°	270°	Equinox	Harvest Festival
6 November	- 16.3°	119°	214°	Samhain	All Souls, All Saints
21 December	- 23.9°	135°	225°	Midwinter	Christmas
5 February	- 16.2°	119°	241°	Imbolc	Candlemas
23 March	+ 0.4°	90°	270°	Equinox	Easter[4]

These correlations are very obvious and tell us a lot of important things all at once: firstly, the ancient Celts clearly had a sufficient degree of astronomical knowledge to relate their festivals precisely to cosmic events; secondly, the resulting festivals were of sufficient importance to have survived over a very long period of time; and thirdly, their power and significance must have been very considerable for church authorities to have aligned subsequent Christian festivals so closely to these originally Druidic calendrical stations of the year.

The Mythological Cycle

Going by the names and nature of the Gods and Goddesses associated with it, there is a very clear mythological pattern to the annual cycle. The four original major festivals commemorate Mother, Son, Father and Daughter, in that order. With the four other festivals added, they make a complete journey.

Imbolc

If the year begins at Midwinter (24th of December, according to Graves), then the first major festival of the year is Imbolc or Oimelg, on or about the 1st of February. The festival is widely dedicated to the Goddess Brigit, also called Brigid, Bridget, Bríd or Bride, and very closely associated with the Christian Saint Brigid or Bridget. This is the time of the first lambing. In practical terms, it meant the beginning of the break on winter's grip, with fresh milk and new cheese brightening up the dull winter diet.

The Christian festival of Candlemas, which is officially dated the 2nd of February, celebrates the purification of the Virgin Mary and the presentation of Christ to the Temple. As in Lupercalia, the Roman festival of February 15th, the lighting of candles was an important part of the celebration. Some Protestants later objected to the celebration of motherhood implied by Candlemas, branding it "Popish," but perhaps recognizing the deep underlying Pagan element and finding it disturbing. Imbolc is the celebration of the Mother, who will cross the long bridge over Midsummer and become the Daughter at Samhain.

The Vernal Equinox

As the first fox and badger cubs were born in the wild, the first spring flowers appeared in abundance. Catkins formed, like lambs' tails. The first ploughing was done, ready for the spring planting of barley and black oats (grey oats were for the autumn planting). Rye or clover was planted in poor soil. Barley was used as a main food staple, for bread, and to make beer. Some of the larger animals would be sent out to graze. The spring pastures were often still wet and cold, and supplementary hay or turnips might still be needed in the fields.

Beltan

Beltan, also Beltane or Beltaine, is the celebration of the God Bel, also called Beli, Belin or Belinos, perhaps related to the Cananite name Ba'al in the Old Testament of the Bible, which is actually a title, meaning "master." The variant Belenos is found in early inscriptions in Gaul and northern Italy. Beli Mawr ("Great Beli") appears in the *Mabinogi* as a British king and founder of the Welsh dynasties. Bel was the name of a Babylonian God, and Belili was a Sumerian Goddess of the Moon, trees and the Otherworld, a sort of amalgam of Diana and Hecate, so the name element *Bel-* appears to be of very great antiquity. It appears in the Latin *bellus* (also *bella* and *bellum*), meaning "beautiful," and perhaps in the Irish Gaelic *bile*, which has four significant meanings: a tree, usually large and sacred; a roof-tree or rafter; a scion or very distinguished person, particularly a judge or arbitrator; the corn marigold. Mediaeval Latin *billa* and *billus*, perhaps borrowed from the Irish, meant "branch" and "trunk" respectively.

The principal attested Druidic ceremony at Beltan was the driving of livestock between two fires for healing and purification after their winter confinement and in preparation for sending them into the summer pastures. Livestock emerging from the rigors of winter would, indeed, be prone to disease, particularly if the grazing land was still cold and wet and the grass still thin and dark from winter. Humans would also walk between the fires, or jump over a single fire. The higher the leaps over the flames, the higher the crops would grow. They would celebrate in lots of other ways, too, including what the 16th-century Christian pamphleteer Philip Stubbes euphemistically refers to as a night of "pleasant pastimes" before the daytime ceremony:

> All the young men and maids, old men and wives, run gadding over night to the woods, groves and hills, where they spend all the night in pleasant pastimes. In the morning they return bringing with them birch and branches of trees, to deck their assemblies. There is a great Lord over their pastimes, namely Satan, Prince of Hell. The chiefest jewel they bring is their Maypole. They have twentie or fortie oxen, every one having a sweet nosegay of flowers on the tip of his horns, and these oxen drag the Maypole (this stinking idol, rather) which is covered with flowers and herbs, bound round with string from top to bottom and painted with variable colours.[5]

(We generously ignore "Satan, Prince of Hell" and "stinking idol" as big-oted insults and aberrations.) Bel is the young-god counterpart of the old-god Brân (or Lugh, or the Dagda), in the same way that Jupiter was the counterpart of Saturn and Zeus was the counterpart of Cronos. As we shall see shortly, he is the oak God who comes before the holly God in the sacred calendar. Beltan is the celebration of the Son, who will cross the short bridge over Midsummer and become the Father at Lughnasadh.

Midsummer

High summer is the permanent season in Afalon or Avallen, the After-world. In the real world, it was a time of long days in the fields. In a good year there might be two or even three hay harvests, each of them critical for surviving the following winter. Even barley and oats might be harvested early if they had prospered through a warm spring. At Midsummer, everything green—weeds included—grows almost fast enough to see the movement, so there would have been a sudden abundance of anything that was both green and edible, and it was important to take advantage of the sudden growth. The Cornish saying is, "*Yn hav, por' kov gwav*" ("In summer, remember winter").

Medicinal flowers would be picked and dried, ready for winter coughs and colds. Borage, with its blue, star-shaped flowers and grey-green leaves, was chewed raw, like wild or cultivated mint leaves, to lighten and exhilarate the mind, particularly before battle. Marjoram was crushed, its oil producing a useful painkiller, its flowering tops yielding a useful purple dye for wool. Other summer-cropped dye plants were woad (blue), madder (brown or red), weld (yellow) and buckthorn berries (green). Bilberries and cranberries would be ripe in the wetlands of the moors: they were too tart to eat with any pleasure by themselves, but were packed with vitamins and easily boiled down into sauces or syrups to accompany meat. Rowan berries and rose hips, pithy and quite tasteless in themselves, are similarly rich in vitamins and were also gathered and boiled down into jams or medicinal syrups, usually with honey.

Lughnasadh

Lughnasadh (also Lughnasa, *Lúnasa* in Irish Gaeilge, *Lùnastal* in Scottish Gàidhlig and *Luanistyn* in Manx Gaelg), which takes place nominally on or about the 1st of August in the solar calendar, was traditionally celebrated in Ireland from mid–July until mid–August, and, remarkably, still survives to this day in some contemporary events. It involved many fairs and markets, some regional as well as local, athletic contests, horse races and other sporting events, and festivals and competitions in music and poetry. There were many harvest activities, including the eating of first fruits, the bilberry being especially venerated, and traditionally the slaying and spit-roasting of a bull or ox. Several of the original Pagan events persist to this day, usually cloaked in Christian names. The hill-top and mountain walks and picnics have been Christianized as "Bilberry Sunday," "Mountain Sunday," or "Garland Sunday." The famous three-day Puck Fair, *Aonach an Phoic* ("Fair of the He-Goat"), held every 10th of August in Killorglin, County Kerry, is a direct continuation of a Pagan Lughnasadh ritual: a wild goat is captured and brought down from the mountainside, where he is crowned (by a chosen local primary school girl, called the "Queen of Puck"), put in a gilded cage, fed to his heart's content (and given generous draughts of Guinness sometimes, as I have witnessed), and paraded widely about the area, before being returned safe and well (considerably fatter and often less sober) to his mountain home. For the three days, the pubs are legally allowed to stay open until 3.00 a.m., as opposed to the normal 2.00 a.m. (In my experience, rural pubs in Ireland open and close whenever they choose.)

The eponymous God of the festival is Lugh, who appears in several guises and forms in both the Goidelic and Brythonic traditions. Lugh instituted the festival in honor of his foster-mother, Tailtiu, after whom the Teltown Fair is named. He is the foster-son of the sea God, Manannán mac Lir. He is the father of the hero and demi–God, Cú Chulainn. He has many additional names or attributes, among them: *Lámfada* ("Long Arm" or "Long Hand"); *Lonnbéimnech* ("Ferocious Striker"); *Conmac* ("Hound-Son"); and *Ildánach* ("Many-Skilled"). Lughnasadh is the celebration of the Father, who will cross the long bridge over Midwinter to become reincarnated as the Son at Beltan.

The Autumn Equinox

By the time of the Autumn Equinox, most of the main harvests were completed and some early planting of winter barley, wheat and grey oats might begin. In traditional Celtic society, the autumn harvests were absolutely critical, literally a matter of life or death. The surest way to judge the ripeness of the crop was by pulling a few ears and rolling them between the finger and thumb to see how plump and yielding the grain felt. The longer it was allowed to stand and ripen fully, the greater the final yield, but the longer it stood unharvested, the greater the danger that it might be spoiled or destroyed by rain, wind, flood, or even—after a lightning strike—by fire. Judging the exact, critical and propitious moment for the harvest was a delicate task, one in which the Ovates and Druids no doubt played an essential role.

Once begun, harvesting and gathering food and other essentials for winter would occupy every member of the *tuath*. Stalks would be scythed by hand and gathered in loose stooks, to be gathered into larger stacks later. Hand threshing and winnowing separated useful grain from chaff. Grain was stored in woven baskets and sacks. In the woods, ceps, blewits, chanterelles and other edible fungi would be collected and dried ready for winter. The final hay harvest would determine how many and which animals would be allowed to live through the coming winter. With luck, calving would continue right through the summer and autumn, because every cow delivered of a healthy calf would continue to give nourishing milk through the lean months. Cattle were the most valuable of all the livestock, and their number was the most obvious indicator of the tribe's overall wealth. Goats were easiest to keep, because they were hardy, could eat almost anything, and could tolerate the rigors of tough or mountainous country. Sheep needed more management, because they generally required better pasturage, but they were more valuable for meat than goats and, especially, for wool used to make clothing. (Celtic woolen cloaks were of such high quality that they were exported to Rome and across the whole Empire.) Pigs gave excellent meat (Celts preferred wild boar, but home-grown pork was a good alternative), but they were big eaters and susceptible to cold weather (and, paradoxically, to sunburn), so they had to be adequately housed in winter (and given shade in high summer). Horses were immensely valuable, for transport and for warfare, but they also needed a lot of feed and upkeep in the winter. We don't know for certain what the Gaulish practice was, but it seems unlikely that the Celts of Britain and Ireland ate horse flesh: it was probably taboo, with the horse-Goddess Epona so widely venerated. Horse meat is regularly eaten in modern France and Brittany, but not at all in Britain or Ireland (other than when unscrupulous suppliers secretly and illegally adulterate minced beef with it).

Samhain

Samhain (pronounced approximately *sa-wayn* usually, but *sa-mayn* is also heard in Scottish Gàidhlig) is the Goidelic word for November. In Scottish Gàidhlig the full name of the month is *An t-Samhain*, pronounced approximately *an-ta-wayn*. In Irish Gaeilge, *Lá Samhna* (*laa-saw-nuh*) is the first of November or All Hallows, and *Oíche Shamhna* (*oykh-yuh-haw-nuh*) is Hallowe'en, the "e'en" or "evening" of All Hallows.

Two Pagan traditions have grown up around Samhain, directly connected to each other, and, although they are both well known, my personal view is that neither has anything much to do with Drudism or even Paganism, although I know many Pagans will be shaking their heads as they read the paragraphs below and disagreeing vehemently, so deeply have these two traditions become embedded in our general culture. Bear with me, if you can.

The first false Pagan tradition, in my view, is Hallowe'en, and everything it has now come to represent. The Christian ceremony of All Saints, as the name suggests, celebrates the souls of all the Christian Saints, and prays especially for the souls of those Saints who, for whatever reason, are still waiting in Purgatory to be released so that they can ascend into Heaven. Druids don't believe in Purgatory (nor do some Christians—there is no mention of Purgatory anywhere in the Bible), nor in the Christian vision of Heaven. All Saints, also called All Hallows and Hallowmass, was and remains established in the Christian calendar on the 1st of November. However, according to legend, a Breton bishop, called Bishop Odo, overheard tragic wailing coming from a deep cave, and decided that what he was hearing were the cries of agony and misery from all the *other* souls in Purgatory (i.e., those who were *not* saints, and therefore had no special prayer day of their own) bewailing their fate and begging that prayers might be said for them, too. So, the Church instituted a second prayer day, All *Souls* on November 2nd, to follow All *Saints* on November 1st. Now everybody in Purgatory was covered by prayer, whether they were saints or not. The ordinary (Christian) people soon began leaving little gifts of food and drink in graveyards on the evenings before All Saints and All Souls, honoring the dead in Purgatory. Special cakes or loaves were made, which were called "soul-cakes." Christian traditions began sprouting up, saying that if you forgot or declined to bake soul-cakes or leave grave gifts, the dead would come after you in anger, seeking revenge. The whole trick-or-treat nonsense began from that fairly obscure Christian ritual. My own view is that Druids should have nothing whatsoever to do with Hallowe'en, or, for that matter, All Saints or All Souls, all of which, as far as I am concerned, are Christian rites that have little or no relevance to our Druidic beliefs. We should stick to celebrating Samhain as a Druidic festival, not a Christian one, or a mock Gothic event derived from Christian traditions.

The second false tradition grew out of the first one. The preoccupation with the dead roaming freely among the living and spooking everybody because they had a bad case of munchies for soul cakes led to the now very widely-held belief that the Veil separating the living, mundane world from the Afterworld or Otherworld grows especially thin at Samhain. Suddenly, for one day only, the ancestors and the Gods and the Goddesses can all come into the world visiting, and therefore, for that one day only, the world is charged with divine presence. Consequently, this day marks the beginning and end of the Pagan year. I think this is nonsense. In my view, which I know many will disagree with, this continuation and extension of what was originally a minor (and fairly recent) Christian rite only serves to take us even further away from a genuinely Druidic viewpoint. I believe that ancestors, spirits, Gods and Goddesses pass through the Veil and into our hearts and lives every single second of the year, and they don't need a special dispensation or pass on October the 31st or November the 1st or November the 2nd, days which I think were chosen by Christians for their own purposes, in order to come into our living world. Nor do I think we have any reason to fear the dead, or "protect" ourselves from their presence. In fact, I would go further and say that the very idea of deities, ancestors and the dead being remote and apart from us most of the time, and only within reach for one day or one special festival, goes directly against the truth of *anam* or soul, which is that life and spirit are in all things, always, and that our ancestors and the dead are always with us, always present, always willing to be with us if we call for them.

Hallowe'en or Samhain pumpkins began as hollowed-out turnips in England in Elizabethan times. At Hinton St. George in Somerset they were called "punkies," and the lighting of the little tallow candles inside them was accompanied by the lighting of bonfires. After the failed attempt to blow up the British Parliament in 1605, the tradition began of adding a mannequin of one of the leading plotters, Guy Fawkes, to the bonfires. Guy Fawkes Night or Bonfire Night on the 5th of November is now a major British family and community tradition, when fireworks and bonfires are lit across the whole country, rather like Independence Day celebrations on July the 4th in America, although our bonfires always have a "Guy" or stick-and-rags figure placed on top of the fire to represent the burning of Guy Fawkes at the stake. Again, I don't see any reason why modern Druids should join in festivities celebrating the torture and execution of a dissenting English Roman Catholic by a Protestant British government in the early 17th century.

In the Irish tales, Samhain (along with Beltan) is one of the times when powerful, significant or magical events take place. It is at Samhain that the Dagda or Father-God mates with the Morrígan, the Great Queen, re-establishing the celestial marriage. It is at Samhain that the triple ritual killing of a king would take place, so that another might succeed him. Oenghus becomes a swan to rescue his beloved Caer at Samhain. Every year at Samhain, an evil goblin-like creature called Aillen destroys the halls of Tara, seat of the High King of Ireland, and every year the hero Fionn or Finn defeats the goblin's sleep spell by holding the point of his own spear against his forehead, thus staying awake long enough to counter the spell and restore the sacred palace. These legends are all to do with kingship (or queenship), inheritance and continuity, and certainly with spiritual power in both life and death, but they have no obvious connection with the Purgatory themes of the Christian rituals.

Samhain is the celebration of the Daughter, who will cross the short bridge over Midwinter to become the Mother at Imbolc.

Midwinter

Midwinter has a mish-mash of different festivals crammed into it, leading to potential confusions. For the most obvious reasons, when you get to the shortest day and the longest night, and you live in a world where you depend absolutely on the return of the Sun so that warmth and growth will return to the Earth, what you pray for is that the Sun will, indeed, regain her strength. That's why the Romans called their Midwinter festival *Dies Natalis Invicti Solis*, "The Day of the Birth of the Unconquered Sun." Prayers were offered to the Grandfather-God Saturn, if that's not too disrespectful a way to address him, the Roman equivalent of the Greek Cronos, the Father of Time, and therefore the controller of seasons, years, months and days. For that reason, the Midwinter festival was also known as the *Saturnalia*, and it had some jolly customs and rituals. It lasted for seven days, later extended to twelve, during which slaves and servants had very light duties only, or even switched places with their masters and mistresses to be waited on, usually to everyone's amusement and edification, although some disagreements (and even murders) occasionally resulted. It was a time of great feasting and drinking, popular items being figs, dates, plums, pears, fresh pomegranates and melons from Africa, cakes and pastries, nuts of every kind, and mulled wine. Courts, markets, government offices and schools were all closed for the holidays. Houses were decorated with branches, flowers (dried, or fresh if they were available) and painted ornaments. Families gave presents to each other wrapped in colored cloth, especially toys, sweetmeats and other treats to children. Special *Saturnalia* hymns were sung. Family members who lived abroad or far away would try to get back to the ancestral home for *Saturnalia* celebrations. There were superstitions about taking down the house decorations by the end of the twelve days of celebration.

Does any of this sound familiar? It should, because in the 3rd century the Christian Church decided that it needed to establish a birth date for Jesus Christ and start commemorating the event. There was no evidence of when he was actually born (some time in March has been postulated), so the Church authorities plumped for the *Saturnalia*, as a very popular festival, and simply grafted Jesus's birthday into the middle of those celebrations, which—whatever our religion, or none—have now become established in the western cultural tradition.

In the Celtic Druidic mythological cycle, Midwinter was the most significant transition of the year. The Daughter makes the short journey across the Bridge of Midwinter to become the new Mother. The Father ends his long decline by making the long journey across Midwinter to Beltan, where he will be reborn as the resurrected Son, and the cycle can continue again for all eternity.

The Solar Calendar of Months

It is clear that the ancient Druids used the month as a meaningful unit of time. Whatever reservations we may have about Roman infuence on the Coligny Calendar, its division into months, with the first half of each month marked MAT ("Good") and the second half marked ANMAT ("Un-Good," i.e., "Bad"), seems genuinely Celtic. However, the Celts almost certainly used lunar months (which are approximately 29 days long, so there are 13 months in every year), and probably, in a similar way to many other cultures, counted a day as the period from sunset to the following sunset, so "a day" really meant "a night and a day." That's why Samhain begins on the eve or evening of the 31st of October, rather than on the day of the 1st of November.

It is also highly likely that the MAT-ANMAT ("Good," "Un-Good") format is Celtic and original, except that it almost certainly refers to the pattern of the lunar month. As the Moon waxes towards the full, life becomes easier and better and sweeter—MAT—and it reaches its peak at Full Moon, when we are flooded by light, prosperity and good feeling. But then the Moon gradually begins to wane, and life becomes a little tougher and less sweet—ANMAT—until by New Moon everything seems to be either in stasis or in confusion, everything seems blocked or thwarted, and the Moon is far away, invisible. When New Moon passes, the MAT sequence begins again, to our great relief. I am so attuned to this cycle, and so familiar with its impact on me, that I can tell you on any given day exactly where we are in the lunar calendar.

But reconciling lunar months with solar years of approximately 365 days plus about a quarter of a day is fiendishly complicated. They only match up exactly every 18.9 years or so, which the Druids knew, and could calculate exactly, and which they observed in the many stone circles and alignments around them. (There is evidence in some megalith alignments that prehistoric scientists—no other word is possible—were even aware of the great cycle created by the slight tilt of the Earth's axis, which takes over 26,000 years to complete.) We know that the Druids named months, attributing a letter to each month, that letter also being the name of a tree. The Song of Amergin, briefly discussed in Chapter 5, was originally a secret codification of these month names and their sacred power and significance.

Robert Graves made a very careful and intelligent reconstruction of the solar calendar that might reflect this original calendrical tree-alphabet, which we shall look at very shortly, but it is worth noting that Isaac Bonewits was not the only person who thought that Graves was a "sloppy" scholar, and there have been many disagreements about the sequence, the exact dates, and some of the correspondences and sacred meanings which Graves identifies or infers. Although it has become very popular as a New Age calendar, there is no evidence that the ancient Celts or Druids used a solar calendar at all—in fact, it is almost certain that their calendar would have been lunar. To be fair, Graves himself (who could be unpleasantly dogmatic when he chose) was fully aware of the difficulties with the reconciled solar calendar and recognized that there would be many discrepancies.

If, for example, we take the solar year of 2016 and compare the Full Moons to the solar festival dates, we can see immediately that the solar and lunar alignments are all over the place, and would be difficult for a professional mathematician to follow, let alone an early Celtic plowman, even with Druidic assistance. (Dates for Midsummer, Midwinter and the Equinoxes vary from year to year.)

FESTIVAL	RITUAL SOLAR DATE	NEAREST FULL MOON	DISCREPANCY
Imbolc	1st February	24th January	– 8 days
Equinox	20th March	23rd March	+ 3 days
Beltan	1st May	22nd April	– 9 days
Midsummer	24th June	20th June	– 4 days
Lughnasadh	1st August	19th July	– 13 days
Equinox	22nd September	16th September	– 6 days
Samhain	1st November	14th November	+ 13 days
Midwinter	22nd December	14th December	– 8 days

So, here is the solar Celtic Druidic calendar, as reconstructed by Robert Graves, with the letter/month names, but we recognize that the solar dates do not and cannot ever align directly and completely with corresponding lunar months. You will see immediately that the sequence is quite different to our familiar ABC, and that the alphabet does not have exactly the same letters. Note also that two letters, S and C, have doubles or alternatives:

LETTER	NAME	PRONOUNCED	TREE	SOLAR DATES
B	Beth	*beh*	birch	24th December to 20th January
L	Luis	*loo-ish*	rowan	21st January to 17th February
N	Nion	*nee-un*	ash	18th February to 17th March
F	Fearn	*fyarn*	alder	18th March to 14th April
S	Saille	*sigh-yuh*	willow	15th April to 12th May
SS/Z	Straif	*strife*	blackthorn	"
H	(H)Uath	*(h)oo-uh*	hawthorn	13th May to 9th June
D	Duir	*doo-eer*	oak	10th June to 7th July
T	Tinne	*cheen-yuh*	holly	8th July to 4th August
C	Coll	*koll*	hazel	5th August to 1st September
CC/Q	Quert	*kayrsht*	apple	"
M	Muin	*moo-een*	vine	2nd September to 29th September

(LETTER)	(NAME)	(PRONOUNCED)	(TREE)	(SOLAR DATES)
G	Gort	*gorsht*	ivy	30th September to 27th October
Ng	Ngetal	*nyay-tal*	reed	28th October to 24th November
R	Ruis	*roo-eesh*	elder	25th November to 22nd December
*	*	*	*	23rd December

The 23rd of December is the "day" of the ritual phrase "a year and a day." It is the turning point of the year, and contains within it the entire story of birth, life, death and resurrection in the five vowels (seven if you add doubles), as follows:

AA	(Omega)	(*aw-may-guh*)	(palm)	birth
A	Ailm	*al-um*	silver fir	birth and childhood
O	Onn	*on*	gorse	adolescence
U	Ura	*oo-ra*	heather	maturity
E	Eadha	*ay-uh-huh*	poplar	old age
I	Idho	*ee-oh* or *yoo*	yew	death
II	Y	*ee*	mistletoe	death and resurrection

Graves argues that this vowel sequence spells out the once secret, sacred name of God, AA/A/O/U/E/I/II, AAAOUEII, Yahweh, or Jehovah.[6]

Beth begins the year because birch is the tree of new beginnings, and the older name for the letter, *Boibel*, is related to the stag or bull and the God Hercules. The seven tines of the stag's antlers are the seven months in prospect and in retrospect, because *Beth* is the seventh month after *Duir* and *Duir* is the seventh month after *Beth*.

Luis is the rowan, also known as the mountain ash and the quicken ("bringer of life"). It was often burned by ancient Druids before or during battle to produce a magic defensive "wall" of smoke. It is associated with a "wide flood on the plain" because "February Fill-Dyke" (an Anglo-Saxon nickname) was the season of floods.

Nion is the ash. Spelled *aesc* in Old English, it meant both "ash tree" and "spear." It is a "wind on the deep waters" because March winds dry up February's floods.

Fearn is the alder, the tree of the God Brân. It is the month when deer and cattle first give birth, and the birth month of Hercules, who was conceived the previous Midsummer. He lies, like a new-born fawn or calf, glistening on the grass, like "a shining tear of the sun."

Saille the willow, from whose bark the chief ingredient of aspirin, the pain-killing salicylic acid, was first derived, is the month when birds nest. The hawk of *Saille* was sacred to Boreas, the North Wind.

Uath or *Huath* is "fair among flowers" because the month is ruled by the blossom of the hawthorn. The Goddess Olwen ("White Track") has hair yellow as broom, fingers pale as wood-anemones, cheeks the color of roses, and white trefoil springs up from the grass wherever her feet tread.

Duir, the oak of summer, is "the god who sets the fire asmoke" because the traditional sacrificial fires of green oak lit on Midsummer Eve produced acrid smoke that stung the eyes.

Tinne, the holly month, was written like the Norse rune for the letter T, in the shape of a spear-point. (A capital-T shape, incidentally, was in all probability the shape of the "cross" on which Christ was crucified, and holly is Christ's tree.)

Coll was the nut month, and the hazel nut was the most prized of all. The salmon (who ate the hazel nuts of wisdom) was and remains "the King of the river-fish," as Graves puts it.

Muin, the vine, was and still is extremely rare in Britain, but the Celtic aristocracy learned from the Romans how to import wine in large quantities, and were very familiar with the mythology surrounding the plant. Wine has always been the drink of poets. British Poet Laureates were traditionally paid in wine, not in cash.

Gort, the ivy month, is also the month of the boar. It was in the form of a boar that the Egyptian Sun-God Set killed the God Osiris, lover of Isis. Fionn mac Cumhnaill shape-shifts into a boar before killing Diarmuid, lover of the Sun-Goddess Greine.

Ngetal, the month of the reed, is in Graves's words, "the month when the terrible roar of breakers and the snarling noise of pebbles on the Atlantic seaboard fill the heart with terror."[7]

In *Ruis*, the month of the elder tree, the wave returns to the sea and the year returns to its end and beginning. In the Irish tales, both Cú Chulainn and Fionn fight against the sea with sword and spear, and, like the English king Cnut or Canute, are not surprised to discover that it is a fight that they can never win.

Lastly, the vowels (AA)AOUEI(II) are "the secrets of the unhewn dolmen," the natural ("unhewn") and divine name of the living spirit, the *anam*, that is in all things. They spell out the eternal, never-changing sequence of birth, growth, life, death and resurrection.

Now we can revisit the ancient *Song of Amergin*, in a slightly tidied-up arrangement, below which I put my "translation" or explanation of the original poem:

> I am a stag of seven tines,
> I am a wide flood on a plain,
> I am a wind on the deep waters,
> I am a shining tear of the Sun,
> I am a hawk on a cliff,

I am fair among flowers,
I am a God who sets the head afire with smoke,
I am a battle-waging spear,
I am a salmon in the pool,
I am a hill of poetry,
I am a ruthless boar,
I am a threatening noise of the sea,
I am a wave of the sea.
Who but I knows the secrets of the unhewn dolmen?

I am B, *Beth*, birch, the proud stag with seven tines,
I am L, *Luis*, rowan, a flash-flood on the plain,
I am N, *Nion*, ash, a wild wind over the flood waters,
I am F, *Fearn*, alder, a new-born glistening tear of the Sun,
I am S, *Saille*, willow, the hawk nesting on the cliff,
I am H, *Huath*, hawthorn, blossoming among flowers,
I am D, *Duir*, oak, stinging your eyes with my sacred smoke,
I am T, *Tinne*, holly, shaking my sacred spear in battle,
I am C, *Coll*, hazel, the salmon who swims in the pool of wisdom,
I am M, *Muin*, vine, a hill of wine-rich poetry,
I am G, *Gort*, ivy, a deadly, ruthless, king-killing boar,
I am Ng, *Ngetal*, reed, the terrifying roar of the wild ocean,
I am R, *Ruis*, elder, the receding wave of the unconquerable sea.
Who but I knows the sacred sequence uncarved in ancient stone
    of A, *Ailm*, silver fir, birth,
    of O, *Onn*, gorse, growth,
    of U, *Ura*, heather, age,
    of E, *Eadha*, poplar, death,
    of I, *Idho*, yew, resurrection?

11. Modern Rituals and Liturgy

The world has changed very dramatically during the time in which modern Druidism has evolved. In the 19th century, and still in the 20th to a great extent, access to the knowledge and wisdom on which the Druidic reconstruction is founded was restricted to a small group of people, often scholarly and well heeled. That has all changed. Through the internet, vast amounts of material are now freely and widely available. Meetings which might have taken weeks or months of planning and considerable expenditure in time and money a hundred years ago can now take place instantly, across the whole world. Tony Taylor, cofounder of The Henge of Keltria, comments:

> The World Wide Web is an opportunity for Druids of various paths to link together in concert to help each other promote Druidism. Through the pages at our website we offer information from novices and experienced practitioners as well as links to other Druid organizations throughout the world. We now reach larger audiences that may not have the opportunity to discover the possibilities offered by Druidism any other way.[1]

Most Druid organizations now post ritual and ceremonial texts on their websites, some of them in great volume and variety, so it is comparatively very easy to access ritual material for just about any occasion and to suit just about any individual or group. The purpose of this section is to make some general comments about ritual and ceremonial practice in this chapter, and then in Chapter 12 to give a few selected examples of ritual text available through the internet. As always with Druidism, what you choose to do with it is up to you. You can join an organization of your own choosing. You can check out what groups are active close by you. You can find material online for your own use, or you can be inspired to write your own, following the examples from others.

There's a sort of Do-It-Yourself aspect to modern Druidism for many of us, particularly perhaps for solitary Druids like myself who won't allow others to rein them in and keep control. I think, for example, of how my wife and

I were married or hand-fasted, which was very much a self-directed, tailor-made, customized, bespoke operation. Once you have read the details of it, you may understand why I am hesitant to suggest ritual specifics to others.

We hand-fasted first just the two of us, face to face, each to the other, in the innermost circle of Avebury, sharing a pledge kiss, exchanging vows, and exchanging rings which depict the Ring of Brodgar in Orkney, her ring also containing a small moonstone. This was a private ceremony. The Order of WhiteOak hand-fasting ceremonial ritual (and probably several others) includes love-making, which in my view makes it also a private ceremony. (There have been and still are cultures where Uncle Ned, Aunt Nellie and the bucktooth cousins all watch while the bridal pair consummate the nuptials, but that's not for me, and in any case we were in Avebury Stone Circle in the middle of the day surrounded by other visitors.) The second part of the ritual, back in America some while later, was to hold a public hand-fasting ceremony, officiated by our friend and teacher and medicine-woman, helped by other members of our prayer family, beneath a venerable and very beautiful walnut tree, our *nemeton* for that occasion, on the banks of the Willamette River in Oregon, surrounded by family and friends, followed by a reception with music, food, wine, singing, dancing, face painting, kilts, poetry, more wine, and silly games. The completion of the circle, quite a while later, was to fly back to Britain, drive to the northernmost tip of Scotland, take the two-hour ferry across to Orkney, drive to the Ness of Brodgar, touch our Ring of Brodgar rings against each other and against the stones of the real and actual Ring of Brodgar, repeat our kisses and pledges, and finally complete the ritual. In other words, our hand-fasting was a triple-phase ceremony that took about four years and covered more than 32,000 miles.

The Prayer Space

For most Druids, the purpose of ritual is to restore our connection with nature, indeed with life itself. We also know that ancient Druidic practice was to worship in the open air, "before the Eye of Day," very often in places which were perceived as being charged with natural energy (particularly from rock or from water, or powerful trees), or places at which the spirits of the ancestors might gather, or *gorseddau* where important events or meetings had taken place, or places guarded or sanctified by a particular spirit, God or Goddess. As noted earlier, the word *nemeton*, often translated as "sacred grove," was used anciently to indicate such places.

It would be perfectly possible to conduct prayer, ritual or ceremony on a crowded commuter train heading into the city, or in a broom cupboard, but it should be obvious that a different kind of space would be preferable.

A sea shore, a glade in the deep forest, beside a thundering waterfall, or on a moor beneath a wide-open sky: these are the kinds of spaces that suggest themselves. But our situations and environments differ, and our holy places will differ too, depending on our circumstances. For me, prayer space always includes something from the natural world: flowers, a tree or trees, a rock or rocks, water. My indoor altar at home has photographs of my grandparents, parents and children, but also feathers and fur, some bones and small animal skulls, herbs, dried plants, small stones and seashells. My many outdoor prayer spaces are magnificently inviting: as I noted earlier, I am fortunate enough to live on a small Hebridean island that teems with wildlife and many rugged, natural spaces where other people are unlikely to intrude.

So, the first step in any ritual will usually be to establish and enter or re-enter the prayer space. The most natural and ancient shape for such a prayer space is a circle. It can be opened or indicated with a pointed finger, a sacred blade like a sword or athamé, a Druidic wand or staff, flower petals, water, or salt, or words, or steps, or any combination of those. Clockwise or sunwise rotation is called *deosil* in Wicca and Paganism generally, although a more accurate spelling in the original Gàidhlig is *deiseal*, pronounced approximately *jay-shal*. The opposite direction, anti-clockwise or anti-sunwise, is called *widdershins* in Lallans or Lowland Scots, and *tuathal* (*too-uh-hul*) in Gàidhlig. The original Irish spellings are exactly the same, but pronounced *desh-al* and *thoo-hal* (Munster dialect),[2] and have the additional meanings of "in a rightwards direction" or "to the right" and "in a leftwards direction" or "to the left" respectively. (*Tuathal* in Gàidhlig also means ill-favored or unlucky, or confused or agitated—the expression "*Chuir e tuathal mi*" means literally, "It put me anti-clockwise," but a better slang translation might be, "It threw me for a loop.") The *deiseal* direction is favored in Buddhism and Hinduism, as well as in Paganism. It has been conjectured that the modern practice of driving on the left in Britain and Japan has its origins in the habit of passing on the left-hand side of a temple or church or other holy place, in other words circling the holy place *deiseal*. The Scottish folklorist Màrtainn Màrtainn described some *deiseal* beliefs and customs in his *A Description of the Western Isles of Scotland* (1703):

> Some of the poorer sort of people in the Western Isles retain the custom of performing these circles sunwise about the persons of their benefactors three times, when they bless them, and wish good success to all their enterprises. Some are very careful when they set out to sea, that the boat be first rowed sunwise, and if this be neglected, they are afraid their voyage may prove unfortunate. I had this ceremony paid me when in Islay by a poor woman, after I had given her an alms. I desired her to let alone that compliment, for that I did not care for it; but she insisted to make these three ordinary turns, and then prayed that God and MacCharmaig, the patron saint of the island, might bless and prosper me in all my affairs. When a Gael goes to drink out of a consecrated fountain, he approaches it by going round the place from east to west, and at

funerals, the procession observes the same direction in drawing near the grave. Hence also is derived the old custom of describing sunwise a circle, with a burning brand, about houses, cattle, corn and corn-fields, to prevent their being burnt or in any way injured by evil spirits, or by witchcraft. The fiery circle was also made around women, as soon as possible after parturition, and also around newly-born babes.[3]

The circle can be small enough for a single person in a suburban bedroom, or large enough for a thousand people at an ancient monument like Stonehenge or Avebury. Most will obviously be somewhere in between. For several years, I lived close by the Twelve Apostles stone circle just to the north of Dumfries in Scotland, which is the seventh largest stone circle in Britain and the largest on the Scottish mainland. It was a very natural place for me to pray, especially since the local landowner, who is a friend, allowed his sheep and cattle to roam in the same field, so that I was often accompanied by inquisitive livestock during my prayers, which provided an entertaining diversion—I thought of them (and spoke with them) as fellow members of the congregation. Some years ago, after decades of visiting and creating prayer circles of every kind and in many different countries, I had a lightning-like moment of inspiration and revelation at the Twelve Apostles, and metaphorically thumped myself on the head for having taken so long to see it. (I think I did actually give myself a real slap.) Every time we create or enter a sacred circle, we simultaneously enter all the other circles we have entered previously or will enter in the future. In reality, there is only one circle. So, standing in the Twelve Apostles, or in Stonehenge, or in the circle I have drawn in my bedroom, or in the woods on my little Hebridean island, I am at one and the same time in every sacred circle, as if they were stacked vertically above and below and through me. I am perched on a limb of Yggdrasill. Time and space no longer have any conventional meaning. Standing in my little circle on the bedroom carpet, I am simultaneously at the center of Stonehenge, Avebury, the Twelve Apostles, Carnac, the Olympic Peninsula, Mount Hood, Crater Lake, the Ring of Brodgar, Boscawen-Un, Castlerigg, Long Meg and Callanais. All the ancestors and Gods and Goddesses I have ever invoked are in the circle with me, have always been there, and will always be there. Every prayer I have uttered is still a living prayer for all time, and the Word of immense holy power moves through infinite universes without hindrance. This was an enriching and massively empowering revelation, and I still wonder that it took me more than sixty years to receive it.

The prayer space needs to be closed as well as opened. In a sense, it never truly closes, since we carry the prayer and, more importantly, the result of our prayer into the everyday world once we are done. But, as many other Druids have observed, Druidism is a way of life as much as it is a religion, and it underpins not just acts of high ceremonial but also driving the car, washing the dishes and feeding the dog. In my view, the circle may (in fact, should) be closed *widdershins* or *tuathal*, although some would disagree. Needless to say, since Druids are environmentalists first and foremost, we leave any natural spaces as we found them, leaving no litter or detritus behind us; whatever you bring in, you take out.

The Invocation

Again, it is stating the obvious to say that the point of prayer or ritual is to be speaking to something or somebody. Even for those Druids who think of modern Druidism as predominantly a moral and ethical philosophy rather than as a religion, accepting prayer and ritual means accepting that we are communicating, even if it is only with the better nature within ourselves. And, as with any conversation, it is good manners to use the name of the person with whom you are speaking. For most Druids, invocation is the deliberate act of inviting a deity or a spirit to join and take part in the activity within the prayer space. In my view, it is best to do this simply. Here are some examples, taken from the Dun Brython group (https://www.dunbrython.org), which is "a group of polytheists aiming to research, recover and redistribute Brythonic spirituality to the best of our knowledge and wisdom."[4] In their sincerity and simplicity, these poems are excellent examples of invocation:

For Rigantona at Calan Mai

Rigantona, the gates of your world are open
As are the blossoms on the boughs
Scenting the air with Summer
As you ride across the land.

Rigantona, you are radiant in the dawn
As sunlight on the morning dew.
You are radiant at the middle-day
As the Sun climbs higher in the sky.

Rigantona, the evening twilight
Is suffused with your radiance.
As you are blessed we seek your blessing
Dwellers in your hallowed lands.

(Rigantona is a Brittonic reconstruction and name variant of the Goddess Rhiannon, wife of Pwyll and mother of Pryderi, associated with horses and the Gaulish Goddess Epona. Calan Mai is Welsh for the *Calends* or first day of May.)

Brigantica

Bride of our hearth
Bless this place
With warmth

With shelter
With fire that burns for us.

Bride of our streams
Of wells and water courses
Asperge our land
With rain
With dew.

Bride of the candles
Lit for your remembrance
Bright be your blessings
As the Sun climbs higher
In his Winter rising.

Bride of our company
Of links and friendship
Across Brigantia, the isles
Of your peoples:
Veil us within the bounds of belonging.

(Brigantica or Brigantia is the tutelary Goddess of the ancient Celtic northern British tribe the Brigantes, whose most famous monarch was Queen Cartimandua in the 1st century CE.)

Gwyn's Feast

Gwyn ap Nudd;
King under the hill,
Stag masked runner in the woodland,
Lord beyond the wall;
I offer you this meat as it is proper for me to do so
I offer you this drink as it is right for me to do so.

(Gwyn or Gwynn is the son of Nudd or Lludd, a warrior God who fights with Gwythr for the love of the Goddess Creiddylad every May Day until the end of time.)

The language of these poems is simple, but sincere and charged with a devotional energy so clear that you can almost hear it off the page. Invocations need not be poetic or fancy, just as long as they are polite. One of my regular prayer places is on the shore of Loch Nell in Gleann Lònain or Glen Lonan in Argyllshire, next to a hawthorn tree which, under the influence of the wind that almost always blows across the loch, has grown into a sort of twin, with two main trunks connected to each other at the base. Whenever I go there, I simply say, "Hello, Hawthorn Twins. I hope you're well. It's a beautiful day. I'm here to pray, and I ask you to join me."

If you don't know the name of the spirit or deity you are invoking, try simply listening for it. You will be astonished at how often you clearly "hear" the name of a particular tree, rock or stretch of water. If you don't, be patient and continue to be respectful. The name will come one day. If you are invoking a particular God or Goddess, be aware that they may have many names. Research them, find out about them, as you might if you suddenly became friends with someone very important or famous (as the Gods and Goddesses surely are). But be careful. True utterance has great power, but foolish or insincere utterance can cause great damage. In the Irish vernacular mythology, Nechtan, father (or husband) of Boann the eponymous Goddess of the River Boyne, guards Tobar Segais, "the Well of Wisdom." Boann approaches the well improperly, and is wounded as a result, and there is catastrophic flooding and subsequent destruction.

Ceisiwr Serith, a Druid interviewed by Ellen Evert Hopman, explains with elegant simplicity how we should approach invocation:

> In ancient times, most Pagans did not serve as priests or priestesses. There were professionals to do that. What the everyday Pagan did was to honor his ancestors, the deities he was personally attached to, and the local land spirits. You can be a good Pagan and do just that. In fact, you can't be a very good Pagan without doing that. Don't let your Coven, or your Grove, become a substitute for your home worship.... The prayers we have show us that there is a standard format to Pagan prayer, at least to Indo-European prayer. First the God is identified. With so many Gods to pray to, it is important to make this clear right off the bat. You can be straightforward: "I pray to Mithras," or more subtle, "God of Contracts, I pray to you." This is followed by titles and descriptions of the God. What you are doing here is explaining why the deity should pay attention to you. You are leading up to your own request. Did the God do something like this in the past? Then he is more likely to do it for you, so remind him of it. Plus the reminders of the God's deed amount to praise. Gods like praise.[5]

In the ceremonies of the Welsh, Cornish and Breton *gorseddau*, which are large, public events, the calling or invocation is done very formally, with a Horner blowing a horn (a literal cow's or bull's horn) to the four cardinal points, East, South, West and North, in that order (because time runs in the same order, i.e., *deiseal*: dawn, day, sunset, night). As Graham Harvey points out, practice may vary between different groups:

> Most Pagan rituals begin with greetings to the four cardinal directions: north, east, south, west (not necessarily in that order). Some also greet "the center" and sometimes "the above" and "the below" also. These greetings may be performed by one experienced or chosen person or by one person per direction.... The directions may be addressed simply as directions, or as the (personified?) four winds who rule them, sometimes by their Greek names: Boreas, Eurias, Notus, Zephyrus. Others address the traditionally associated elements: earth, air, fire and water. Yet others address associated creatures, bear or gnome, hawk or sylph, stag or salamander, salmon or undine.[6]

The call is to all the ancestors, to all the Gods and Goddesses, and even to the God or Gods of those who have faiths other than or in addition to their Druidism (for example, several members of the Welsh and Cornish gatherings are Methodists and several Druids of the Breton *Gorsez* are Catholics). That's quite a crowd of spirits and deities to invite all together into one place, which is why the ritual is so formal. Even though solitary Druids and smaller gatherings of henges or branches may have much simpler rituals or less formal routines, the principle is exactly the same: we always begin prayer with a respectful invitation to the Gods, spirits or ancestors we wish to join us.

The Call for Peace

We also call for peace at the beginning of every rite. It is vital to do this if there are two or more people involved, because the sacred circle becomes a consecrated space of considerable power, in which resentments or malice or negativity can become not only irksome but actually dangerous, so it is essential to establish trust and mutual confidence. (Even as a solitary Druid, I begin with a call for peace, because it is a reminder of my need to find peace and harmony within myself before inviting sacred beings to share my prayers, my hopes and concerns.) In the Brythonic *gorseddau*, as we saw earlier, the Archdruid or Grand Bard asks three times, with great solemnity, "Is there peace?" Only when the assembly has affirmed three times that there is peace, is the *gorsedd* allowed to continue. Many groves and branches make the call for peace to the four cardinal directions, as with the invocation. Emma Restall Orr explains the importance of this part of ritual:

> When we call to the north, the south, east and west, "Let there be peace!" it is a demand on our own ability both to perceive the world around us with fuller awareness and to pour into the world the beauty of peace. And, as around us, so within: the call for peace is a reminder to let go of the crises of conflict in our daily lives as we move into the sacred space of the circle.... A shared circle is also a place of absolute trust, a trust that is based on the harmony between every soul present. Where there are people who don't know each other, it is the role of the Druid leading the rite to ensure that the sense of trust is shared.[7]

Ritual Elements

There are many elements involved in Druidic ritual, including literally the four elements which were anciently thought of as the prime materials from which all matter was composed: earth, air, fire and water. (The fifth element, or *quinta essentia* in Latin, from which the word quintessential is derived, is spirit or soul, *anam* to use the Celtic term.) We are perfectly aware that modern science describes the nature of matter in much more complex terms, explaining how the atoms of different elements (we still use that word in modern science, but now with a much broader meaning) combine chemically with other atoms to form molecules. But no matter how thoroughly we understand particles, quarks, electrons, protons and neutrons, etc., we recognize the significance and power of earth, air, fire and water because those ancient "elements" have been part of sacred ritual in Druidism as well as in many other religions for thousands upon thousands of years. Emma Restall Orr again:

> The temple of the sacred circle is usually consecrated, using incense and water which together represent the four elements the Druid works with. Within the incense is *earth*, in the dried herbs and berries, resin, bark and oils that make up the mixture that is burnt, expressing the *fire*, sending plumes of beautiful smoke into the *air*, to be breathed by the wind and the circle's participants. The *water* is often from a sacred spring, but always it is fresh, representing the waters of life. At times the chalice may have herbs or petals infusing their essence into the water. When the circle is consecrated, the Druid calls to her Gods, the elementals, the *devas* of the Earth, to bless the smoking censer and the chalice, then, as she moves slowly sunwise, letting the incense swirl, scattering water with fingertips, there is a shift in the energy and the vibration changes. The fifth element, *spirit*, comes into play. The circle, blessed, is ready for the rite.[8]

Incense, as used by almost all Pagans, as well as by Native Americans, is often called "smudge," from the Scottish Gàidhlig word *smùid*, pronounced approximately *smoo-ij*, which means "smoke." The related word *smùdan* (*smoo-dun*) can mean either a small block of wood, a kiln, or smoke, especially smoke raised as a signal. Dried sage leaves, tied in a bundle (often called a "smudge stick" in America, but not so much in Britain), are very commonly used for smudging, which includes personal "de-toxing" as well as cleansing sacred spaces. Cedar is also popular, and other sweet herbs are often added. There have been some clashes between authorities and either Pagan or Native American smudge users over its use, for example in college dormitories, where candles and incense may be banned on health and safety grounds. Smudge can be very pungent (usually pleasantly so), and the tendency of Druids to worship in outdoor spaces makes its use more practicable and less contentious. The sense of smell is located close to the hippocampus in the human brain, the site of memory, which is why smells so often trigger powerful memories and associations, both recent and distant. My wife and I use smudge and incense frequently in our little cottage, not just on ceremonial occasions, but also as a regular cleansing, detoxifying and purifying agent.

I have already mentioned my home altar, and Emma Restall Orr mentions a chalice in the passage above, so now seems like a good time to say something about the equipment, paraphernalia and accoutrements of worship and ritual. As with so many other topics in modern Druidism, there are no fixed rules. Individuals and groups choose whatever works best for them. When I pray, I wear jeans, a t-shirt, and sensible boots for the woods or seashore: the Gods see me all the time, and they know that I always come to them with humility and respect, no matter what I am wearing. Others, solitary or in groups, prefer ceremonial robes, or some might choose to worship "sky-clad" (although that is much more likely in Wiccan rites than in Druidic ceremonies, I believe). If I use anything outside of myself in ritual, it is most likely to be natural (usually wood, bone, horn or antler) and roughly made. Others may prefer athamés or ceremonial swords, carved wands, metal censers or candle-holders, or any amount of beautifully crafted equipment and paraphernalia. It is all a matter of personal or group preference.

However, most Druids who are members of a branch or henge may also have their own personal altars at home, for individual worship. I have briefly described my altar above. Emma Restall Orr gives a fuller general description:

> The art of creating and tending an altar is an important part of Druidry. It need not be big, but big enough for a candle or two and the other bits and pieces. It may even be in the garden or in a secluded spot in the wild beyond. With the candles place offerings which represent for you the beauty and strength in your life, all you would give thanks for and to, the natural world and the ancestors. It isn't necessary to make it all at once: allow it to evolve and beautiful objects to present themselves. These may be stones, shells, feathers, cones, photos of your family, a chalice of water, a bowl of earth. The altar should be tended daily. You may bring to the altar flowers, foliage or fresh fruit, a hunk of bread, a little of your meal. With the candles lit, spend a period of time quietly before it. You may like to meditate, but the important part is to stop running, to relax, to ponder on the beauty and simply to be, for a short while, every day.[9]

I have already mentioned that my wife, who is American, belongs to a group which combines Native American traditions (including a sweat lodge) with Celtic traditions. Even though we now live 8,000 miles away from that group, our connections (partly thanks to Facetime and other modern systems of communication) remain very close: we are family. I have always been struck by how often members of the group give each other small gifts, not just for birthdays and high holidays, but for everyday occasions and all sorts of reasons, and often no reason at all. And it is the nature of the gifts as much as the frequency of the gift-giving which is remarkable. They are not store-bought or gift-wrapped. They are not expensive or hi-tech, but they are as valued as if they had come from Macy's or Fortnum and Mason. They are pebbles, feathers, a twist of sage, a drawing sketched on a scrap of paper, a dried flower, a piece of driftwood, a seashell, a few cones of incense, or some mistletoe berries: and they often end up on a personal altar, or even journey between several personal altars within the family, carrying love and laughter and family unity with them, no matter how small and insignificant they may appear to be.

Ritual Purposes

Druidism, like all other religions, has rituals and ceremonies to mark the universal stations of life. They will vary enormously from group to group, but are likely to include: birth, naming, Druidic baptism; acceptance into membership of a group, branch or henge; coming of age; marriage, usually called "hand-fasting" in Pagan traditions; Moon rites, solar or planetary rites, calendrical rites; rites of celebration, anniversaries, achievements and commemoration; rites of dedication; rites of separation and loss, rites of passing, funerary rites. Ceremonials and ritual events may be limited to members, or they may be public events, like the Welsh, Cornish and Breton *gorseddau*.

Most of the larger Druid organizations have created huge amounts of ritual and liturgical material intended originally for their own use, but which they sometimes make available (usually through the internet) to anybody who may find them useful or of interest. By and large, Druids are very generous with intellectual property, and quite happy to share their texts, but theft is as unacceptable to Druids as it is to anybody else, so permission should be sought for the use of any substantial text in ritual, and its use should be appropriately acknowledged. Some organizations reserve at least part of their ritual or liturgical material for initiates only, with access to the rites included in the protocols of elevation to higher levels of qualification and status.

Most of the rituals are essentially requests to the deities to bless or support us. Marriage or hand-fasting, also known as matrimony or wedlock, for example, has ceremonial rites in every world religion (as well as secular equivalent protocols) and all of them, widely as they may differ in content as much as in appearance, are essentially asking God, the Goddess, or other deities to bless and make holy a physical, emotional and social union. Every culture will have its own laws, rules, regulations and customs, and these may be disputed between cultures or within cultures. To continue the marriage example, polygamy (marriage to several partners) is acceptable in some religions and cultures and not acceptable in others (and legal in some places, illegal in others); same-sex marriage is welcomed and approved by some, and rejected as immoral by others. For our purposes here, the political and theological debates are of secondary importance. The essential guiding principle for Druids is ancient and very simple: *y gwir yn erbyn ar byd*, truth against the world, truth above all things. If the ritual is accepted by all participants as true, fitting, fair and worthy in the sight of the Gods and Goddesses, the ancestors and the spirits, then it is the correct ritual. But if we think back to William Price, and the shock and horror he created when he proposed cremation rather than burial as a fitting way of dealing with the remains of the dead, we can see that Druids and the rest of society may often disagree about what is or is not true, fitting, fair and worthy, and that being in the right doesn't always guarantee an easy way forward.

Philip Carr-Gomm captures the underlying moral basis of religious ritual or magic in a creative and poetically imagined colloquy (conversation between teacher and pupil):

Standing alone, her figure outlined by the silver moonlight on the water, is your teacher—Elidir. You and your fellow pupils sit on the smooth rocks around her, and she invites a young man to step forward. His name is Brendan. Elidir unfurls a rug embroidered with Celtic knotwork and together they sit down and begin a conversation … "I'm glad you've come here now—on such a beautiful night. This is the best place to learn about the magic of Druidcraft," begins Elidir. "Here, at every moment, Nature shows to you the fundamental law of life and of magic—the Law of the Returning Tide." For a moment, Elidir is silent, and you find yourself watching the gentle surf, listening to the rhythmic sound of the waves upon the beach. Then Elidir continues. "The Law of the Returning Tide says that whatever you cast into the sea of life returns to you— often changed, often in an unrecognizable form, but nevertheless what comes to you in your life is usually the direct result of what you have given out into the world. Most people are only vaguely aware of this law, or don't fully accept it, but magicians use it all the time. They deliberately and consciously project positive ideas, energies, images, feelings, thoughts, prayers, chants and spells into the world, knowing fully that they will reap the benefits of these—sometimes quickly but sometimes not for years or even lifetimes. Using your knowledge of this law and the techniques of Druidcraft you can actually work at creating your future lives."[10]

And I wouldn't still be a Druid if I hadn't had many, many years of experience of seeing ritual and ceremonial prayer producing results. I have had a few prayers answered in such a peculiar, back-to-front, inside-out way that it has taken me a long time to understand what was going on, but all of my prayers have eventually been answered, some of them literally years after the asking.

To me, "magic" and "prayer" are just slightly different aspects of the same thing, and both are very real, and very powerful. Many people associate the word "magic" with trickery, legerdemain and cunning deceit. (To escape that connotation, some modern Pagans use the 18th-century spelling "magick" to distinguish ritual and sacred magic from mere theatrical entertainment or stage magic.) Some accept the definition of magic as an attempted harnessing or invocation of supernatural assistance to achieve a particular purpose, but don't themselves believe in deities or supernatural beings, so, as far as they are concerned, magic and prayer are both naive, foolish and meaningless activities—just talking to yourself—or, even more dangerously, listening to beings who aren't really there, voices in your head. Those of us who think of our Druidism as a religion, rather than merely a philosophy, have to believe in magic as we believe in prayer; the conversations we have with deities, ancestors and spirits are real, powerful, meaningful, and effective, or they are nothing.

Margot Adler's definition of the word "magic" is prosaic, but useful. She describes magic as a natural application of emotion and concentration to effect changes in consciousness towards intended results, not as something supernatural, i.e., beyond or above nature, but natural, part of nature, *within* nature:

Magic is a convenient word for a whole collection of techniques, all of which involve the mind.... We might conceive of these techniques as including the mobilization of confidence, will, and emotion brought about by the recognition of necessity; the use of imaginative faculties, particularly the ability to visualize, in order to begin to understand how other beings function in nature so we can use this knowledge to achieve necessary ends.[11]

I believe that much of the ritual and liturgical text and protocols used in Druidism is used to stimulate the "imaginative faculties" Adler describes, and I think her use of the phrase "ability to visualize" is also very useful: visualization is a powerful step towards actualization.

As an aside, I still enjoy Isaac Bonewits's descriptions of the "colors" of different kinds of magic. Typically Bonewits, he began in a kind of tongue-in-cheek way to debunk the constant esoteric arguments about the differences between "white magic" and "black magic," effectively by saying, "Hey, let's talk about all the other colors of magic we can do." But what may have been started tongue-in-cheek actually turns out to be a very useful description of the many different kinds of magic and the many different contexts in which they appear. As he often did, Bonewits flipped the initial flippancy upside-down and turned it into something actually quite profound: he developed his description of multi-colored, multi-faceted magic in impressive detail. Red magic deals with the body, healing and hurting, blessings and curses. Orange magic is about mental health, confidence, pride, ego and identity. Yellow magic is about the mind and the senses, and learning. Green magic is about plants, nature and fertility. Blue magic is about spiritualism, theology and social science. Indigo magic is about weather and meteorology. Purple magic is about love, passion, all high emotion. Ultraviolet magic is about psychic power, influence and politics. Brown magic is the magic of the forest and the hunt, of wild places, and of ecology.[12] Some years later, Terry Pratchett, in *The Colour of Magic* (1983), wittily added another color to the magical spectrum, which he called Octarine, a "rather disappointing greeny-purple-yellow."

Similarly, some rituals are to do with seeing patterns, or creating patterns, the ancient practice of *imbas forosnai* which I described briefly in Chapter 2. We may be asking a particular God or spirit for vision and guidance, for a revelation or foresight of what is to come. One of my favorite stories about this kind of pre-vision comes from a completely separate context and has no obvious connection with Druidism (the story is actually about a Christian minister), but, in its simplicity, clearly describes for me the *imbas forosnai* which always surrounds us and is available to us if we know how to search for it, or can simply let go and let it find us. This is the story:

Chad Varah (1911–2007) was the British Anglican clergyman who founded the Samaritans organization, the "suicide hotline" service for those in despair and desperation, which now has branches across the world. When Varah began the Samaritans in 1953, they had only one telephone. It was in the crypt of the church of St. Stephen Walbrook in London, a space which Varah was just borrowing, and the phone had never been used since it was installed, so it was covered in grime and cobwebs. Varah wanted to find a memorable number that potential callers could keep in their heads and recall even when in great distress. In those days, London telephone numbers were prefixed by district abbreviations, and Varah knew that the number would begin with the letters MAN, since they were in the Mansion House district. That seemed appropriate, so it was only the following digits that needed to be decided. In a moment of what he almost certainly would have attributed to God, but which we might call *imbas forosnai*, Varah was "inspired" that the number should be 9000. He went down to the ancient, dusty telephone to call the Post Office and request the number MAN 9000. He found, to his relief and slight surprise, that the telephone was working. Via the operator, he was connected to a sales clerk, who agreed that supplying a new number would be straightforward. His first question was to ask Varah the existing number of the telephone that he was calling from. Using his handkerchief, the minister wiped off the cobwebs and grime from the telephone, thus discovering to his astonishment that the number he was calling from was MAN 9000.[13]

Closure

When the main ritual is completed, it is important to bring matters to closure. This is just as important for a solitary Druid on a tiny Hebridean island as it is for a congregation of hundreds in the middle of Calanais or Stonehenge. The deities, ancestors and spirits who have been invoked need to be thanked for their attendance, and invited to watch over us and be with us for the future. The Brythonic *gorseddau* close their ceremonies with a second triple call for peace: in the same way that the ceremony cannot begin unless peace is agreed and declared, nor can it end unless and until peace is agreed and declared. The sacred circle needs to be closed, with thanks and blessings, or, if it is kept open, with assurances of proper and adequate guardianship. Lastly, the ceremonial site needs to be cleared and cleaned, out of respect for the environment.

These steps in ritual, small or large, which I have outlined above, can be summarized very simply as follows:

1. Establish a place of prayer, or a sacred circle.
2. Invoke, by name, the Gods, Goddesses, ancestors or spirits, whom you would like to join you. Praise and thank them for the qualities they bring to the circle.
3. Call for peace, and declare that there is peace before the main body of the prayer or ritual begins.
4. Identify and demonstrate the elements, earth, air, fire and water,

which you think may be helpful to your present purpose, and place or distribute them appropriately.

5. Identify, for the deities assembled as well for the participants, the purpose of the rite. Choose words with great care. If the rite involves requests, identify to whom the request is being made, and why it is being made.

6. When the main rite is completed, thank all summoned deities, ancestors and spirits for their participation and assistance.

7. Call again for peace, and declare that there is peace before the ceremony closes.

8. Close the sacred circle with thanks and blessings to all who have been involved.

9. Clean up, tidy up, leave the space pristine.

12. Sample Rites and Texts

From the Druid Network

The Druid Network publishes many rituals. The sample below is the Druid Network International Full Moon Peace Intention Ritual. It is a recent initiative, written by Neil Pitchford, Pauline Pitchford and Mark Rosher, intended as a widely available ritual in which everyone and anyone can join, based on the simple but powerful idea that prayer is effective, and the more people there are praying for good things, the better.

It is claimed in the classical writings that the Druids held the power to stop armies engaging in combat and that may have been because one of their priorities was peace. Today's Druids wield nether the power or influence of the classical Druids but our priorities remain the same. The achievement of peace is a central aim within today's Druidic communities. It is with this in mind that The Druid Network has, at this time, now engaged in spiritual work to help bring about peace, not just on the local scale like the classical Druids, but on a worldwide scale enabled by the technology of today.

We therefore invite anyone and everyone to engage with us in our aims, through the use of our International Full Moon Peace Intention Ritual. This ritual, which will be held on the full moon of each month, is suitable for use on its own or in conjunction with any other type of ritual. It can be done on an individual basis or through a community based ritual. Travel is unnecessary, just putting aside a place and time is all that is required. Ideally, the aim is for people to engage with the ritual at the time of the full moon. However, life does not normally allow for such specific timing, therefore we would request that you aim to do the ritual within the 12 hour period either prior to or just after the full moon if you cannot do the ritual at the specific timing of the full moon.

We have worded this ritual to have no specific political or religious favour, it is a ritual for peace without taking sides.

The Ritual

First we would suggest that everyone starts with the calls for peace in each direction.

> May there be peace in the east,
> may there be peace in the south,

may there be peace in the west,
may there be peace in the north,
may there be peace in the whole world.
After that we suggest each individual or group proceed with whatever ritual opening they usually use and when that is complete use the following:
We honour the fallen,
Those who chose to take arms and fight,
Those who chose to meet war with peace,
And those for whom a wakeful choice was never an option,
All those whose fate it was to die in conflict.
We honour and remember them.
(Pause to honour and remember those known and unknown who have died in conflict.)
We stand in the web of life, each of us connected to each other.
Our thoughts and deeds ripple outwards across that web.
(Pause to reach out and feel our connections to each other and the web of life)
Today we stand for peace, today we act for peace.
Let each of us be a channel for peace.
Peace in our hearts.
Peace in our lives.
Peace in the world.
(Pause and focus on being a channel for peace and radiating that peace out across the world)
After that we suggest closing your ritual in whatever is your normal fashion.[1]

Description of Some Henge of Keltria Rituals

The following description by Tony Taylor from The Henge of Keltria is not ritual text, but describes some of the organization's rituals:

We also celebrate the sixth night of the moon with a ritual called the "Mistletoe Rite," which is also open to non-initiates. It provides a communion of food, drink and fellowship. The Nature Spirits are invited to consecrate the food and the Ancestors are asked to consecrate the drinks for the ritual. Two chalices, one of water and one of mead, are blessed by the Gods and Goddesses of the Grove. The participants partake of these foods and libate everything that is brought. We discuss topics of religious significance, questions and answers are addressed, and perhaps some storytelling or other related activity. The Mistletoe Rite is also an opportunity for the Grove to do healing work.

Another ritual is the Vervain Rite. Vervain was gathered in ancient times when neither sun nor moon were in the sky. This is the magic working ritual for initiates only. We gather after sunset on one evening during the third quarter of the Moon. The principal content of that ritual is one of the mysteries revealed during initiation. Two other rituals that we celebrate are considered Tribal Rites. They are "The Feast of Age" and "The Feast of Remembrance." For the Feast of Age we borrowed a mythological story and transformed it into a ritual. It is usually celebrated between Lughnasad and the Autumnal Equinox, which are traditional harvest times. The mythological Feast of Age was hosted by Manannán Mac Lir, God of the Headlands, and Goibhniu, God of Brewing. Manannán provided magical pigs which, when eaten, gave the Gods immortality. Goibhniu brewed ale which, when consumed, gave the Gods invincibility. Finally we honor the cloak of Manannán which was often loaned to mortals so they could pass unseen. We ritualize the cooking of the pork and partaking of it and the ale. A cloak is passed to each person who wraps up in it and declares the immortality of spirit, the invincibility of our convictions and the ability to pass through the mundane world without arousing attention. The Feast of Remembrance can be observed on any traditional celebration of the dead. It is usually held near Samhain or Memorial Day, which is a modern-day secular American holiday. It celebrates, remembers, and mourns all who sacrificed their lives in the name of their religion, from the Druids at Mona/Anglesey and the Native Americans to the Jewish brethren who died in the Holocaust. We remember anyone, throughout history, put to death because of their religious beliefs.[2]

Sample Order of WhiteOak Rituals

The Order of WhiteOak publishes many rituals on its website. The samples given below are representative.

Beltaine Rite

Let two large ritual fires and one small fire be constructed by nine persons carrying nine sacred woods or let the fires be of oak. The fires shall be sacred fires, lit by the sun passing through a crystal, or kindled by a "thunderstone" (flint), or by a fire drill (using powdered mistletoe as tinder) or from "wild fire" caught from a lightning strike. Let the fires be of nine sacred woods or all of oak. The nine sacred woods shall be; Oak, the tree of the High Gods. Willow, a tree sacred to poets. Hazel, the tree of Wisdom. Alder, the tree of protection. Birch, the tree of new beginings. Ash, the tree that spans the three worlds. Yew, the tree of immortality. Elm the favorite of the Elves. Rowan, guardian of the home and cattle. Apple, the tree of love, favorite of the deer. Pine, the tree of peace. Let the first sacred fire be kindled in the small pyre on the perimeter in preparation for the rite. Let the tuath rise before dawn to watch the lighting of the fires. The two large fires shall be consecrated to Belenos and to Belisama, deities of the Sun. Let a Druid bring fire from the small pyre to the flame of Belenos. Let a Druidess bring fire from the small pyre to the flame of Belisama. Let the tuath chant the names of these Gods while the Druids pour oil, ghee or butter on the flames. The Druid and Druidess shall intone these words; "Hail summer, season of light and of life. Blessed are those who stand here today, witness to the ancient rite. To everyone who passes between the flames, whether human or beast, may health and prosperity come! May the fires bring us fields of ripe corn and fruit in abundance. May the fires bring us streams of white milk, freedom from conquest, fair justice and righteous law, comfort and abundance in every home. May the fires bring us rivers of fish, forests filled with strong woods, great abundance of clean water, ornaments of silver and gold, rich soil, sheep with fine fleece, fat pigs and healthy cattle. May every disease and unhappiness be purged from those who walk here, in the name of Belenos and Belisama!" Then shall the tuath walk between the two fires. Let those who are too young or too weak be carried, even the aged and the infirm. Then shall the animals be led through the flames as a blessing on them. Then shall music be played and let there be dancing around the fires. Let torches lit from the sacred flames be carried around the perimeters of the land to bless it. Let torches lit from the sacred flames be carried around the fields to bless them. When the fires have burned lower let the young of the tuath leap the flames, for it is the height of their leaping that will ensure the height of the corn. And later let those who are able leap across the coals. Let the day be spent in feasting and merry making and let everyone who wishes it carry an ember home to re-kindle their hearths and altars and bless their gardens and fields. (© Ellen Evert Hopman 1999)

Death Rites

At the time of death the Anam Chara shall stay with the dying person. The Anam Chara shall be well known to the dying one or a person who has a soul mission to help the dying. When possible harp music shall be played for the dying as it eases pain and brings spiritual comfort.

When the death rattle begins let three drops of water be placed on the tongue or the lips of the dying one by the Anam Chara saying;

"Go easy to the land of the ancestors. Let the waters carry you across to the Blessed Isles where your family and loved ones await."

Burial Rites

The burial shall be accompanied by well-chosen articles associated with the life of the deceased. A favorite torque, a mantle, golden jewelry, drinking horns, magical wands and staffs, boughs of oak and sprays of mistletoe and any other precious object the deceased might have chosen or that is chosen lovingly by others.

A hole shall be dug and stones brought from near or far and placed near the grave. The body shall be placed on a stretcher or a bier and carried to the location of the earthen hole. It shall be dressed in fine clothing or covered in fine cloths and sacred herbs and flowers.

The people shall visit the body for a day, praying, singing, telling stories and praises of the deceased until nightfall. At night the Druids and those of the kin group who wish to remain in vigil shall sit with the body until dawn. During the night the Druids shall listen and watch for messages from the deceased for it is known that the spirit often remains with the body, even after death.

At dawn, at the time of the rising of the birds, the Druids and kin shall lovingly place the body in the grave. A Bard or a poet shall sing these words or any song or poem from ancient tradition;

"Come spirits across the ocean join with your brother/sister who waits here Take him/her across to the bright land Take her/him across moor and meadow Take her/him across a calm sea Take her/him across a blissful ocean Peace and joy on the day of her/his death As he/she finds her/his way to the white sun."

And then shall every person present begin to cover the body with soil, a handful or a shovelful at a time. And then shall a cairn be lifted from the collected stones, over the body of the deceased. And let every stone be placed with a prayer for the well being of the deceased, for their family and kin and for their spiritual family. Or in place of the cairn or beside it let there be planted a tree in memory of the deceased. And all care shall be taken to ensure the tree's survival. Afterwards let a great feast be prepared with music and celebration and stories of the deceased and praise of their accomplishments (© Ellen Evert Hopman 1999).

Embalming

In researching ancient Egyptian embalming methods and the herbs used, the following were included. We know that there was much sea traffic from the Mediterranean up the coast of Iberia and Armorica, to Alba and on to Eire. It is not outrageous to think that Druids might have been aware of this knowledge:

Myrrh
Sandalwood
Attar of Roses
Cedar
Salt
Cinnamon
Frankinsence
Ladanum
Saffron
Orris (Iris) root
Storax
Gum mastic.

These herbs would have been used in embalming mixtures and to wash body cavities. I suggest that they be incorporated into a dusting powder or a wash for the corpse. (Saille, for the Order of the Whiteoak, Ellen Evert Hopman 1999[3])

Sample ADF Ritual

ADF have on their website (www.adf.org) a huge and extremely valuable, carefully thought-out body of ritual texts and protocols. They take the whole of Indo-European culture as their ideological base, so their rituals are derived from many sources. Here is a sample of rites and prayers for the Roman pantheon:

Religio Romano: Simple Daily Home Rites and Prayers
(Originally published in *Oak Leaves* No. 13.)

Early Romans were simple farmers and shepherds, and their gods and religious practices revolved around their homes, farms, and immediate community. Every household had some kind of shrine for the home deities, the *Lararium*, and would perform daily prayers to honor the *Lar*, the guardian spirit of the household, and the *Penates*, the guardian spirits of the pantry or cupboards. In previous articles, I have discussed the basics of Roman hearth religion (see OL 10). I am now offering to share some very simple household prayers and rites suitable for a Roman household.

Morning Lararium Prayer

The *Paterfamilias* was traditionally responsible for leading the household each morning in a prayer to the deities of the household (the *Lar* and *Penates*) to thank them for keeping watch over the welfare and prosperity of the home and to ask that the coming day be fruitful and safe. In ancient times, the *Paterfamilias* was the male head of the household; however, in modern times, this need not be so. Just as the *Paterfamilias* of the community is responsible for the spiritual welfare of the community, the *Paterfamilias* of the household is responsible for maintaining a proper relationship between the deities and the household.

This particular prayer is designed to be performed before the *lararium* early in the morning after the *Paterfamilias* has been cleaned and purified, but before breakfast. The *Paterfamilias* stands before the *lararium* with arms outstretched and greets the household spirits:

> *Salve Lar Familiaris!* Greetings, household Lar! *Salvete Di Penates!* Greetings, Divine Penates!

> If you are making an offering, do so while speaking these lines; otherwise, omit the passages in brackets.}

> *Vos precor {hoc sacrificio obmovendo bonas preces} uti sitis volentes propitii mihi, {liberisque mei,} domo meo, familiaeque meae.* I humbly ask that you may bestow your blessing upon me, {my children,} my home, and my household. *{Mactete hoc sacrificio}* {Be thou increased by this which I give to you.} *Ita est!* So be it!

This is a great time for a few moments of daily meditation, particularly giving thought to what your plans, expectations, and hopes for the day may be and how the kindred spirits may be included and helpful during the day. A daily offering is not necessary, but is always an option, particularly if you seek especial favor that day. Moreover, this would be an ideal time for making a prepared or extemporaneous prayer or vow to a deity (or deities) for assistance in a particular situation. For example, when I had to leave my car at the shop for the day, I prayed to and made a vow to *Mercurius* (as one who is associates with commerce and fair business deals) *Vulcanus* (as one who is associated with metalwork and the forge fire), and any other deity who may have been able to assist me in keeping the cost of the repairs to a minimum. (It seemed to work, by the way; I had a loose spark plug, which was easily reconnected, and my mechanic didn't charge me a dime!)

Daily Meal Prayer

At the evening meal (or whatever is the main meal of the day), it is appropriate to honor *Vesta*, the living flame, who is associated with the cook fire and the *Penates*. If, like me, you live alone and have irregular, quick meals, make a point of offering to *Vesta* a bit of whatever it is you're eating whenever you do sit down for a meal. Ideally, a place should be set for *Vesta* at the table with a serving of all that which the family is eating, then after dinner, but before dessert, the contents of the plate are cast into the fire on the hearth. As the offering is made, a short prayer to *Vesta* is made:

> *Salve, Vesta mater!* Greetings, Mother Vesta! *Accipe hoc sacrificium factum meo artificio de tua auxilia beata.* Accept this offering, made by my own handiwork with your blessed help. *Te precor humiliter uti sis volens propitia foco meo, domique familiaeque meae.* I humbly beseech you to bless my hearth, and the home of my family. *Macte hoc sacrificio.* Be thou increased by this which I give to you.

> Throw the offering to the hearth (or place it in the offering bowl, as the case may be.)

> *Dea propitia sit!* May the Goddess be favorable!

Prayer When Leaving Home

Janus is the deity most commonly associated with doors in the Roman religion. He protects our homes from that which would bring harm to it or those within it. Not only is it a good idea to invoke *Janus* as a protector of the home, but *Janus* is also the gatekeeper between us and the realm of the deities. Establishing a good relationship with *Janus* may aid in enlisting his help in opening the gates in more elaborate rituals. It's not a bad idea to invoke him every time you enter and leave your home.

As you cross the threshold and close the door behind you, say:

Semper salve valeque, Jane Clusive! Greetings always, *Janus,* closer of doors!

Extend your hands in supplication and say:

Me absente te precor uti sis domum, meam vigilans et ab injuria protegens. I humbly beseech you to watch over my home in my absence, and protect it from harm.

Lock the door, then kiss your hand and touch this hand to the door, saying:

Ita est! So be it!

Prayer Upon Returning Home

As you approach the entrance to your home, greet *Janus,* saying:

Salve Jane Patulci! Greetings, *Janus,* opener of doors!

Extend your hands in supplication, saying:

Tibi gratias ago quod in me absentia domum meam vigilasti et ab injuria protexsti. Thank you for watching over my home in my absence and keeping it safe from harm.

Kiss your hand, touch this hand to the door, and unlock it, saying:

Gratias tibi ago! I give you thanks!

Prayer of Ablution (Cleansing):

This is a short prayer than can be used whenever you shower, wash your hands, before a ritual or anytime you feel the need for purification. While washing, say:

Haec aqua a corpore impuritates, simile modo velut plumbum ad aurum mutando, eluat. May this water cast out all impurities from my substance as from lead to gold. *Purget mentem. Purget corpus. Purget animum.* Purify my mind. Purify my body. Purify my spirit. *Ita est.* So be it.

If they were going to be attending or participating in a formal ritual, Romans would cover their heads, *capite velato,* to protect themselves from any evil omens en route to or during the ritual. If this prayer is used as an ablution prior to a ritual, it would be proper to cover your head with a shawl or length of cloth. As you do so, say:

Purus(-a) sim May I be pure. *Immunis ex impurtates sim* May I be free from all impurities. *Mei facti fidi et justi sint* May my deeds be true and just.

Stand straight, your hands in a supplicant position, and say:

Juppiter mihi induat pietate. May *Jupiter* enwrap me with Pietas. *Ita est!* So be it!

Conclusion

These are the first Latin prayers I have written, and they are ones I have begun to use on a regular basis. It's not necessary to address the Roman deities in Latin, and I wouldn't recommend anyone doing so without first learning some basics of Latin pronunciation. However, if you understand how to pronounce the Latin and feel more comfortable using it (speaking in Latin always reminds me of the days of Latin Masses and feels more formal to me), I believe the gods prefer it. The most important thing to remember, however, is that the more often you perform these small, daily rites and prayers, the closer you will grow to the deities. Your relationship will grow and you will feel their presence a little more each time you pray to them. Use the prayers in English or put them into your own words once you are comfortable with them. The Gods will hear you and appreciate your efforts and your piety.[4]

Poems

Finally, I humbly submit a few of my own poems as possible texts for meditation on Druidic themes and topics. As will be obvious from reading them, several take as their starting point a specific place or feature on the little Hebridean island where we live. The first poem is in Cornish and is followed by a literal English translation.

Bennath gernewek

Re dhrollo dhis howldrevel hardh ha nowydh
an sterennow a omdenn dres an Tamar.

Re dhokko dha golonn dhe benn an als
gwyns an Atlantek ha'y goelannes gwyls.

Re dheffo dhis lowender hag enor yn taran
mordros Godrevi war garregi loes.

Re dhrollo dhis kres yndan gwith agan hendasow
kosoleth goth gorthugher dres Goen Brenn.

Re wystlo dhis kewerans dha denkys wir
an howlsedhes kogh dres Penn an Wlas.

Re gerdhy yn kres war lergh lor leun
dhe'th treveth gosel lenwys a gerensa.

A Cornish blessing
(translation from Cornish)

May the stars that fade beyond the Tamar
bring you a bold and new dawn.

May the breath of the Atlantic and her wild gulls
carry your heart to the cliff top.

May there come to you joy and honor in the thunder
of Godrevy's sea-sound on grey rocks.

May the ancient stillness of evening over Bodmin Moor
bring you peace under the protection of our ancestors.

May the scarlet sunset beyond Land's End
pledge you the fulfillment of your true destiny.

May you walk in peace on the track of the full Moon
to your quiet homestead filled with love.

The tree song

Good health to the traveler who wanders the byways,
who gathers his firewood and eats under the sky,

whose horse knows the woods and the untrodden highways,
who sleeps deep and easy while the world hurries by.

> Good luck to the holly, the hazel, the hawthorn,
> the blackthorn, the whitethorn, the apple and the pear,
> the oak and the ash and the beautiful willow,
> the bright bonny birch that brings in the new year.

Good health to the badger, the fox and the vixen,
the swan who swims stately and flies wild and free,
the stag king who bellows his might on the mountain,
the robin who sings songs of joy in his tree.

> Good luck to the holly, the hazel, the hawthorn,
> the blackthorn, the whitethorn, the apple and the pear,
> the oak and the ash and the beautiful willow,
> the bright bonny birch that brings in the new year.

Good health to the forest alert in the still night,
the dark lovely woods where the creatures all stir
as the sweet Goddess passes wrapped up in her moonlight
and blesses all beings of feather and fur.

> Good luck to the holly, the hazel, the hawthorn,
> the blackthorn, the whitethorn, the apple and the pear,
> the oak and the ash and the beautiful willow,
> the bright bonny birch that brings in the new year.

Eala Bhàn

When Oenghus mac Oc first saw Caer,
she swam as a beautiful swan
with a hundred and fifty swan companions,
and her name was Eala Bhàn.

A silver chain connected them
as they swam at Samhain-tide,
but gold were the links at Caer's white throat
and he wanted her for his bride.

Ethel Anbual, father of Caer,
forbade Oenghus mac Oc
from marrying his lovely daughter
and sweeping her away in his cloak.

The wind blew cold on the tarn's dark water
in little rippling waves,
and the swan feathers spun like snowflakes falling
on the icy slab of a grave.

Eala Bhàn looked to the sky,
where the God shone like the sun,
and she spoke not with her voice but her heart
when she said, "You and I are one."

Oenghus mac Oc flew down to her then,
shedding the clothes he had on,

and splashed in the cold water beside her
in the princely form of a swan.

Ethel Anbual mustered his men
and rushed to the tarn's wild shore,
bearing arms and uttering curses
that Oenghus would live no more.

But the swan couple beat their beautiful wings
and took to the golden air,
and Caer's silver-linked swan maidens
accompanied them there.

Three times they flew around the tarn,
its waters black and deep,
until Ethel Anbual and his men
fell into a charmèd sleep.

Then Oenghus mac Oc and Eala Bhàn
flew to the god's own *sídh*,
at Brugh na Bóinne where the river flows
down to the western sea.

"I love you, Eala Bhàn, my bride,
and whatever you choose to be,
I will shape myself to be with you
for all eternity."

Evensong

How huge the sky, how sweet and soft the air!
Two fields below, the timid, leaf-eared deer

tiptoe to the burn to drink, their pool eyes
deep, dark and lustrous as the evening sky.

Pipistrelles, little flying moustaches,
flick black on grey, snapping up midges.

I breathe, my rib-cage and the sky-cage one,
inhaling silent stars and crescent Moon,

conjuring, working the old Druid trick
of leaving time, of being dead and quick,

taking in and breathing out with one breath
the honeysuckle headiness of death.

Such stillness! The passing moth does not dare
disturb my ecstasy of silent prayer

but flutters to the south white as chalk dust
and fades into the softly rising mist.

Hope
(after Robert Louis Stevenson)

The world gives, takes away, brings lovers near,
separates them into distant, strange lands.

Fate's butterfly flutters on storm-blown strands
and flicks away all that was once held dear.

Lust even more than love fades into dust,
its roiling heat cooling to indifference.
All that languishing, that fierce longing must
dwindle meekly into mild temperance.

And yet to love is the great amulet
that makes the world a garden, lets us brave
a whole eternity of sad regret.

Hope, the sweet gift that lovely love first gave,
outwears the accidents of life to let
the hand of love reach beyond the blank grave.

Night walk

Night here is primeval, the starfield
vast enough and clear and far
to steal the breath entirely away.
Silence leaps from the lumpy rocks,
daring a single sound to intrude.
Tree and leaf and fox and otter
have a pact of stealth. They only stir
when the Neanderthal spirits give them leave,
their pods and pads and skittering claws
laid gently on the ancient, sleeping ground.
Only the sea, even more ancient,
dares to murmur, but even she
whispers demurely, her dark wrack
swaying gently in the starlit shallows.

I walk like a caveman, could be naked,
but there are houses further along the shore
and I am here to speak with the Goddess,
not to frighten children or horses.
My limp and my trusted rowan staff
keep me anchored to the passive turf.
Without them, I might fly up into the darkness,
never to return, even with my pocketful
of Druid magic and shifting tricks.

My breath takes me by surprise,
as though the world stopped long ago
but somehow I have soldiered on
when all around me eternity
like Vaughan's ring of endless light
hangs from the vault of starlit heaven
and all Earth's ages have collided here
in these unchanging stones, this track
of clear, cold, loving moonlight.

Tree guardians

Our cottage, on a low rise in the clachan,
feels the wind like a pony in a field.
We sit inside by the peat-laden stove,

but outside, beating at the wetted windows,
the pines, ashes, rowans and a ragged bunch
of bushes and shrubs flail and thrash.

They make a roar that cannot be dismissed.
Like the dripping pony we hunker down,
while the screaming wind, wild as whips,

lashes the trees to Hebridean frenzy.
Oh, blessed is the storm, and welcome,
when we are safe and dry and warm at home.

Our guardians, to whom we offer prayers
every day, cold or warm, calm or raging,
are the venerable ash who towers

over the driveway, ancient, battle-scarred,
full of tales and talkative as a brother,
and his sister the quiet rowan tree,

who guards the kitchen door, sheltering
the little feeding birds on calmer days,
whisper-singing her Old Irish songs.

When the wild white horses beat their hooves
in Balvicar Bay, and the rain blasts in,
forcing folk to turn their stung faces away,

our guardians nod and hold their ground,
our Manannán mac Lir and Arianrhod,
our living protectors and loving friends.

Appendix A: Glossary

abaton   a sleeping chamber in ancient Celtic sanctuaries, used for healing and divinatory dreaming (Greek, literally "do not tread," meaning a wild or inaccessible place)

anam   soul, spirit, identity, individual nature (Irish Gaeilge, cognate of Latin *animus*)

anam cára, anamchara, Anam Chara (*an-am-ka-ra, an-am-kha-ra*)   literally "soul friend," originally used in Irish Christian monasticism to signify a monk's tutor, used by modern Druids to signify a close friend, supporter, guide or teacher (Irish Gaeilge)

athamé (*a-tha-may*)   ceremonial dagger, usually with a black handle, used mostly in Wicca and related forms of witchcraft (from Late Latin *artavus*, "quill knife")

awen, Awen   poetic or divine inspiration, symbolized as the *Awen* of three descending rays

barrow   a large earthen burial or grave mound, usually either circular or oval in shape

BCE   Before the Common Era, replacing the outdated BC (before Christ)

Brythonic   relating to the Brittonic or British nations and languages, i.e., Wales (*Cymru*) and Welsh (*Cymraeg*), Cornwall (*Kernow*) and Cornish (*Kernewek*), and Brittany (*Breiz*) and Breton (*Brezoneg*)

CE   of the Common Era, replacing the outdated AD (*Anno Domini*, "in the Year of the Lord")

cèilidh, céili (*kay-lee*)   gathering, either for food and drink and conversation, or for music and dancing (Scottish Gàidhlig, Irish Gaeilge)

clàrsach   harp (Gaelic)

colloquy (*koll-o-kwee*)   a formal philosophical or religious discussion between a teacher and pupil, common in ancient cultures as well as in modern Paganism (from Latin *con*, "with" and *loquor*, "speak")

cromlech *see* **dolmen**

deiseal (*jay-shal, de-shal*)   clockwise or sunwise, also (incorrectly) spelled *deosil* (Scottish Gàidhlig, Irish Gaeilge)

dolmen   a prehistoric burial chamber typically made of two or three upright stones and a larger capstone (Brythonic Celtic), also called a cromlech (Goidelic Celtic)

fír fer, fíre fer (*feer fayr, feer-uh fayr*)   fair play, justice, balance and adjustment, literally "truth of men" (Irish Gaeilge)

fitness of things   appropriateness, harmony with Nature, balance in justice

Goidelic   relating to the Gaelic nations and languages, i.e., Scotland (*Alba*) and *Gàidhlig*, Ireland (*Éire*) and *Gaeilge*, and the Isle of Man (*Mannin*) and Manx or *Gaelg*.

gorsedd, gorsedh, gorsez (*gor-seth, gor-sez*)   event, place of wonder or importance, or gathering of Bards, Ovates or Druids (Welsh, Cornish, Breton)

imbas forosnai (*eem-bas-for-aws-nay*)   divine foresight or poetic inspiration (Old Irish)

lunula   a pendant, badge or brooch in the shape of a crescent Moon, made usually of silver as worn by traditional Druids (Latin *luna*, "the Moon")

Mabinogi (Mabinogion)   Welsh vernacular stories, first written down about 1050 CE, containing a great deal of mythological information (Welsh—*Mabinogion* is now universal, but is grammatically incorrect)

megalith   literally "big stone," a rock, sometimes shaped or decorated with carvings, placed either alone or with others in an alignment or circle (Greek)

menhir   literally "long or tall stone," a megalith usually standing by itself (Celtic)

nemeton   sacred space, usually by or near trees, rocks or water (Old Irish *nemed*, cognate with Latin *nemus* and Greek νεμω)

Ogham (*ow-um* in Old Irish, *og-um* in modern Irish)   an ancient alphabet used by the Druids, made up of combinations of straight lines either drawn or cut on a surface (in Druidic tradition, devised by the God Ogmios)

Paneurhythmy (*pan-yoor-rith-me*)   a program of exercises performed to music, to achieve inner balance and harmonization, devised by the Bulgarian spiritual leader Peter Deunov and introduced to Britain by Philip Carr-Gomm

polyamory   relationships with multiple partners with the knowledge and consent of all involved

psychosynthesis   a system of psychology, derived from Jung and others, that goes beyond analysis and includes self-actualization

ríastrad   battle frenzy or "warp spasm," associated with Cú Chulainn (Irish Gaeilge)

sí, sídh, sídhe (*shee, shee-uh*)   a fairy mound, fairies (Irish Gaeilge)

troyll (*troyl*)   gathering, either for food and drink and conversation, or for music and dancing (Cornish)

tuath (*too-uh*)   family, tribe, people, group, or territory (Irish Gaeilge)

tuathal (*too-uh-hul, thoo-hul*)   anti-clockwise, anti-sunwise (Scottish Gàidhlig, Irish Gaeilge)

tumulus   an earthen burial mound or grave mound, usually smaller than a barrow (Latin)

twmpath (*toom-path*)   gathering, either for food and drink and conversation, or for music and dancing (Welsh)

vision quest   a period spent alone in a wild place, fasting and without water, to pray and invite sacred visions (Native American)

Wicca   modern witchcraft, derived by Gerald Gardner from Old English *wicce* and *wicca*, originally meaning male witch and female witch respectively

widdershins   anti-clockwise, anti-sunwise (Lallans or Lowland Scots)

y gwir yn erbyn ar byd (*uh-gweer-un-ayr-bin-ar-beed*)   truth against the world, truth above all else, honesty and sincerity (Welsh)

Appendix B:
Contact Information

This list of Celtic and Druidic organizations is accurate at the time of writing, but it is by no means exhaustive. New organizations come into being and new groves and henges are created within organizations all the time.

The Ancient Order of Druids (AOD)
Email: United Kingdom: Barrywood39@aol.com
Email: International Grand Lodge of Druids: gs@igld.org
Website: http://www.aod-uk.org.uk

The Ancient Order of Druids in America (AODA)
Website: http://www.aoda.org

Ár nDraíocht Féin (ADF/A Druid Fellowship)
Email: adf-office@adf.org
Website: www.adf.org

The British Druid Order (BDO)
Mailing address:
BDO
P.O. Box 29
St. Leonards-on-Sea, East Sussex TN37 7YP, UK
Website: http://www.druidry.co.uk

Council of British Druid Orders
Website: http://www.cobdo.org.uk

The Druid Clan of Dana
Mailing address:
The FOI
Clonegal Castle
Enniscorthy, Eire
Website: http://www.fellowshipofisis.com

The Druid Network
Website: http://www.druidnetwork.org

The Druid Order
Email: http://www.druidorder@macmate.me
Website: http://www.druidorder.macmate.me

The Fellowship of Isis
Website: http://www.fellowshipofisis.com

The Gorsedd of Bards of Caer Abiri
Website: http://www.druidry.co.uk/getting-involved/the-gorsedd-of-bards-of-caer-abiri

The Gorsedd of Bards of the Isles of Britain
Mailing address (UK):
BDO
PO Box 29
St. Leonards-on-Sea
East Sussex TN37 7YP, UK

Mailing address (USA):
The Bards of Caer Pugetia
PO Box 9785
Seattle, WA 98109, USA

Gorsedd y Beirdd
Website: http://www.gorsedd.cymru

Gorsedh Kernow
Email: secretary@gorsedhkernow.co.uk
Website: http://www.gorsedhkernow.org

Gorsez Breizh (The Gorsedd of Brittany)
Website: http://www.gorsedd.fr/?lang=en

The Grove of Aes Dana
Website: http://www.stonehenge-druids.org

The Henge of Keltria
Mailing address:
Henge of Keltria
P.O. Box 48639
Minneapolis, MN 55448–0369, USA
Website: http://www.keltria.org

The Loyal Arthurian Warband (LAW)
Website: http://www.warband.org.uk

Order of Bards, Ovates and Druids (OBOD)
Mailing address:
OBOD

PO Box 1333
Lewes, East Sussex BN7 1DY, UK
Email address: office@druidry.org
Website: http://www.druidry.org

The Order of WhiteOak (*Ord na Darach Gile*)
Website: http://www.whiteoakdruids.org
Tribe of the Oak, a White Oak teaching Grove: http://www.tribeoftheoak.com

Reformed Druids of North America
Email: mikerdna@hotmail.com
Website: http://rdna.info

The Secular Order of Druids
Website: http:/Pagan.wikia.com/wiki/Secular_Order_of_Druids

Chapter Notes

Chapter 1

1. Adler 1979, Preface, v–vi.
2. https://www.druidnetwork.org/constitution, accessed 05/16/2017.
3. Harvey 1997, 214.
4. Ellen Evert Hopman, email correspondence 5/22/2017.
5. Handford 1951, 137.
6. Orr 2000, 9.
7. Philip Carr-Gomm, email correspondence 8/4/2017.
8. Markale 1999(a), 198.
9. https://www.antifascistnews.net, accessed 05/17/2017.
10. Harvey 1997, 67.
11. Carr-Gomm 2002, 35.
12. Hopman 2016, 187–188.
13. Encyclopedia Britannica, 2003, 306.
14. Adler 1979, 35.
15. Rees and Rees 1961, 340.
16. Email correspondence, 5/22/2017.
17. Jones and Jones 1949, 3.
18. Cited in Piggott 1968(b), 94.

Chapter 2

1. Hopman 2016, 203–204.
2. Ross 1970, 230.
3. Cited in Tolstoy 1985, 167.
4. Markale 1999(a), 219.
5. Email correspondence, 5/22/2017.

Chapter 3

1. Gimbutas 1974, 216.
2. Email correspondence 5/22/2017.

3. Herm 1976, 14.
4. Grant 1992, 17.
5. Cited in King 1994, 63.
6. Jones and Jones 1949, 97.
7. Cited in King 1994, 66.
8. Mattingly 1948, 61–62.
9. Cited in Cunliffe 1997, 183.
10. Cunliffe 1997, 187.
11. Green 1995, subtitle.
12. Cited in Green 1992, 28.

Chapter 4

1. Cited in Matthews 1997, 15.
2. *Ibid.*, 15.
3. *Ibid.*, 16.
4. *Ibid.*, 21.
5. Graves 1948, 125.
6. Email correspondence 5/22/2017.
7. Cited in Matthews 1997, 31.
8. http://themagicalbuffet.com/blog1/?p=168, accessed 5/23/2017.
9. http://www.sacred-texts.com/neu/celt/rac/rac24.htm, accessed 6/6/2017.
10. Cited in Matthews 1997, 16.
11. Rees and Rees 1961, 181.
12. Mercatante 1988, 2.
13. Piggott 1968(b), 112.
14. Markale 1999(a), 124.
15. *Ibid.*, 195.

Chapter 5

1. Graves 1948, 13.
2. Cited in Matthews 1997, 33.
3. Cited in Wright 1924, 65.

4. Green 1992, 132.
5. Email correspondence 6/15/2017.
6. Thorpe 1966, 196.
7. *Ibid.*, 208.
8. Cited in Tolstoy 1985, 47.

Chapter 6

1. Email correspondence, 5/22/2017.
2. Email correspondence, 8/4/2017.

Chapter 7

1. Cited in Wright 1924, 79.
2. Hopman 2016, 267.
3. http://druidorder.macmate.me/history, accessed 5/19/2017.
4. *Ibid.*
5. Cited in Adler 1979, 18.
6. *Ibid.*, 300–301.
7. *Ibid.*, 300–301.
8. https://www.ADF.org, accessed 5/19/2017.
9. *Ibid.*
10. Hopman 2016, 113–114.
11. http://www.keltria.org/Blog1, accessed 5/19/2017.
12. Email correspondence 6/17/2017.
13. http://www.whiteoakdruids.org/aboutwhiteoak.cfm, accessed 5/25/2017.
14. http://www.druidry.org, accessed 5/19/2017.
15. http://www.druidry.org/join/membership-orders-training-course, accessed 5/19/2017.
16. Hopman 2016, 145–146.
17. https://druidnetwork.org/about-the-druid-network/charitable-status/the-druid-network-charity-press-release-092010ce/, accessed 05/16/2017.

Chapter 8

1. Massey 1907, 752.
2. https://en.wikipedia.org/wiki/Rostrenen, accessed 5/22/2017.
3. http://www.druidry.org/events-projects/mount-haemus-award/fifth-mount-haemus-lecture, accessed 5/23/2017.
4. *Ibid.*
5. Carr-Gomm 2002, 61–62.

6. *Ibid.*, 62.
7. Valiente 2007, 80.
8. Nichols 1990, 10–11.
9. From *Real Magic*, 1971, cited in Adler 1979, 67–68.
10. Bonewits 1976, 12.
11. Cited in Adler 1979, 335.
12. *Ibid.*, 368.
13. *Ibid.*, 59–60.
14. *Ibid.*, 130.
15. Hopman 2016, 231.
16. Cited in Adler 1979, 152.
17. *Ibid.*, 365.
18. *Ibid.*, 207–208.
19. *Ibid.*, 303.
20. Hopman 2016, 240–241.
21. http://www.ADF.org, accessed 5/29/2017.
22. Carr-Gomm 2002, 152–153.
23. Hopman 2016, 2.
24. *Ibid.*, 63–64.
25. *Ibid.*, 133.
26. *Ibid.*, 134.
27. Restall Orr 2000, 3.
28. Said at the "Fire in the Hearth" conference, Ottawa, July 2009, cited at https://en.wikipedia.org/wiki/Brendan_Myers, accessed 5/30/2017.

Chapter 9

1. Email correspondence, 6/15/2017.
2. https://en.wikipedia.org/wiki/Nemeton, accessed 6/7/2017.
3. Groome, Francis H. (1903), *Ordnance Gazetteer of Scotland*, V, 1, Caxton Publishing Company, London, cited at https://en.wikipedia.org/wiki/Drumelzier, accessed 6/9/2017.
4. Ó Dónaill 1981, 83.
5. Hopman 2016, 78–79.
6. *Ibid.*, 268.

Chapter 10

1. Stevenson 1870, 4.
2. Scullard 1979, 83.
3. Thom 1971, 15.
4. Thom and Burl 1980, 11.
5. Cited in Green V.J. 1978, 53.
6. Graves 1948, 216.
7. *Ibid.*, 210–211.

Chapter 11

1. Hopman 2016, 118.
2. Anne K. Kennedy Truscott, email correspondence 6/5/2017.
3. https://en.wikipedia.org/wiki/Sunwise, accessed 5/31/2017.
4. https://www.dunbrython.org, accessed 5/31/2017. *For Rigantona* and *Brigantica* are by Greg Hill; *Gwyn's Feast* is by Lee Davies, used with permission.
5. Hopman 2016, 92–93.
6. Harvey 1997, 5.
7. Restall Orr 2000(b), 40 and 42.
8. *Ibid.*, 43.
9. *Ibid.*, 36.
10. Carr-Gomm 2002, 24–25.
11. Adler 1979, 8.
12. Bonewits 1974, 122–124.
13. Fadiman 1985, 560.

Chapter 12

1. https://druidnetwork.org, accessed 6/11/2017.
2. Hopman 2016, 115–116.
3. https://www.whiteoakdruids.org/ritualswhiteoak, accessed 6/7/2017.
4. https://www.adf.org/print/rituals/roman/religio-romano.html, accessed 6/6/2017.

Bibliography

Adkins, Lesley, and Roy A. Adkins. 1996. *Dictionary of Roman Religion*. New York: Facts on File, Inc.

Adler, Margot. 2006. *Drawing Down the Moon: Witches, Druids, Goddess-Worshippers and Other Pagans in America*. London: Penguin.

Almond, Mark, Jeremy Black, Felipe Fernández-Armesto, Rosamond McKitterick, Geoffrey Parker, Chris Scarre, and Richard Vinen. 2001. *The Times History of Europe*. London: Times Books.

Anwyl, J.B., ed. 1934. *Spurrell's English–Welsh, Welsh–English Dictionary*. Carmarthen: Spurrell.

Armit, Ian. 2005. *Celtic Scotland*. London: Batsford.

Berresford Ellis, Peter. 1987. *A Dictionary of Irish Mythology*. London: Routedge & Kegan Paul.

Bessy, M. 1961. *Histoire en 1,000 images de la magie*, trans. M. Crosland and A. Dave. Paris: Point Royal.

_____. 1964. *A Pictorial History of Magic and the Supernatural*. London: Spring Books.

Bonewits, Philip E.I. 1974. *Real Magic: An Introductory Treatise on the Basic Principles of Yellow Magic*. London: Sphere.

Bord, Janet, and Colin Bord. 1978. *A Guide to Ancient Sites in Britain*. London: Latimer.

Bouquet, A.C. 1954. *Sacred Books of the World*. London: Penguin.

Branston, Brian. 1957. *The Lost Gods of England*. London: Thames & Hudson.

Burl, Aubrey. 1976. *The Stone Circles of the British Isles*. New Haven, CT: Yale University Press.

_____. 1979. *Prehistoric Avebury*. New Haven, CT: Yale University Press.

_____. 1983. *Prehistoric Astronomy and Ritual*. Princes Risborough: Shire Publications.

Campbell, N. 1963. *Pageant of Saints*. Oxford: Mowbray.

Carr-Gomm, Philip. 1993 (2006). *The Druid Way*. London. Element Books and Thoth Publications.

_____. 2002(a). *In the Grove of the Druids: The Druid Teachings of Ross Nichols*. London: Watkins Books.

_____. 2002(b). *Druidcraft: The Magic of Wicca & Druidism*. London: Thorsons, HarperCollins.

_____. 2002(c). *Druid Mysteries: Ancient Wisdom for the 21st Century*. London: Rider, Random House.

_____. 2004. *The Druid Craft Tarot*. New York: St. Martin's Press.

_____. 2005. *What Do Druids Believe?* London: Granta.

_____. 2010. *Journeys of the Soul: The Life and Legacy of a Druid Chief*. UK: Oak Tree Press.

_____, ed. 1996. *The Druid Renaissance*. London: Thorsons, HarperCollins.

_____, with Stephanie Carr-Gomm. 1996. *The Druid Animal Oracle*. London: Connections.

_____, with Stephanie Carr-Gomm. 2008. *The Druid Plant Oracle*. New York: St. Martin's Press.

Castleden, Rodney, 2012 .*The Element Encyclopedia of the Celts*. London: HarperCollins.

Chippindale, C. 1983. *Stonehenge Complete*. London: Thames & Hudson.

Clayton, Peter. 1976. *Archaeological Sites of Britain*. London. Book Club Associates.

Clouter, Gregory A. 2003. *The Lost Zodiac of the Druids*. London: Vega.

Crowley, Vivienne. 1989. *Wicca: The Old Religion in the New Age*. Wellingborough: Aquarian Press.

Cunliffe, Barry, Robert Bartlett, John Morrill, Asa Briggs, and Joanna Bourke. 2001. *The Penguin Atlas of British & Irish History*. London: Penguin.

Cunliffe, Barry. 1979. *The Celtic World*. London: The Bodley Head.

———. 1997. *The Ancient Celts*. Oxford: Oxford University Press.

Dames, Michael. 2002. *Merlin & Wales: A Magician's Landscape*. London: Thames & Hudson.

Davies, John. 1990 (1993). *A History of Wales [Hanes Cymru]*. London: Allen Lane Penguin Press.

de Bhaldraithe, T. 1959. *English-Irish Dictionary*. Dublin: Baile Átha Cliath Oifig ant Soláthair.

Devereux, Paul. 1990. *Places of Power*. London: Blandford.

Dickins, Bruce, and R.M. Wilson, eds. 1951. *Early Middle English Texts*. London: Bowes & Bowes.

Drake-Carnell, F.J. 1938. *Old English Customs and Ceremonies*. London: Batsford.

Duval, Paul-Marie. 1976. *Les dieux de la Gaule*. Paris: Persée.

Fadiman, Clifton, ed. 1985. *The Little, Brown Book of Anecdotes*. Boston: Little, Brown and Company.

Falkus, Malcolm, and John Gillingham, eds. 1987. *Historical Atlas of Britain*. London: Kingfisher Books.

Fleuriot, Léon. 1980. *Les Origines de la Bretagne*. Paris: Payot.

George, Ken. 1993. *Gerlyver Kernewek Kemmyn [Cornish–English, English–Cornish Dictionary]*. Truro: Kesva an Taves Kernewek.

Gimbutas, Marija. 1974. *The Goddesses and Gods of Old Europe*. Berkeley: University of California Press.

———. 1990. *The Language of the Goddess*. London: Thames & Hudson.

Ginzburg, C. 1991. *Ecstasies: Deciphering the Witches' Sabbath*. London: Thames & Hudson.

Grant, Michael. 1975. *The Twelve Caesars*. New York: Barnes & Noble.

———. 1992. *Readings in the Classical Historians*. New York: Charles Scribner's & Sons.

———, transl. 1956. *Tacitus: The Annals of Imperial Rome*. London: Penguin.

Graves, Robert. 1948. *The White Goddess*. London: Faber & Faber.

———. 1957. Suetonius, *The Twelve Caesars*. Harmondsworth: Penguin Books.

Green, Miranda J. 1992. *Dictionary of Celtic Myth and Legend*. London: Thames & Hudson.

———. 1995. *Celtic Goddesses*. London: British Museum Press.

Green, V.J. 1978. *Festivals and Saints' Days*. Dorset: Blandford, Poole.

Hadingham, E. 1983. *Early Man and the Cosmos*. London: Heinemann.

Handford, S.A., transl. 1951. *Caesar: The Conquest of Gaul*. London: Penguin.

Harbison, Peter. 1988. *Pre-Christian Ireland*. London: Thames & Hudson.

Harvey, Graham. 1997. *Listening People, Speaking Earth: Contemporary Paganism*. London: Hurst & Company.

Hemon, R. 1978. *Nouveau Dictionnaire Breton-Français*. Brest: Al Liamm.

Herm, Gerhard. 1976. *The Celts: The People Who Came Out of the Darkness*. London: Book Club Associates.

Hitching, Francis. 1977. *Earth Magic*. New York: Marrow.

Hole, C. 1940. *English Folklore*. London: Batsford.

———. 1947. *Witchcraft in England*. London: Collier-Macmillan.

———. 1965. *Saints in Folklore*. New York: Barrows.

———. 1976. *A Dictionary of British Folk Customs*. London: Granada.

Holmes, Julyan. 1998. *An Dhargan a Verdhin [John of Cornwall's The Prophecy of Merlin]*. Truro: Kesva an Taves Kernewek/The Cornish Language Board.

Hopman, Ellen Evert. 1995. *A Druid's Herbal for the Sacred Earth Year*. Rochester, VT: Destiny Books.

———. 2008. *A Druid's Herbal of Sacred Tree Medicine*. Rochester, VT: Destiny Books.

———. 2016. *A Legacy of Druids: Conversations with Druid Leaders of Britain, the USA and Canada, Past and Present*. Winchester, UK: Moon Books.

James, T.G.H. 1969. *Myths and Legends of Ancient Egypt*. New York: Gosset & Dunlap.

Jones, Gwyn, and Thomas Jones, eds. 1949 and 1974. *The Mabinogion*. London: Everyman's Library; London: J.M. Dent & Sons.

King, John. 1994. *The Celtic Druids' Year*. London: Blandford.

———. 1998. *Kingdoms of the Celts*. London: Blandford.

Kinsella, Thomas. 1969. *The Táin*. Dublin: Oxford University Press.

Lacey, R. 1976. *A Dictionary of Philosophy*, Routledge & Kegan Paul, London.

Lemprière, J. n.d. *Lemprière's Classical Dictionary*. London: Routledge and Sons.

LeRoux, Françoise, and Christian-Jean Guyonvarc'h. 1978. *Les Druides*. Rennes: Ouest France Université.

MacManus, Seumas. 1921. *The Story of the Irish Race*. New York: Devin-Adair.

Markale, Jean. 1986. *Women of the Celts*. Rochester, VT: Inner Traditions.

———. 1994. *King of the Celts*. Rochester, VT: Inner Traditions.

———. 1995. *Merlin*. Rochester, VT: Inner Traditions.

———. 1999(a). *The Druids*. Rochester, VT: Inner Traditions.

———. 1999(b). *The Great Goddess*. Rochester, VT: Inner Traditions.

Matthews, John. 1991. *Taliesin*. London: The Aquarian Press.

———. 1997. *The Druid Source Book*. London: Blandford.

Mattingly, H., trans. 1948 and 1970 (translation revised by S.A. Handford). *Tacitus: The Agricola and the Germania*. London: Penguin.

Mercatante, Anthony S. 1988. *The Facts on File Encyclopedia of World Mythology and Legend*. New York: Facts on File.

Michell, John. 1977. *A Little History of Astro-Archaeology*. London: Thames & Hudson.

Nichols, Ross. 1990. *The Book of Druidry*. Wellingborough: The Aquarian Press.

Ó Dónaill, Niall, ed. 1981. *Gearrfhoclóir Gaeilge-Béarla [Gaelic–English Dictionary]*. Dublin: Baile Átha Cliath.

O'Rahilly, Thomas F. 1946. *Early Irish History and Mythology*. Dublin: University College.

Ordnance Survey. 1996. *Ancient Britain: A Map of the Major Visible Antiquities of Great Britain Older Than AD 1066*. Southampton: Ordnance Survey.

Orr, Emma Restall, 2000. *Thorson's First Directions—Druidry*. London: Thorsons.

Paterson, Jacqueline Memory. 1996. *Tree Wisdom*. London: HarperCollins. 1996.

Piggott, Stuart, 1968(a), *Ancient Europe*. Chicago Aldine.

———, 1968(b), *The Druids*. London: Thames & Hudson.

Powell, T.G.E. 1958. *The Celts*. London: Thames & Hudson.

Rees, Alwyn, and Brinley Rees. 1961. *Celtic Heritage*. London: Thames & Hudson.

Richmond, Ian. 1947. *Roman Britain*. London: Bracken Books.

Ross, Anne. 1970. *Everyday Life of the Pagan Celts*. London: Batsford.

Scullard, H.H. 1979. *Roman Britain*. London: Thames & Hudson.

Sharkey, John. 1975. *Celtic Mysteries: The Ancient Religion*. London: Thames & Hudson.

Squire, Charles. 1979. *Celtic Myth and Legend, Poetry and Romance*. New York: Bell Publishing.

Stevenson, John, transl. 1870 and 1903 (revised by L.C. Jane). *Bede's Ecclesiastical History of the English Nation*. London: Dent & Sons; New York: Dutton & Co.

Stobie, Denise. 1999. *Exploring Celtic Britain*. London: Collins & Brown.

Thom, Alexander. 1967. *Megalithic Sites in Britain*. Oxford: Oxford University Press.

———. 1971. *Megalithic Lunar Observatories*. Oxford: Oxford University Press.

———, and Aubrey Burl. 1980. "Megalithic Rings: Plans and Date for 229 Sites." *British Archaeological Reports* 81.

Thorpe, Lewis, transl. 1966. *Geoffrey of Monmouth: The History of the Kings of Britain*. London: Penguin.

Tolstoy, Nikolai. 1985. *The Quest for Merlin*. London: Hamish Hamilton, 1985.

Treharne, R.F., and Harold Fullard, eds. 1938. *Muir's Historical Atlas, Ancient and Classical*. London: George Philip and Son.

Valiente, Doreen. 1989. *The Rebirth of Witchcraft*. London: Robert Hale.

van der Hoeven, Joanna. 2014. *The Awen Alone*. Winchester, UK: Moon Books.

Waring, P. 1978. *A Dictionary of Omens and Superstitions*. London: Souvenir Press.

Weatherhill, Craig. 2009. *Cornovia: Ancient Sites of Cornwall and Scilly*. Wellington: Halsgrove.

Wright, Dudley. 1924. *Druidism: The Ancient Faith of Britain*. Burrow; Wakefield: EP Publishing, 1974.

Index

Numbers in **bold italics** indicate pages with illustrations

Abaris the Hyperborean 20
abaton 48
aborigines, Australian 6, 11, 14–15
Adler, Margot 18, 133, 135, 204–205
Áed Dub mac Suibni 81
Áedán mac Gabráin, King of Dál Ríada 86
Aedui 74–75
Aericura 54
Aes Dana, Grove of 10
Æsir 12
Afagddu *see* Morfran
Afalon (Avallen, Avalon) 21, 182
Africa 15
The Afterworld 18, 22
agricultural cycle 38, 176–179
Ahimsa 31
Aided Diarmata 80
Ailill 19
airbacc giunnae see tonsure
airbe druad 59, 61
Alexander Severus 41, 55
Alisanos 50
altar 49, 146, 201–202, 211
Ambrosius Aurelianus 78–79, 83
Amergin (Amhairghin, Amorgain, Amor-
  ghain) 52, 70–72; Amergin Glúingel 70–
  71; Amergin mac Eccit 71; Amergin of
  Magh Seóla 71–72
Ammianus Marcellinus 40, 63
An Druidh Uileach Braithreachas see An-
  cient Druid Order
Anacalypsis 96
anam 6, 8, 20, 22, 26, 34, 50, 129, 186, 191, 200
anam cára, anamchara, Anam Chara 211, 221
Ancamna 47
The Ancient Druid Order 103–105
The Ancient Order of Druids (AOD) 103
The Ancient Order of Druids in America
  (AODA) 95
Andraste (Andate, Andarte) 45, 50

Anglesey *see* Mona
anguinum 58
Anishinabe nation 18
Anna Perenna 38
Annwn (Annwfn) 20–21, 45, 63
Anu (Ana, Anna) 45–46
Anubis 15
Aonach an Phoic 184
Apache 11
Aphrodite 12
Apollo 12, 44
Apollo Grannus 48, 54
Ár nDráiocht Féin (ADF) 4, 107–108, 129–131,
  133, 136–137, 164, 212–215, 224
Arawn 21, 45–46
Arbor Low 152
Archdruid 29, 56, 65, 79, 92, 97, 116, 118, 119–
  120, 130, 132, 143, 200
Arderydd, Battle of 85–86
Arduinna 50
Ares 12
Arianrhod 45–46, 53–54, 219
Arnemetia 45, 50
Artemis 12
Arthur, King 22, 39–40, 43, 78, 83–84, 116,
  141, 154, 155, 225
Artio 50
Arverni 74
Ásatrú 12
Ásatrú Folk Assembly (AFA) 12
Assembly of the Wondrous Head 19
athamé 125, 195, 202, 221
Athena (Athene, Pallas Athene) 12, 44
Athirne 71
Atlantis 1, 95
atua 14
Aubrey, John 90–91, *91*, 103, 153
Audacht Morainn 42, 109–110
augury 34
Augustus 75

235

Aurelian 41
Avebury (Caer Abiri) 10, 91–92, 127, 149, *149*, 152, 153, 163, 194, 196
Aveta 48
awen (*Awen*) 27–30, *28*, 34
Ayers Rock *see* Uluru

Badbh 45, 50
Baldur 12
Balor 7, 51, 73
ban-drui 59, 73
ban-sídhe see *ban-drui*
ban-tuatha see *ban-drui*
Banbha 37, 46
Bantu 15–16
Bard 62–64
bardd teulu 64
Barddoniaeth Dafydd ab Gwilym 93
Bardsey Island 159–160
Bé Chuille 72
Bechbretha 42
Bec mac Dé 80–81
Bechuma *see* Bé Chuille
Bede 176
Bel (Belinus, Beli Mawr) 38, 45, 179, 181–182, 210
Belatucadrus 44, 51
Beltan (Beltaine) 19, 38, 45, 179, 181–182, 183, 186, 187, 189, 210–211
Bergusia 54
Berthou, Erwan 115, *116*, 116–117
Berthou, Gwilherm 127–128
Bighorn Medicine Wheel 11
Biróg 73
Bitruriges 74
The Black Book of Carmarthen 85
Blake, William 104
Blodeuwedd 46
Boann 47, 49, 162, 199
Bodhmall (Bodmall) 74
Bonewits, Isaac 107, 131–137, 144, 188, 205
The Book of Shadows 125
Boudicca 41, 50
Boyne (river) *see* Boann
Brahma 16
Brân (Bendigeidfran, Brân Fendigaidd) 19, 45–46, 51
Branwen 46
Branwen, Daughter of Lyr 25
Brehon laws 23, 42, 109–110
Breitheamhin 64
Brigantica (Brigantia) 197–198
Brighid (Bríd, Bride, Bridget) 37, 44, 46, 180
Brittany (*Breizh*) 62
Brodgar, Ring of 149–150, *150*, 194
Brú na Boinne see Newgrange
Bryn Celli Du 162
Buddhism 16, 31, 121, 195
bull worship 38
Burl, Aubrey 179

Cadair Idris 158–159, *159*
caduceus 65
Caer Ibormeith 47
Caesar, Julius 4, 19, 44, 56, 63, 65, 67, 74
Cahokia Mounds 11, 171–172
The California Redwoods 172–173
Callanish (*Calanais, Tursachan Chalanais*) 150–151, *151*
Calpair 60, 69
Camlann, Battle of 22
Capitan, El 171, *171*
Carman 72
Carnac 163
Carr-Gomm, Philip 10, 13, 95, 111, 123–124, 126, *137*, 137–138, 203–204, 222
Cartimandua 41, 198
Cassandra 54
Castlerigg 151
Cathbad (Cathbhadh) 58, 60–61, 75–76
cèilidh (*céili*) 30
Celtic art 39
Celtic pantheon 44–55; of forests and wild places 49–50; Gods and Goddesses 45–47; of healing 47–48; the Triple Goddess 53–55; of war 50–51; warrior heroes 51–53; of water 49
Celtic physical attributes 39–40
Celtic tribal society 7, 23–24, 176–179
cerddorion 64
Cerne Abbas Giant 155
Cernunnos 44, 49–51
Cerridwen (Ceridwen) 79, 103, 117
Chalice Well 155
chameleon 15–16
Chartism 97
chivalric code 24
Christianity 1, 8, 15, 17, 19, 25, 31, 38, 60, 92, 95, 99–100, 102–103, 105–106, 109, 114–115, 117, 121, 123–124, 131–133, 135, 140, 143, 156, 158, 160–161, 163, 177, 179–180, 181, 183, 185–186, 187, 205, 221
Chubb, Cecil 122
Ciarán 80
Cicero 56
Cicht 76
Ciotha 76
Ciothruadh 76
clàrsach 63
Clement of Alexandra 20
clerwr 64
Clíodna 48, 54
The Clootie Well 160–161
Cluta (Clutha, Cliota) 49
Cocidius 51
Coibes Uisci Thairdne 42
coincidences *see* synchronicity
Coligny Calendar 177, 188
Columba, Saint 60–61
Conaire 19
Conall Cernach 52

Conann, King 72
Conchobar mac Nessa 47, 52, 58, 71, 75
Condatis 49
Confucius (Kung Fu Tze) 17
Conn 62, 73
Cormac mac Art 26, 58, 60, 76–77
Cornwall 19, 62
Council of British Druid Orders 111–112
Coventina 48
Crater Lake 11, 172
Creidhne 47
cremation 97–98
croesaniaid 64
Cronos 12, 182
Crowley, Aleister 121
Cú Chulainn 19, 44–45, 51–52, 54, 61, 74–75, 183
Cú Rói 19, 52, 71
Culhwch 39–40
Cumhal (Cumhall) 73–74
Cunliffe, Barry 44, 110, 147
Cunomaglus 50

Da Derga 46
The Daghda (Dagda) 46–47, 62, 162, 186
Dál Riada 86, 160
Damona 54
Danu (Dana) 45–46, 49
Dark Matter 8
Darwin, Charles 1, 114–115
Dathi, King 77
"death tales" 19
Deidre 47, 60, 75–76
deiseal (deosil) 195, 199, 222
Denali 167–168
Devereux, Paul 158, 167
Devi 16
The Devil's Tower 11, 173, *173*
Dian Cécht 47
Diana 12
Diarmait, King 80–81
Dinas Emrys 160
Dindsenchas, The Metrical 59
Dio Cassius 40–41, 50
Diocletian 41, 55
Diodorus Siculus 39, 56
Dis Pater 44
Dísitrú 13
Diviciacus (Divitiacus) 74–75
divination 34, 56
dlui fulla 7
Dôn 46
Donn 46
Douarnenez, Baie de 163–164
The Dream of Oenghus 47
The Dreaming 14
The Druid Network (TDN) 112–113, 208–209
Druidcraft 13, 138, 204
Druidesses 41, 55, 59, 72–74, 76–77
Drumelzier 161–162

Drumeton 66
Dun Brython 197–198
Dunadd 160
duotheism 17–18
Dyfed 43, 54
Dylan 46, 54

Eccet Salach 71
Egyptian pantheon 15, 114
Eisteddfod (Esedhvos) 29, 97, 100–102
Eithne 73
Ellison, Robert Lee "Skip" 129–131, *130*
Emer 61
environmentalism 105, 143
Éogan mac Durthacht 76
Éostre 12
Epona 39, 45–46, 54, 197
Ériu 37, 45–46, 70
Esus 51
Étain 47, 53
Ethnea 60, 69
Euhages *see* Ovates
Excalibur 116
excommunication 7

Fand 61
fascism 117, 119, 127–128
Fedelma 54, 60, 69
Fedlimid mac Daill 47, 75
feminism 3, 12, 135, 143
Ferghus mac Róich 52, 76
Fergus Lethderg 72
Festival des Cornemuses 99
festivals 179–187
feth fiada (Fâed Fiada) 61
Fiacha Muilleathan, King 76
Fianna 52, 73
filidh (Filid) 33, 62
Findchóem (Fionnchaomh) 52
Finnchaemh 77
Finnegas 52–53, 79
Fiodhgha, Tuatha na 59
Fionn mac Cumhaill (Finn McCool) 34, 44, 52–53, 73, 79, 186
Fionnbharra (Finbarr) *see* Amergin of Magh Seóla
Fir Bolg 128
fír fer (fíre fer) 23–25, 32, 65
First Nations 14
fitness of things 25–26, 65
Flann 19
Fodhla (Fódla) 37
Fomorians 51, 73
fosterage 74
Freemasonry 89–90, 100, 103
Freyja 3, 12
Frigg (Frigga) 12

Gá Bólga (Gae Bolg) 45
Gaia 8–10, 30, 105

Gàidhlig (Scottish Gaelic) 2
Ganesh 16
Gardner, Gerald 13, 100–101, 123–125, 138, 223
Gavida 73
geis (geisa, gessa) 19, 32
Geoffrey of Monmouth 21, 82–85
Gildas 78
Giraldus Cambrensis 27–28
Gitchi Manitou 18
Glastonbury 22, 111, 112, 127, 140, 141, 154–155
Glastonbury Tor 22, 126, *154*, 154–155
God and Goddess 37
Gododdin 42–43
Gofannon 47
Goibhniu 47, 209
The Golden Dawn 100, 121, 143
Goll mac Morna 73–74
Gorlois 84
gorsedd (gorsedh, gorsez, gorseddau) 28–29, 62–63, 65, 93–94, 100, 101–102, 121, 149, 194, 199–200, 203, 206, 222
Gorsedd Beirdd Ynys Prydain 63, 101–102, 116, 118, 225
Gorsedd Prayer 93–94
Gorsedh Kernow 63, 94, 101–102, 104, 128–129, 140, 143, 222, 225
Gorsez Breizh 63, 102, 116, 118–119, 128–129, 140, 199, 222, 225
Grand Bard 29
Graves, Robert 57, 70, 125, 133, 177, 180, 188–191
Great Mother Goddess 18
Greek pantheon 11–12
Green, Miranda 44–45, 110
Greer, John Michael 142–143
Guest, Lady Charlotte 97
Gundestrup cauldron 49–50
Gwenc'hlan (6th-century Druid) 81
Gwenc'hlan (15th-century Bard) 81
Gwenc'hlan (20th-century Grand Druid) see Le Scouëzec
Gwenddolau 85–86
Gwenddydd 85–86
Gwion Bach 79
Gwydion 46
Gwynedd 46, 86
Gwynn (Gwyn, Gwyn ap Nudd) 44, 198

Hades 12, 19
Hadrian's Wall 45
Halley, Edmund 91
Halstatt 39
hand-fasting 135, 149, 150, 152, 194, 203
Hanuman 16
Harvey, Graham 6
Hathor 15
Haumia 14
Heimdall 12
Hekate (Hecate) 55
Hen Wlad Fy Nhadau 118

The Henge of Keltria 108–109, 193, 209–210, 225
Hera 12
Hercules 44, 46
Herm, Gerhard 38
Hermes 12
Higgins, Godfrey 1, 95–96, 104, 115, 123
Hindu pantheon 16
Hinduism 31, 109, 132, 195
Hineahuone 14
History of the Kings of Britain (Historia Regorum Britanniae) 21, 82–87
Hobbes, Thomas 90
Hohokam 11
Hopman, Ellen Evert 34, 37, 58, 95, 108, 109–110, 138–140, *139*, 199, 210–212
Horus 15
humanism 17
Hutton, Dr. Ronald 13–14

Ialona, Ialonus Contrebis see Alisanos
Ianuaria 48
Iceni 41
Icovellauna 48
Igraine 84
imbas forosnai 33–34, 205, 222
Imbolc (Oimelg) 38, 179, 180, 186, 189
India 1
Iovantucarus see Lenus
Isis 15
Islam 1, 15, 17, 19, 31, 38, 132
Iunones 53

Jainism 31, 124
Jenkin, Ann Trevenen 104, 143
Jenner, Henry 102
Judaism 1, 17, 31, 38, 132
Jung, Carl 33
Juno 53
Jupiter (Juppiter) 12, 44, 182

Kamba 15
karma 16, 20, 22, 32
Kentigern, Saint 86
Kerloc'h, Per Vari 140
Kikuyu 15
Kingsley, Charles 114–115
Kinsella, Thomas 52
Klamath nation 11
Klix-in 166
Kredenn Geltiek 102, 119, 127
Krishna 16

La Tène 39
Ladmirault, Paul 117
Laegaire, King 60
Lailoken see Merlin
Lakshmi 16
Lampridius 41
Latis 49

Laurie, Erynn Rowan 23
Leabharcham 75–76
Le Fustec, Jean 115–116
Leinster, The Book of 72
Lenus (Mars Lenus) 47
Le Scouëzec, Gwenc'hlan 128–129, *129*, 140
Leviathan 90
Lia Fail 62
Liath Luachra 74
Lickona, Thomas 30
life after death *see* metempsychosis
Lindow Man 80
liturgy 203
lizard 15–16
Llew Llau Gyffes 46, 54
Lochru 60
Loki 12
Long Meg and her Daughters 151–152
Lucan 51, 66, 146
Lucetmail 60
Luchta 47
Lugaid mac Con 26
Lugh (Hugh, Ludd) 38, 44, 46, 57, 73, 179, 182–183
Lughnasadh (Luanistyn, Lughnasa, Lughnasad, Lúnasta, Lùnastal) 38, 46–47, 72, 179, 182–183, 189, 209

Mabinogi (*Mabinogion*) 25, 39–40, 43, 97
Mabon (Maponus) 37, 44–45, 47
Mac Cinnfhaelaidh 73
Mac Da Thó 51
MacCana, Proinsias 44
MacGregor-Reid, George Watson 100, 104, 119–123
MacGrené 46
Macha 45, 50
Maconochie, Alexander 24
Macsen Wledig *see* Maximus
madman's wisp *see* dlui fulla
Madron (Modron) (Goddess) 37, 45, 54
Madron, Madron Well (place) 156–158
Mael 60, 69
Maes Howe 162
magic 3, 13–15, 19, 20, 29, 43, 46, 48, 52, 54, 57–63, 67, 70–71, 73, 76, 77, 79, 82, 84, 87, 121, 124, 126, 132–134, 136, 138, 186, 190, 203–205, 209, 218
magus rotarum *see* Mogh Ruith
Malory, Sir Thomas 87
Manannán mac Lir 46, 49, 53, 150, 183, 209, 219
Manawydan ap Llyr 46, 49
manteis see Ovates
Maori 6, 11, 14
Marchal, Morvan 119
Markale, Jean 10–11, 31–32, 66
Mars 12, 44
Massey, Gerald 104, 114–115, 117
Math 46, 54

Mathgen 61
Matholwch 25
Mathonwy 46
Matres Domesticae 53
Matres Griselicae 53
Matres Nemausicae 53
Matrones (*Matronae*) 37
Matrones Aufaniae 53
Maughfling, Rollo 111–112
Maximus 78
Medb, Queen 44–45, 54, 71, 179
The Medicine Wheel 173–174
Mercury 12, 44, 65
Merlin (Merlyn, Myrddin) 68, 81–87, 117, 160, 161–162
metempsychosis 19–22
Midhir 47
Midhir and Étain 47, 53
Míl Espáine 70
Milesians *see* Míl Espáine
Minerva 12, 44, 48
mistletoe 57
Mithras 15
Mòd Nàiseanta Rìoghal (Royal National Mod of Scotland) 99
Mogh Ruith (Mag Ruith, Mog Ruith) 60, 76–77
Mona (Môn) 66, 81, 146
monotheism 17–18
Monument Valley 167, *174*, 174–175
moral philosophy 5, 23–35
Morfran 79
Morganwg, Iolo 29, 60, 63, 92–95, *93*, 97
Moritasgus (Apollo Moritasgus) 48
The Morrígan 37, 45, 51, 186
Morte Darthur 87
Mount Haemus 103, 119, 144
Mount Hood 169–170, *170*
Mount St. Helen's 169
Mount Shasta 11, 172
Muichertach 19
Muirne 73–74
Mullo (Mars Mullo) 48
Mungu (Mulungu, Murungu) 15
Mycenean culture 38
Myers, Brendan Cathbad 144
Myrddin *see* Merlin

Nantosuelta 54
Naoise 47, 76
Native Americans 6, 11, 14, 18, 59, 164–165
nature of reality 8
Nechtan (Nectan), Saint 49
Nectan's Glen 156, *157*
Nehalennia 49
Nemetodurum 66
nemeton 9, 50, 66, 145–146, 150, 194, 222
Nemetonia 50
Nemhain 45, 50
Nennius (Nyniau) 27

Neptune 12, 49
Newgrange 162
Newton, Sir Isaac 91
Ngai 15
Niagara Falls 167, *168*
Niamh 53
Nichols, Ross 31, 101, 123–127, 137–138
Ninian, Saint 66, 161
Ninian's Cave 161
"noble savage" 90
Nodens 44, 48–49
norma magica see tonsure
Norse pantheon 11–12, 21
Nuadu (Nuada, Nuada Argat Lámh) 47–48, 73

Odin (Woden, Wotan) 3, 12, 151
Oenghus (Mac Óc) 47, 162, 216–217
Ogham 42, 66
Ogmios 44, 46
Oimelg *see* Imbolc
Oirfidigh 64
Oisin 53
Ollamh le Ceól 64
Ollamhain Re-Dan 64
Ollscoil na hÉireann (National University of Ireland) 23
Olympic Peninsula 168–169
Omaha nation 18
Orates *see* Ovates
Order of Bards, Ovates and Druids (OBOD) 10, 18, 95, 110–111, 119, 137, 139, 225
Orphic oracle 38
Orr, Emma Restall 9, 113, 143–144, 200–201
Osiris 15
The Otherworld 18
Ovates 33–34, 64–65

Pádraig (Saint Patrick) 60
Pagans, Neo-Pagans 4, 6, 11, 133, 135, 136, 138, 139, 142, 143–144, 149, 150, 152, 154–156, 158, 160–161, 163, 165, 179, 180, 183, 184–185, 195, 199, 201, 203–204, 221
Pan 44, 50–51
Papatūānuku 14
parole 24
Parvati 16
pencerdd 64
Pendragon, Arthur Uther *141*, 141–142
Persephone 12
The Pheryllt 103
Pliny the Elder 57–58, 177, 178
Plutarch 41
Pluto (Dis) 12
polytheism 3, 17–18
Pomponius Mela 57
Poseidon 12, 49
"prayer family" 11, 165–166, 202
Preiddeu Annwfn 43
Price, William 96–98

Pryderi 46
prydydd 64
Pwyll 20–21, 46, 54, 63, 197
Pythagoras 20, 25, 63, 72

Ra (Amun-Ra) 15
racism 12–13
Rama 16
Ranguini 14
raven 19
The Red Book of Hergest 43, 85
Reformed Druids of North America (RDNA) 105–107, 132, 136, 226
reincarnation *see* metempsychosis
Relbeo 72
respect and responsibility 17, 30
restorative justice 26
Rhiannon 46, 48, 51, 54, 63, 197
Rhydderch Hael 85–86
ríastrad 52
Rigantona 46, 51, 197
Ritona (Pritona) 49
rituals 4, 9, 14–15, 57, 60–62, 193–207
Robins, Don 80–81
Rollright Stones 152
Roman pantheon 11–12
Romantic Revival 1, 15, 60, 89–90, 98–100
Ronan 80
Rongo 14
Rosicrucian Order 100, 124
Rosmerta 54
Ross, Anne 26, 80–81
roth ramhach see Mogh Ruith
Rousseau, Jean-Jacques 90
rowan 76
Ruadrí Ua Conchobair, King 77

Sabrina 49
The Sacred Headwaters 166
sacred sites 10, 14, 66; *see also* nemeton
Samhain 19, 38, 77, 179, 180, 184–186, 188, 189, 210, 216
Saoyú-?ehdach 166–167
Saraswati 16
Satanism 133–134, 181–182
Saturn 12, 182
Saturnalia 187
Scáthach 45, 51, 74
science 1, 3, 8–9, 17, 64, 87, 90, 104, 114, 134–135, 165, 188, 200, 205
Seanachidhe 64
Sedona 11, 175
Sekmet 15
Sequana 49
Sequani 74
Sétanta *see* Cú Chulainn
shape-shifting 67–68
Sí an Brú see Newgrange
Silbury Hill 152–154
Silures 39

Silvanus 44, 50–51
Simon Magus 77
sin 31–32
Sín 19
Sinagua 11
Sinann 49
Sioux nation 18
Sirona 48, 54
Siva (Shiva) 16
"sky-clad" 124, 131, 202
Smertrius 47–48
smudge 201
snaidm druad see *airbe druad*
solitary Druids 4
The Song of Amergin 70, 191–192
"songlines" 14
Souconna 49, 74
South Cadbury 155
staff *see* wand
Stanton Drew 152
status of women 24–25, 40–42, 69, 74
"stink eye" 7
stone circles 9
Stonehenge 10, 83–84, 90–92, 112, 120–123, 126, 140–142, 147–148, *148*, 150, 153, 162, 172, 179, 196, 225
Strabo 39–40, 63, 66
Stregheria 13
Stukeley, William 1, 10, 91–92, *92*, 104, 115, 154
Sucellus 54
Sulis 48
Swahili 15
synchronicity 32–33, 35

Tacitus 39–41
Tadg mac Nuadat 73
Tailtiu 38, 46, 77, 183
Táin Bó Cúailnge 44, 179
Taldir-Jaffrennou, François 118–119
Taliesin 43, 79–80
Tamesas 49
Tāne 14
Tangaroa 14
Taoism 16
Tara 26, 60, 162–163, 186
Taranis 44, 50–51
tarbhfess 48
Tarvostrigaranus 50
Tāwhirimātea 14
Taylor, Tony 108, 193
TDN (The Druid Network) 5
Telo 49
Tennyson, Alfred Lord 21
teuluwr 64
Teutates (Toutatis) 51
Thom, Alexander 179
Thor 3, 12
Thoth 15
"three worlds" (Earth, Sky, Sea) 17

Tighernach, King 71
Tintagel 84
Tir (Týr, Tiw) 12
Tír na nÓg 53
Tlachtga 76–77
Tolstoy, Nikolai 82
tonsure 59–60
Tower of London 19, 46
Toynbee, Arnold 105
training and induction 4
transmigration of souls *see* metempsychosis
the tree alphabet 67, 188–192
triads 29
Tribe of the Oak 4, 109–110
Trioedd Ynys Prydein 43
triple killing 80–81
Trisantona 49
Trostan 59
true and correct utterance *see y gwir yn erbyn ar byd*
tuath 9, 26, 38, 41, 48, 51, 59, 78, 129, 184, 210–211, 223
Tuatha Dé Danann 9, 46, 49, 61, 70, 128, 162
tuathal 195, 197, 223
Tursachan Chalanais see Callanish
Twrch Trwyth 50

Uatis *see* Ovates
Ucuetis 54
Uffington White Horse 155–156
Ulster cycle 51–52, 75
Uluru 14–15
United Nations Universal Declaration of Human Rights 30
Unkulunkulu 15
Uraicecht na Riar 42, 64–65, 109
Urien, King of Rheged 79, 86

Valhalla 21
Vanatrú 13
Vanir 13
Vates *see* Ovates
Venus 12
Verbeia 49
Vercingetorix 75
vernacular texts 1, 19, 42–44, 58–60; Irish tales 43–44; Welsh tales 42–43
Vernostonus 51
Vishnu 16
Vita Merlini 82
Vitiris 51
Vopiscus 41
Vortigern, King 78, 82

Wakan Tanka 18
Wakanda 18
wand 65
war frenzy, warp spasm *see ríastrad*
Wayland's Smithy 156
Weatherhill, Craig 80–81, 145–146

West Kennet Long Barrow 152–154, *153*
White, T.H. 68, 79
The White Book of Rhydderch 43
WhiteOak (White Oak, Whiteoak), The
  Order of 4, 109–110, 126, 139, 194, 210–212,
  226
Wicca 13–14, 23, 53, 55, 110, 125, 130, 131–133,
  138, 195, 202, 221
widdershins 195, 197, 223
Williams, Edward *see* Morganwg, Iolo
women in early Celtic society 40–42
Woodhenge 11
World Drum 10

y gwir yn erbyn ar byd 26–27, 65, 94, 132,
  203, 223

Yann ab Gwilherm *see* Berthou, Erwan
Yao 15
Yavapai 11
Yellowstone 170–171
The Yew of Fortingall 35
Ygern, Ygrain *see* Igraine
Ynys Enlli *see* Bardsey Island
Ynys Mon *see* Mona
Ynys Wedrenn *see* Glastonbury
Yr Afallennau 85
Ys 163

Zambese 15
Zeus 12, 182
Zoroastrianism 121
Zulu 15